WOMEN, THE KORAN AND INTERNATIONAL HUMAN RIGHTS LAW

THE EXPERIENCE OF PAKISTAN

STUDIES IN RELIGION, SECULAR BELIEFS
AND HUMAN RIGHTS

VOLUME 4

Titles in this series are listed at the back of this volume.

WOMEN, THE KORAN AND INTERNATIONAL HUMAN RIGHTS LAW

THE EXPERIENCE OF PAKISTAN

By
NIAZ A. SHAH
Visiting Fellow
Lauterpacht Research Centre For *International Law*
Faculty of Law
University of Cambridge

MARTINUS NIJHOFF PUBLISHERS
LEIDEN/BOSTON

A CIP Catalogue record for this book is available from the Library of Congress.

Printed on acid-free paper.

ISBN 90 04 15237 7

Koninklijke Brill NV incorporates the imprints Brill Academic Publishers, Martinus Nijhoff Publishers and VSP.

http://www.brill.nl

Printed and bound in The Netherlands.

To my parents and those who love humanity

Acknowledgements

Before acknowledging the support of my relatives, colleagues and friends, I must record the shock I experienced at the loss of my supervisor during my PhD, Stephen Livingstone. His loss is irreparable and painful. I am deeply grateful for his comments on the earlier draft of my PhD thesis. This book would have not taken on its current shape without Tom Hadden's constant sharp, precise, honest and unflattering but fair comments. Yvonne Galligan was always there to warn me not to lose focus. The detailed comments of Lynn Welchman were significantly helpful.

I am grateful to Mel Dubnick, Ciaran O'Kelley, Cillian McBride, M. Shujaullah, Colin Harvey, Kevin Boyle, Brice Dickson, Therese Murphy, Javaid Rehman and Amanda Wetzel for their valuable comments and help at different stages. I deeply appreciate the support of Elizabeth Meehan and academic-cum-politician John Barry. I am also grateful to Stephen McGrath and Trevor Leonard for editing an earlier draft of this book. The help and resourcefulness of chief law librarian John Knowles and Florence Gray must not go without being acknowledged. Working with Eleanor Solo in the Division for the Advancement of Women, United Nations, New York, and other colleagues was a genuine pleasure. It provided me with first-hand experience of and insights into the working of CEDAW which informed the writing of this book.

The company of my friend Owen McEldowney always gave me the feeling of belonging to the Irish Island whereas the company of Oliver Beck invariably remained my mainstay in the highly individualised and competitive Western society. The support of my parents, sisters and brothers is my enduring strength to work for human rights.

Table of Contents

Human Rights in Islam: An Introduction

The issue of women's human rights has become a separate category of analysis (Bunch, 1995; Friedman, 1995) in relatively recent human rights scholarship and is at the centre stage in the discourse on human rights. Religion plays a pivotal role in the way women are treated around the world, socially and legally. 'The two major challenges to all human rights and especially those of women in the twenty-first century will be the forces of religious extremism and economic globalisation' (Charlesworth and Chinkin, 2000:249). C. W. Holland (1997:273) argues that: 'religious fundamentalism poses the most acute problems for women's equality'. This is very true of the Islamic statutory laws practised in many Muslim jurisdictions wherein men and women are treated unequally. The general areas of tension between human rights standards and Islamic law (as interpreted and practised by Muslim states) are the unequal treatment of women and religious minorities, freedom of religion and the theoretical underpinning of slavery in the Koran.[1] This study, however, focuses on the equality rights of women in the Koran, the statutory Islamic law of Pakistan and compares these with international human rights standards attempting to find a 'common understanding' between the two systems. Before proceeding with the issues related to women's rights in the Koran and the international human rights regime, it is necessary to outline general Islamic approaches in the area of human rights and some schemes attempting to reconcile both standards. It will then be possible to locate the position of women's rights in the Koran: whether and to what extent they can be reconciled with international human rights standards.

---

[1] Currently, slavery in the traditional sense is not practiced in the Muslim world despite the fact that the Koran allows it. Muslim states have not outlawed it but it is simply not practiced.

DIFFERENT POSITIONS OF MUSLIM STATES AND SCHOLARS

In Islamic human rights scholarship, a distinction should be made between the positions of Islamic states and that of the scholars of Islam. The scholars of Islam may be broadly divided into two categories: conservative and liberal/reformist (cf. Stowasser, 1987, who has divided them into three groups: modernists, conservatives and fundamentalists or integrists). The conservatives argue that Islam has a separate and distinct system of rights and duties, and hence, they resist imposition of any foreign human rights system and influences. The liberals recognise the tension between Islamic and human rights standards and search for reconciliation. Usually, Muslim states follow the conservative interpretation of Islamic law and this is why a majority of the Muslim countries have taken the position that international human rights law is not applicable or partially applicable in their domestic jurisdictions (Baderin, 2001). The two most prominent examples are Iran and Saudi Arabia (Mayer, 1994). And those Muslim states which have ratified human rights instruments have done so with significant reservations, arguing that international human rights law would be implemented domestically to the extent that it does not conflict with either their constitutions or *Sharia* law (Baderin, 2001).[2] Pakistan is a case in point (see Chapter 5.8). However, there are exceptions such as Afghanistan, which ratified the 1979 Convention on the Elimination of All Forms of Discrimination against Women without reservation in March 2003. The Muslim states also argue that Islam is both a religion and scheme of law that includes its own rules of international law known as the *siyar*. Since Muslims believe Islamic law is divinely inspired, it has to be treated as though it supersedes all man-made laws. Thus, whenever there is conflict between Islamic and international law, Muslims are bound to follow their religious law (Mayer, 1990). Afshari (1994) has divided Islamists engaged in the debate on human rights and cultural relativism into old traditionalists and new traditionalists. The former try to accommodate the discriminatory rules emanating from *Sharia* into their human rights schemes, whereas the later tend to create, through reinterpretation of Islamic tradition, an indigenous Islamic cultural foundation for human rights.

---

[2] *Sharia* law is the result of interpretation of the Koran and the *Sunnah* of the Prophet over the ages by Islamic jurists. It is not divine in the strict sense but based on divine sources.

Like Muslim states, the position of liberal Muslim scholars is also not unanimous. Mayer (1990:2) contends that:

> In their writings on the relationship between Islamic and international law, Muslims have espoused a wide range of opinions on rights – from the assertion that international human rights is fully compatible with Islam to the claim that human rights are the products of alien, Western culture and represent values that are repugnant to Islam. In between these extremes, one finds compromise positions that in effect maintain that Islam accepts many but not all aspects of international human rights or that it endorses human rights within certain reservations and qualifications.

Halliday (1995:154-55) has pointed out four Islamic reactions to human rights law. First, that human rights are compatible with Islam; second, that they are not compatible; third, that true human rights could be realised properly only under Islam; and fourth, that human rights are an imperialist agenda and must be rejected. Mortimer (1983) has added another class as well, that human rights are a hidden anti-religion agenda. Heiner Bielefeldt (1994:597) refers to this as a 'variety of Muslim voices' in human rights.

DIFFERENT ISLAMIC APPROACHES TO HUMAN RIGHTS

As indicated above, there are several approaches towards human rights in the Islamic tradition and its relation to the international human rights regime, but four of them are discussed here: secular, non-compatible, reconciliatory and interpretive.

A. The Secular Approach

A few secular minded Muslim scholars advocate the approach of applying international human rights law in Muslim states (Afshari, 1994). They seem to presume that Islamic law presents no obstacle to signing up to human rights law and both may co-exist. For example, Afshari (1994:236) advocates strict adherence to the Universal Declaration of Human Rights (UDHR): 'I write from a secular and universalist perspective as a non-religious Middle Easterner'.[3] Some national human rights organisations in

[3] A distinction should be made between those Muslim scholars who want to reform Islamic law within limits set by Islam in order to make it compatible with human rights standards and those who support enactment of laws compatible with human rights standards without referring to religion.

Muslim states, such as the Human Rights Commission of Pakistan, also follow this approach, advocating adherence to international human rights standards.

This approach has two main disadvantages. First, a cursory view of Islamic statutory laws in many Muslim states would show some obvious discrepancies between Islamic and international human standards, and co-existence of two contradictory systems is not workable. The unequal treatment of minorities and discriminatory laws of personal status are two clear instances. The second disadvantage of this approach is that it will not get us what we want: to achieve the equal protection and enjoyment of human rights in Muslim states. There are two simple reasons for that. First, Islam is the declared state religion in several Muslim states (see Pakistan Constitution 1973, Article 2; Afghanistan Constitution 2004, Article 2; and Iraq Constitution 2005, Article 2) and second, as argued above, the majority of the Islamic statutory laws of Muslim states are based on the conservative interpretation of the Koran and so are their other official policies. For the bulk of humankind, belief is the most significant of all aspects of life (Boyle and Sheen, 1997) and the international human rights regime recognises the right to freedom of religion. A majority of the Muslim population may want to live by their religious standards instead of a human rights system which is perceived to be based on Western liberal and secular philosophies.

B. The Non-compatible Approach

The proponents of this approach comprise Muslim governments (e.g. Iran) and conservative Muslim scholars who tend to argue that Islam has its own distinct system of rights and duties. They reject the international human rights system and praise the Islamic legal system for its eternity and antiquity. They not only reject the international human rights regime but also look at it as a new form of Western imperialism.

Abdul Aziz Said (1979) argues that Islam is a belief system predicated fully upon *haqq*, which is the Arabic word for 'right'. 'The essential characteristic of human rights in Islam is that they constitute obligations connected with the Divine and derive their force from this connection' (Said, 1979:63). He further argues that:

> The present global system, however, is dominated by a Western attitude of cultural superiority ... what is right for the West is [considered] right for others. This Western moral and philosophical posture projects a parochial

view of human rights exclusive of the cultural realities and present existential condition of the Muslim world (Said, 1979:63).

A. K. Brohi (1976:148) argues that Islamic human rights are 'radically different from the ones that we associate with a modern approach to the problem of [h]uman [r]ights'. He said that:

> There is a fundamental difference in the perspectives from which Islam and the West each view the matter of human rights. The Western perspective may, by and large, be called anthropocentric in the sense that man is regarded as constituting the measure of everything since he is the starting point of all thinking and action. The perspective of Islam on the other hand is theocentric – God-consciousness. Here the Absolute is paramount and man exists only to serve His Maker ... (Brohi, 1978:179-80)

The view of Brohi is based on premodern Islamic thought wherein the emphasis is 'on duties of the believers vis-à-vis the deity, not the protection of individual freedoms' (Mayer, 1990:133). Western individualism is unacceptable in the human rights scheme of Brohi (Mayer, 1990). Riffat Hassan (1982) argues that what Brohi described as 'Western' and 'anthropocentric' may be the view of those who either deny the existence of God or regard it as unrelated to human affairs. No-one who is either Jew or Christian shares this view and since Jews and Christians form a majority in the West, it is unwarranted to make such a sweeping statement.

Abul A'la Maududi (1995:12) has castigated the West and the Western origin of human rights in his Islamic human rights system. In Islam, God grants human rights, not 'any king or any legislative assembly'. He said:

> The rights granted by the kings or the legislative assemblies, can also be withdrawn in the same manner in which they are conferred ... since in Islam human rights have been conferred by God, no legislative assembly in the world, or any government on earth has the right or authority to make any amendment or change in the rights conferred by God (Maududi, 1995:12).

The rights, which have been sanctioned by God, are permanent, perpetual and eternal and are to 'be observed under all circumstances'. At the end of his book, Maududi (1995:39) says that 'this is the brief sketch of those rights which fourteen hundred years ago Islam gave to man ... which every believer regards as sacred as law'. Mayer (1990:133) points out that 'Mawdudi ... espoused ideas that are in fundamental conflict with international human rights law'.

N. J. Coulson (1957) maintains that Islamic religious law sees as its essential functions the portrayal of an ideal relationship of man to his Creator: the regulation of all human relationships, those of man with his neighbour or with the State, is subsidiary to, and designed to serve, this one ultimate purpose (Coulson, 1957). He further elaborates:

> A distinction is indeed drawn between the rights of God … and the rights of men … but most authorities would regard only property rights as belonging essentially to the later class; and in any case, on the higher plane, the whole Sharia is *haqq* [right] of Allah, for all rights and obligations are derived from his commands (Coulson, 1957:50).

Majid Khadduri (1946:78-79), taking the same line of argument, said that 'human rights in Islam are the privilege of Allah (God), because authority ultimately belongs to Him'. All the laws are the commands of God and 'man can only obey them'.

Three distinct points can be gleaned from the foregoing account of human rights in Islam. First, that in Islam the origin of duties and rights is divine and not a human artefact. In the Islamic scheme of human rights, duties are stressed more than rights. To respect the human rights of others (*huquq-ul-ibad*) amounts to fulfilling the duty imposed by divine command. One possesses rights because another observes his/her duty imposed by God. 'The idea of human rights is more applicable to God than man … ' (Piscotri, 1980:142). This is in contrast to international human rights notions, which are the product of human efforts spurred by human misery in the mid twentieth century. On this view, an individual possesses rights because of his/her humanness without owing any corresponding duty (Hayden, 2001). Second, human rights in Islam are theocentric, that is, everything belongs to God and man is here only to serve his Maker. Conversely, international human rights values are anthropocentric where man is the measure of everything. However, the above Muslim writers forget that the international human rights system is focused on treatment of human beings in this world. It does not deal with the relation of man to his Maker and reward and punishment in the next world. In Islam a man may be rightly called a servant of God but a man cannot be a servant of a man. Also, the Koran is not confined to the relation between man and God (*ibadat*) but certainly covers the relation of man to man (*muawalat*) (Stowasser, 1998). 'Obey Allah, and obey the Messenger, and those charged with authority among you' (Koran, 4:59). Commenting on this verse, Ali (1989:203) writes that 'as Islam makes no sharp division between sacred and secular affairs, it expects governments to be imbued with righteousness. Likewise, Islam expects Muslims to respect the authority of such government …'. Ebrahim Moosa (2000-2001:187) argues that:

> From its very inception in seventh century Arabia, the message of Islam demonstrated a preoccupation with the social, moral and spiritual condition of human beings. The deity proclaimed by the Prophet Muhammad to the world was both the "Lord of the World" … and "Lord of the People" … The subject of the prophet's revelation, the Quran, was not exclusively a self-revelation of God to humanity, but an instant where human became the very leitmotif of revelation.

The verses of the Koran reproduced in this study are mainly related to the rights of women, which manifestly reflect that the subject matter of the Koran is not confined to worshiping God and spiritual issues only. It covers human relations as well. Third, human rights in Islam are granted by God and are permanent and eternal; in contrast, its international counterparts are man-made and dynamic. Some may contest the 'man-made and dynamic' nature of human rights norms arguing that they are fixed and cannot be changed, e.g. the right to life, while others, such as Michael Freeman (2004) may argue that God is hidden in human rights.

It seems that most of the above writers argue that the international human rights system, as stated above, is the hegemonic tool of the West so they struggle to make the Islamic rights system look strongly different and defend it against Western intellectual arrogance and cultural imperialism (Piscotri, 1980). These non-compatible approaches to human rights in Islamic culture have lent support to Huntington's paradigm of a civilisational clash and the stand of cultural relativists. Huntington (1993:22-23) argues that 'the great divisions among humankind and the dominating source of conflict will be cultural' and 'it is more meaningful now to group countries … in terms of their culture and civilisation'. He argues that differences in religion and culture can create difference on policy issues such as human rights, immigration, trade etc. In response to his critics he referred to:

> The confrontation at the Vienna Human Rights Conference between the West, led by the United States, denouncing "cultural relativism" and the coalition of Islamic and Confucian states rejecting "Western universalism" (Huntington, 1993a:188).

The most vocal critic of the non-compatible Islamic human rights schemes is Mayer (1990:86) who argues that: 'Islamic schemes do not offer protection for what international law deems fundamental rights' and Muslim authorities 'have no sure grasp of what the concern of human rights are'. Bassam Tibi (1992:225), supporting Mayer's argument, says that the authors of Islamic human rights schemes 'lack any clear theory' and that their approaches are 'by-products of methodological confusion and weaknesses'. Afshari (1994:260) said that Muslim thinkers believe that human rights are the essence of their belief but:

> [T]hey make no clear distinction between human rights in the modern nation-state and human rights in Islam. When a right is recognised in Islam, it is often an ethical and spiritual assertion ... when a right is recognised in a state, it is fundamental entitlement ...

C. The Reconciliatory Approach

The proponents of this approach argue that Islamic human rights norms are compatible with international standards in many respects and that where they conflict, those areas could be reformulated and reconciled with international standards. They do not deny the divine origin of Islamic notions of rights and duties. They believe that there are similarities and dissimilarities and offer their own formulae on how to reconcile the divergent areas. Quite a few scholars have expressed their views on this issue. Only four, Munshipouri, Tibi, An-Na'im and Baderin, are discussed below.

Mahmood Monshipouri's (1998:25) main theme is that the 'fusing [of] secular and Islamic principles can effectively promote human dignity'. Monshipouri (1998:9) argues that to effect social change 'Islamism must accommodate a new awareness of the need for civil society and human rights' whereas 'the Western world must address the need for consideration of culture in the human rights discourse'. He adds:

> The dispute between the two worlds [Muslim and Western in the context of human rights] does not and should not imply a fundamental conflict; instead, one must view the dispute as a cultural dialogue (Monshipouri, 1998:64).

He stands for the enlightened interpretation of Islam to build a bridge between the two apparently opposing groups on the one hand and argues for accommodation of cultural aspects of human rights on the other. Asifa Quraishi (2000:628), however, argues that Munshipouri:

> Judges specific rules of Islamic law against conceptual values of secularism for compatibility but does not articulate the parallel essential values of Islam, let alone place specific secularist human rights norms against them for judgment.

Quraishi (2000:628) further says that 'it is comparisons like these that make Monshipouri's underdeveloped study of Islamist theoretical discourse an obvious weakness'. Monshipouri's argument of fusing secular with Islamic is not convincing as it would be yoking two opposing standards together and the approach may not be acceptable to many Muslims. (This study argues that tensions exist between Islamic statutory laws and human rights norms).

Bassam Tibi (1994:285) has focused on 'the global dimension of human rights law' and 'its compatibility with the Islamic Shari'a in our current historical period'. He believes that:

> The call of Islamic fundamentalists for the implementation of this very Shari'a law leads to contesting secular international morality and thus contributes to the clash of civilizations rather than to building bridges (Tibi, 1994:285).

In a situation of structural globalisation and cultural fragmentation, there is an urgent need, argues Tibi, for establishing globally shared legal frameworks on cross-cultural foundations. Only unbiased cultural dialogue and inter-cultural communication, not subject to policy concerns, could contribute to overcoming these cultural fragmentation-related obstacles (Tibi, 1994:288). He adds that if Muslims are to embrace international human rights law, they need to achieve cultural-religious reforms in Islam, not as faith but as a cultural and legal system (Tibi, 1994:289). He calls on Muslims to make a distinction between the political dominance of the West and the universality of international human rights standards. It is possible to criticise the hegemonic rule of the Western powers while accepting the achievements of the cultural modernity. He proposes that 'an originally European concept be integrated into non-Western cultures, which in the case of Islam we can refer to as the Islamization of human rights' (Tibi, 1999:117).

Tibi's approach of bridging the gap through cross-cultural dialogue is attractive and similar to views expressed by other scholars of Islam as discussed below. Nonetheless, his view of Islamising originally Western human rights conceptions is not reassuring as many Muslims are already sceptical of subtle Western cultural imperialism and this would buttress their views further. Afshari (1994) considers Tibi as a secular scholar advocating cultural pluralism within the emerging global civilisation which most of the Muslims will consider unacceptable.

The most vocal reformer among Islamic scholars is Abdullahi Ahmad An-Na'im although his scheme of reconciliation is not without controversy. He candidly accepts the 'inconsistencies between the Sharia and international human rights' and argues that 'reconciliation can be achieved only through the drastic reform of Sharia' (An-Na'im, 1996:172,179). Like his teacher Mahmoud Taha (1987), An-Na'im (1996:180) believes that the texts of the Koran emphasising exclusive Muslim solidarity were revealed during the Medina stage to provide the emerging Muslim community with psychological support against violent non-Muslims whereas the fundamental and eternal message preaching the solidarity of all humanity was revealed at Mecca.

> The only effective approach to achieve sufficient reform of Sharia in relation to universal human rights is to cite sources in the Quran and [S]unna which are inconsistent with universal human rights and explain them in historical context while citing those sources which are supportive of human rights as the basis of legally applicable principles and rules of Islamic law today (An-Na'im, 1996:171).

He adds that:

> We must be able to set aside clear and definite texts of the Quran and [S]unna of the Medina stage as having served their transitional purpose and implement those texts of the Meccan stage which were inappropriate for practical application but are now the only way to proceed (An-Na'im, 1996:180).[4]

He argues that it is imperative 'to take verses that have been previously abrogated as the new basis of Islamic law' if we are to 'resolve the problems raised by the modern application of the public law of Sharia' (An-Na'im, 1996:180).

[4] The verses of the Koran are divided into two groups: those which were revealed at Mecca before Muhammad's migration to Medina and those which were revealed in Medina. Both differ in respect of the issues they address: the Meccan deal with issues of faith and rituals, whereas the latter deal with politics and state, war etc.

The approach of An-Na'im has not found favour with either conservative or liberal Islamic scholars. For the conservatives, it is clearly against Islamic legal principles as he suggests leaving out the bulk of the Koran revealed at Medina over ten years in favour of abrogated (repealed) verses. A few verses of the Koran were abrogated when they were no longer required and instead new ones were revealed to address a particular issue during the lifetime of the Prophet Muhammad. With the passing away of the Prophet Muhammad, the chain of revelation came to an end and to repeal or change a Koranic verse is the right of God, and there is no room for human involvement as An-Na'im suggests.

> And recite (and teach) what has been revealed to thee of the Book of thy Lord: none can change His Words, and none wilt thou find as a refuge other than Him (Koran, 18:27).

Liberal Islamic thinkers agree with his cross-cultural argument for bridging the gap between the two divides (Tibi, 1994). However, they take issue with his method of reforming the law of Islam. John Voll (1996:X) wrote in his foreword to An-Na'im's book that:

> It represents a radical departure from both the Islamic modernist and the Islamic fundamentalist positions which dominate the contemporary thought in the Muslim world. It is neither an attempt to integrate Western and traditional Islamic thought ... nor a fundamentalist effort to return to pristine principles.

An-Na'im tries to change the understanding of the foundation of Islamic law, not to reform it (Voll (1996:X). An-Na'im (1996:186) himself was conscious of the controversial nature of his approach when he wrote 'whether this particular methodology is accepted or rejected by contemporary Muslims, the need for drastic reform is ... beyond dispute'.

Mashood Baderin, examining the issue of compatibility between international human rights law and Islamic law, formulates the synthesis between the two extremes and argues that though there are differences of scope and application that does not mean that both are fully incompatible and cannot be reconciled. He suggests that it would be easier to address the difference if the concept of human rights is developed from within the themes of Islamic law rather as an alien imposition from outside. He contends that we should:

> Theoretically engage international human rights law in dialogue with Islamic law, facilitating an evaluation of the human rights policy of modern Muslims states within the scope of that dialogue (Baderin, 2003:preface).

Baderin (2003:231) argues for the reconciliation between the two sets of laws through the adoption of a 'margin of appreciation' doctrine (defined as 'the line at which international supervision should give way to State Party's discretion in enacting or enforcing its law') by international human rights treaty bodies and reforming Islamic law by utilization of the Islamic legal conceptions of '*maqasid al-Sharia*' (over all objective of *Sharia*) and '*maslahah*' (public interest/welfare) (Baderin, 2003:231).

Baderin has a very valid point in saying that the concept of human rights should be developed from within Islamic law rather than imposing it from outside. However, his method of reconciliation through the principles of '*maslahah*' and doctrine of 'marginal appreciation' has some weaknesses. First, the doctrine of *maslahah* is associated with one of the sub-schools of the four Sunni Schools of Islamic law, the Malaki School (Esposito and DeLong-Bas, 2001). In Sunni jurisprudence, *maslahah* is considered a minor source of law through which law could be developed (An-Na'im, 1996). Fazl Rahman (1979) and Rashid Rida (1966) argue that the principle of *maslahah* can be used subjectively and abused. Second, the doctrine of marginal appreciation is an established principle of the European human rights regime (Baderin, 2003) and has not been widely accepted so far in international human rights law. Being aware of this phenomenon, Baderin (2003:231), wrote:

> The HRC [Human Rights Committee] has … refrained from adopting the margin of appreciation doctrine due to the fear of its potential abuse by State Parties to limit rights …

The main problem with this doctrine is that according to it the enjoyment of the European Convention rights may be subject to the requirement of national legislation (Barrnet, 2002). For example, the right to marry and found a family under Article 12 of the Convention is subject to national legislation. In the Republic of Ireland, the law prohibits a divorced person from remarriage (Barrnet, 2002). The European Court of Human Rights upheld this principle in the case of *Johnston v. Ireland* (European Human Rights Review, 1986(9):203). Similarly, Muslim states' legislation allows polygamy, which can be condoned under the doctrine of marginal appreciation if

Baderin's method of reconciliation is adopted. Gender equality will never be achieved.

D. The Interpretive Approach

There is a separate group of Islamic scholars within the reformist group who argue that Islamic law can be reformed by the re-analysis of the divine text, the Koran. They do not necessarily seek compatibility between Islamic and international human rights standards but rather argue that the Koran is a living text and can be reinterpreted to meet contemporary needs of given Muslim societies. For instance, many Muslim women now campaign against female genital mutilation but not on the grounds that it is barbaric or even infringe the rights of women, the feminist position. Instead they claim that it is unhealthy, it is no longer necessary due to social change, or the Koran does not advocate it (Bullbeck, 1996).

Fazlur Rahman (1982) argues that all the Koranic passages, revealed as they were in a specific time in history and within certain general and particular circumstances, were expressions relative to those circumstances. However, the message is not limited to that time or those circumstances historically. Muslims living in other circumstances must make practical application in accordance with how that original intention is reflected or manifested in the new environment. In modern times this is what the spirit of the Koran means. Rahman's view is in line with that of Asghar Ali Engineer (1996) who makes a distinction between 'normative' and 'contextual' verses of the Koran. Engineer (1996:45) suggests that certain passages of the Koran are normative: they are universal and their applicability inheres at all times and in all circumstances. In contrast, contextual verse has cultural and social specificity and its application is limited to periods of time and social contexts. Wan Mohd Wan Nor Daud (1989) argues that certain practices encouraged by the Koran may be restricted to that society which practiced them, but the Koran is not confined to or exhausted by one society and its history. These arguments tend to suggest that normative verses may be given preference over the contextual ones which were only applicable in that society, i.e. seventh century Arab society and may not be applicable to the needs of contemporary societies.

Within this group, Muslim feminists strongly argue that the current Islamic legal norms are based on a masculine and patriarchal interpretation of the Koran and suggest re-interpretation of the Koran from the perspectives of females. The development of the feminists' argument is motivated to achieve two main objectives. First, to redress gender inequality in the Islamic legal norms and second, to represent authentic Islam (Mirza, 2000). Amina Wadud (1999:5) has identified three types of Koranic interpretive methodologies: traditional, reactive, and holistic. The traditional method analyses the text of the Koran in a linear manner, starting from the first one moving on to the second, omitting to take into account the structure and thematic coherence of the Koran. This results in insufficient analysis and is traditionally utilised by men to the disadvantage of women. Ideologically motivated writers developed the 'reactive method' primarily as a reaction to the position of women in poor Islamic societies. They advance a Koranic interpretation, which attributes the inferior position of women in these societies to the text. Finally, the 'holistic method', which Wadud favours, is based on the contextualised analysis of the Koranic verses. She suggests an analyses of each verse (1) in its context, (2) in the context of discussions on similar topics in the Koran, (3) in the light of similar language and syntactical structures used elsewhere in the Koran, (4) in the light of overriding Koranic principles and (5) within the context of the Koranic *Weltanschauung* (world view). She believes that if the relevant verses of the Koran are reinterpreted according to this methodology, women's equality can be realised within Islamic tradition.

The central thesis of this study is that the Koranic verses, which are the basis of state-practised gender discriminatory legal principles, if interpreted in their proper context, and gender-biased Islamic statutory laws are reformed according to that interpretation, greater compatibility with international human rights law may be achieved. Context here means three things: (1) historical context (7th century), (2) social context (Arab society), and (3) the Koranic context, which in turn has two meanings. First, when and why was a verse revealed? Second, what is the overall approach (intention) of the Koran towards women? This study argues that the intention of the Koran was to uplift the status of woman gradually, not to relegate women to social and legal subordination as believed and legally practised in much of the Islamic world today. To achieve gender equality, this Koranic spirit and intention must be recaptured through the re-analysis of the pertinent verses of the Koran in their proper context.

The process of reformation on the lines of contextual interpretation of the Koran needs *ijtihad* which literally means striving and exerting. As a term of jurisprudence it means the application by a lawyer of all his faculties to the consideration of the authorities of the law (the Koran and the *Sunnah,* the model behaviour of the Prophet Muhammad) with a view to finding out what in all probability is the law (Rahim, 1911). The current position of conservative Muslim scholars is that the gate of *ijtihad* is closed. This study, taking the line of reformist Muslim scholars, argues that it is a myth that the gate of *ijtihad* is closed and it is possible to reform Islamic law according to the contextual interpretation of the Koran. The question addressed is that who and how *ijtihad* may be carried out? It is argued that courts in Muslim states are competent to be engaged in judicial *ijtihad* (see Chapter 3).

MERITS OF THE INTERPRETIVE APPROACH

Before discussing the merits of this approach, it is important to review some weaknesses of other approaches. The approach of secularists advocating adherence to international human rights standards while ignoring Islamic norms is not workable. As stated above, many Muslim states have declared Islam a state religion and any law incompatible with Islam is considered null and void constitutionally. Also, Muslims may argue that international human rights law recognises the right to freedom of religion and they are required to live by Islamic standards. The approach of the conservative scholars, who dismiss the international human rights regime totally, is untenable since many Islamic human rights standards, as we will see later, match international human rights norms and values and it is possible to gain greater compatibility in areas of conflict.

The 'cross-cultural dialogue', reconciliatory approach may not be well received in Muslim circles because of their ambivalence to Western modernity. Most Muslims accept modern technological advancements but are reluctant to accept cultural advances. Secondly, in many cases the inferior position of women is attributed to religion and problems with essential religious principles cannot be changed through cultural dialogue. Riffat Hassan (1988:16-20) argues that:

> If we do not deal with the theological foundation of these negative attitudes [inferior treatment of women in Islamic society and law] we cannot free women from the burden of guilt and fear, because religion is very powerful and it goes very deep.

The interpretive approach, adopted in this study, is different and has certain advantages over the ones discussed above. First, it is an Islamic approach and should be acceptable to Muslims and any result emerging from it will be implementable in Muslim states. It is an internal evolutionary drive, not an alien imposition. To put it simply, it is an 'insider strategy'. Second, this approach provides answers to the challenges posed by Islamic relativists and supports the universalists' drive. It accommodates the views of the relativists who argue that every culture and religion has its own rights system, as the change would come from within Islamic culture. The theme of reconciliation to international standards in this approach advances the argument of the universalists as to the universal application of human rights. The foremost advantage of the interpretive approach is that it is achievable because Islamic law can be reformed through the mechanism of *ijtihad* (see Chapter 3). It is practical and has the virtue of realism. Muslims will listen to and follow what is based on the Koran and the *Sunnah*. Al-Hibri (1997:3) argues that 'it is important to keep in mind that most women tend to be highly religious and would not want to act in contradiction to their faith'.

> The majority of Muslim women who are attached to their religion will not be liberated through the use of a secular approach imposed from the outside by international bodies or from above by undemocratic governments. The only way to resolve the conflicts of these women and remove their fear of pursuing rich and fruitful lives is to build a solid Muslim feminist jurisprudential basis which clearly shows that Islam not only does not deprive them of their rights, but in fact demand these rights for them (Al-Hibri, 1997:3).

OBJECTIONS TO THE INTERPRETIVE APPROACH

The main attack on the religious/insider strategy of reconciliation comes from within the secularist group. They argue that religious scriptures can be interpreted in multiple ways and each group of interpreters will consider their interpretation valid and right. In their view this leads to confusion and theological impasses, and they therefore consider it better to turn to international human rights standards. For instance, Hina Jilani (cited in Friedman, 1995:22-23) says that trying to reinterpret religious law 'created controversies and no resolutions' so we turned to international human rights law.

It is candidly admitted that this argument is valid to the extent that divine scriptures can be interpreted in so many ways and in many cases it becomes problematic to decide whose interpretation is right. But this is also a blessing as it enables people in different regions and times of history to interpret scriptures in ways suitable to their needs. The argument of the secularists is weak from the perspective of international law as well. First, like religious scriptures, there is no single monolithic interpretation of international human rights law. It is also susceptible to various interpretations. For instance, which interpretation is final: that of State Parties or that of expert committees, such as CEDAW (of the Women's Convention) and the Human Rights Committee (of the Covenant of Civil and Political Rights)? These questions arise when it comes to authoritative interpretation of human rights law (Hessler, 2005). Second, it is not practically possible to apply Islamic law and international human rights law in Muslim states simultaneously. It is a trend with the constitutions of Muslim states to accord Islam the status of state religion and to prohibit legislation against Islam, and because of apparent discrepancies between Islamic statutory laws and human rights norms, the latter will be considered against the constitution (see Shah, 2005). Also, as said above, Muslims may want to live by Islamic standards, a right recognised by international human rights law.

Ghazala Anwar (1999) has reservations about the efficacy of insider methods such as the interpretive approach to achieve the goals of articulating a basis for universal human rights including gender equity. She argues that Islamic reformists share several features with fundamentalists. They do not promote a secular state and they commit too much authority to the Koran and *hadiths* (recorded sayings of the Prophet) and idealise early Islamic history and its selective use for their purposes, and by idealising the past, they tacitly consent to patriarchy.

All of Anwar's arguments have little or no force when we look at them carefully. First, not seeking a secular state does not mean at all looking for a fundamentalist state or being a fundamentalist camp follower. She wrongly assumes that the only available option is a secular versus a fundamentalist state, but there are other options such as a modern/liberal Islamic state where the rights of women can be protected. There are Muslim states such as Saudi Arabia where women cannot drive and there are Muslim states such as Pakistan where a woman became Prime Minister twice. Second, seeking theological feminism or reinterpretation of the Koran from the perspectives of women's rights is not consenting to but dismantling patriarchy. Third, commitment to the authority of the Koran and the *Sunnah* will augment the efficacy of this approach in a Muslim world instead of retarding its progress. If the commitment of authority is shifted to or replaced by international human rights law, which is perceived to be based on the philosophies of Cicero, Kant, Lock, Paine, etc., it is more likely that Muslims will either reject it totally or be hesitant to follow. This will damage its efficacy. A Muslim in the street can ask a simple question: why fail to observe what the Koran and the Prophet said, but follow something which is alien instead? Still further, an intellectual Muslim may ask: is it not possible to live in harmony with others while adhering to ones own religion or is one forced to choose between joining the liberal/secular camp or be criticised and derided as a fundamentalist? Courtney Howland (1999:XI) argues that 'many women will assert their legal rights only to the extent that they believe it consistent with their religious beliefs'.

APPROACH TOWARDS ISLAMIC LEGAL SOURCES AND SCHOOLS

The approach of this study towards different Islamic legal sources is that it mainly relies on the primary source of Islamic law, the Koran, and its various interpretations. The translation of Yousaf Ali (1989) is used throughout the study unless indicated otherwise. The reason for using Ali's translation is that it is considered authoritative in the Muslim world and particularly in the Indian sub-continent where superior courts rely on it in their judgements. For instance, the Supreme Court of India has relied on it in the case of *Shah Bano* (AIR 1985 Supreme Court 945) and the Supreme Court of Pakistan in the case of *Hazoor Bakhash* (PLD 1981 Federal Shariat Court 145). The Dhaka High Court has relied on Ali's translation in the case of *Hefzur Rahman* (47 (1995) Dhaka Law Reports 54). When reference to Islamic statutory laws is made in this study, it is mainly Sunni law and within Sunnite tradition, the Hanafi School of Law, which is an officially adopted and popularly observed school in Pakistan. That transliteration of Arabic words is followed which is adopted in the legal system of Pakistan, e.g. *hudood* (Pakistan) and not *hudud* (Arabic). The choice of spelling the Qur'an as 'Koran' is mine. In the Koranic citation, chapter (*sura*) comes first followed by verse number such as 4:34.

STRUCTURE OF THE BOOK

This study is divided into three parts. Part I looks at the status of women in 7th century Arab society, what reforms Islam effected, whether women were given equal status and what was the Koranic method of reforming Arab society. It also probes how Islamic law evolved over the ages and what were the external factors informing its growth and whether courts are competent to be engaged in judicial *ijtihad*. Part II uses the legal system of Pakistan as a case study investigating the politicising of religion in the process of legislation generally and the so-called process of Islamisation during the Zia-ul-Haq regime (1976-1988). Women's related constitutional provisions, law of personal status and criminal law are analysed to find out their Koranic standing and how the superior courts interpret and apply them. An analysis of case law is made in order to find out whether the courts' interpretation of these laws matches the Koranic standards and protects or undermines women's rights. It examines the influences of politics on Islamisation, the adoption of the conservative interpretation as the official interpretation and how the judicial interpretation of legal norms reflects gender prejudices of the players of the justice system and how society turns Islamic law into a tool of women's victimisation. Part III focuses on the doctrine of gender equality in the international human rights instruments, its claim of universal application and the challenges posed by cultural relativism and feminism. International human rights standards are compared with the Islamic law of Pakistan and the Koranic standards as understood contextually to find out where conflict occurs. The study concludes with suggesting reform of the Islamic law of Pakistan on the lines of a contextual interpretation of the Koran using the mechanism of *ijtihad* on the one hand, and proposing, on the other, to make human rights law more sensitive to issues specific to women and voices from other cultures to achieve maximal universal acceptance and application.

REFERENCES

Ali, Y. (1989) *The Meaning of the Holy Qur'an*. Maryland: Amana Corporation.

Afshari, R. (1994) 'An Essay on Islamic Cultural Relativism in the Discourse of Human Rights' *Human Rights Quarterly*. 16 (2) pp.235-276.

Al-Hibri, A. (1997) 'Islam, Law and Custom: Redefining Muslim Women's Rights' *American University Journal of International law and Policy*. 12 (1). pp.1-44.

An-Na'im, A. A. (1990) *Towards an Islamic Reformation: Civil liberties, Human Rights and International Law*. Syracuse: Syracuse University Press.

Anwar, G. (1999) 'Reclaiming the Religious Centre from a Muslim Perspective: Theological Alternatives to Religious Fundamentalism' In: Howland (eds.) *Religious Fundamentalisms and the Human Rights of Women*. Macmillan.

Baderin, M. A. (2001) 'A Macroscopic Analysis of the Practice of Muslim State Parties to International Human Rights Treaties: Conflict or Congruence?' *Human Rights Law Review*. 1 (2) pp.265-303.

Baderin, M. A. (2003) *International Human Rights and Islamic Law*. Oxford: Oxford University Press.

Barnett, H. (2002) *Britain Unwrapped: Government and Constitution Explained*. Penguin Books.

Bielefeldt, H. (1995) 'Muslim Voices in the Human Rights Debate' *Human Rights Quarterly*. 17 (4) pp.287-617.

Boyle, K. and Sheen, J (eds.) (1997) *Freedom of Religion and Belief: A World Report*. London: Routhlege.

Brohi, A. K. (1976) 'Islam and Human Rights' *All Pakistan Legal Decisions*.

Brohi, A. K. (1978) 'Islam and Human Rights' In: Gauhar (eds.) *The Challenge of Islam*. London: Islamic Council of Europe. pp.117-195.

Bullbeck, Chilla. (1996) 'Less Than Overwhelmed by Beijing: Problems Concerning Women's Commonality and Diversity'. 6 pp.31-37.

Bunch, C. (1995) 'Transforming Human Rights from Feminist Perspective' In: Peters and Wolper (eds.) *Women's Rights Human Rights: International Feminist Perspectives*. Routledge.

Charlesworth, C. Chinkin. (2000) *The Boundaries of International Law: The Feminist Analysis*. Manchester: Manchester University Press.

Coulson, N. J. (1957) 'The State and the Individual in Islamic Law' *International and Comparative Law Quarterly*. 6 pp.49-60.

Engineer, A. A. (1996) *The Rights of Women in Islam*. Islamabad: Vanguard Books Limited.

Esposito, J. and DeLong-Bas (2001) *Women in Muslim Family Law*. 2nd ed. Syracuse: Syracuse University Press.

Daud, Wan Mohd Wan Nor (1989) *The Concept of Knowledge in Islam and its Implications for Education in a Developing Country*. London: Mansell Publisher.

Freeman, M. (2004) 'The Problem of Secularism in Human Rights Theory' *Human Rights Quarterly*. 26 (2) pp. 375-400.

Friedman, E. (1995) 'Women's Human Rights: The Emergence of a Movement' In: Peters (eds.) *Women's Human Rights: International Feminist Perspective*. Routlege. p.18.

Halliday, S. (1995) 'Relativism and Universalism in Human Rights: The Islamic Middle East' In: Beetham (eds.) *Politics and Human Rights*. Leeds University Press.

Hassan, R. (1982) 'On Human Rights and The Quranic Perspective' In: Swindler (eds.) *Human Rights in Religious Traditions*. New York: The Pilgrim Press.

Hassan, R. (1988) *Feminist Theology and Women in the Muslim World*. Interviewed by Mistead, B. 1988. Available at 'Women Living Under Muslim Laws' (Dossier 4, 1988): http://www.wluml.org/english/pubsfulltxt.shtml?cmd[87]=i-87-2595. [Accessed Feb. 2005].

Hayden, P. (2001) *The Philosophy of Human Rights*. Paragon House.

Hazoor Bakhash (1981) *All Pakistan Legal Decisions* 1981 Federal Shariat Court 145.

Hessler, K. (2005) 'Resolving Interpretive Conflicts in International Human Rights Law' *The Journal of Political Philosophy*. 13 (1) pp.29-52.

Holland, C.W. (1997) 'Women and Religious Fundamentalism' *Columbia Journal of Transnational Law*. 35 pp.217-377.

Holland, C. W. (1999) 'Introduction' In: Holland (eds.) *Religious Fundamentalism and the Human Rights of Women*. Macmillan.

Huntington, S. P. (1993) 'The Clash of Civilisations?' *Foreign Affairs*. Summer, pp.22-49.

Huntington, S. P. (1993) 'If Not Civilisations, What?' *Foreign Affairs*. November/December, pp.186-194.

Johnston v. Ireland (1986) 9 *European Human Rights Review* 203.

Khadduri, M. (1946) 'Human Rights in Islam' *The Annals of the American Academy*.

Maududi, S. A. (1995) *Human Rights in Islam*. 2nd ed. Lahore: Islamic Publication.

Mayer, A. E. (1990) 'Current Muslim Thinking on Human Rights' In: An-Na'im and Deng (eds.) *Human Rights in Africa: Cross Cultural Perspectives*. Washington: Brooking Institutions.

Mayer, A. E. (1994) 'Universal versus Islamic Human Rights: A Clash of Cultures or a Clash with a Construct?' *Michigan Journal of International Law*. 15 (2) pp.307-404.

Mirza, Q. (2000) 'Islamic Feminism and the Exemplary Past' In: Richardson (eds.) *Feminist Perspectives on Law and Theory*. Cavendish Publishing Limited.

Moosa, E. (2000-2001) 'The Dilemma of Islamic Human Rights Schemes' *Journal of Law and Religion*. 15 pp.185.

Mortimer. (1983) 'Islam and Human Rights' *Index on Censorship*. 12.

Monshipouri, M. (1998) *Islamism, Secularism and Human Rights in the Middle East*. Lynne Rienner.

Said, A. A. (1979) 'Precepts and Practice of Human Rights in Islam' *Universal Human Rights*. 1 (1) pp.1-18.

Piscotri, J. P. (1980) 'Human Rights in Islamic Political Culture' In: Thompson (eds.) *The Moral Imperatives of Human Rights: A World Survey*.

Quraishi, A. (2000) 'Book Review of Islamism, Secularism and Human Rights in the Middle East By Mahmood Monshipouri' *Human Rights Quarterly*. 22 (2) pp. 625-629.

Rahim, A. (1911) *Muhammadan Jurisprudence*. Lahore: PLD Publishers.

Rahman, F. (1979) 'Towards Reformulating the Methodology of Islamic Law' *New York University Journal of International Law and Politics*. 12 (2) pp.219-224.

Rahman, F. (1982) *Major Themes in the Quran*. 2nd ed. Bibliotheca Islamica: Minneapolis.

Hefzur Rahman ((1995) *47 Dhaka Law Reports 54*).

Rida, M. R. (1966) 'Muhammad Rashid Rida: Legal Doctrines' In: Kerr (eds.) *Islamic Reform: The Political and Legal Theories of Muhammad Abduh and Rashid Rida*. University of California Press.

Shah Bano (1985) *All India Review* 1985 Supreme Court 945.

Shah, N.A. (2005) 'The Constitution of Afghanistan and Women's Rights' *Feminist Legal studies*. 13 (2) pp.239-258).

Stowasser, B. (1987) 'Liberated Equals or Protected Dependent? Contemporary Religious Paradigms on Women's Status in Islam' *Arab Studies Quarterly*. 9 (3) pp.260-283.

Stowasser, B. (1998) 'Gender Issues and Contemporary Quran Interpretation' In: Haddad (eds.) *Islam, Gender and Social Change*. Oxford University Press.

Taha, M. M. (1987) *The Second Message of Islam*. An-Na'im, (trans.) Syracuse University Press.

Tibi, B. (1992) 'Review of Mayer's, 'Islam and Human Rights' *Harvard Human Rights Journal.* 5 pp.221-226.

Tibi, B. (1999) 'The European Tradition of Human Rights and the Culture of Islam' In: An-Na'im and Deng (eds.) *Human Rights in Africa: Cross Cultural Perspectives.* Washington: Brooking Institutions.

Tibi, B. (1994) 'Islamic Law/*Shari'a*, Human Rights, Universal Morality and International Relations' *Human Rights Quarterly.* 16 (2) pp.277-299.

Wadud, A. (1999) *Quran and Woman: Rereading the Sacred Text from the Woman Perspective.* New York: Oxford University Press.

PART 1

ISLAMIC REFORMS AND THE EVOLUTION OF ISLAMIC LAW

CHAPTER 1

The Position of Women in Pre- and Post-Islamic Arabia

This chapter provides an understanding of the status and role of women in Arab society before the rise of Islam and what reforms Islam introduced for lifting up the status of women. The question of 'how' or the 'methodology' of the Koranic reformation process is looked at carefully. By analysing Koranic reformation and its methodology, an effort is made to discover the 'intention' of the Koran regarding women: whether the Koran perceived them as inferior beings with a subordinate role in society or wished to raise their status from subordination.

1.1 CONFLICTING VIEWS OF WOMEN'S STATUS IN PRE-ISLAMIC ARABIA

The position of women in pre-Islamic Arab society is open to dispute. The majority of scholars of Islam maintain that women were held in subjection and that Islam raised their status (Mansfield, 1990).

> The position of woman at the time of Prophet Muhammad was no better than that of animals: they had no legal rights; in youth they were the goods and chattels of the father; after marriage the husband became their lord and master. Polygamy was universal, divorce was easy and female infanticide was common (Fyzee, 1999:5).

Women were treated as 'objects of sale'; they were fully exploited by their fathers, and could be sold in marriage to the highest bidder. The husband was entitled to terminate the contract of marriage on any occasion and on any whim (Pearl, 1979). Another group of Islamic scholars think that Islam robbed the Arabian woman of her ancient liberty. They relied on the poetry and proverbs of the days of *jahiliya* [Age of Ignorance] to show that an ideal Arab woman was an embodiment of modesty, fortitude, virtue and beauty and that men honoured and respected her (Fyzee, 1999).

Both these positions seem partial and incomplete since the evidence put forward in support of a particular view by one writer is contradicted or refuted by other(s). The view of traditional Muslim writers is based on two main sources: the Koran and the *Sunnah* (the model behaviour of the Prophet). They conclude that what is mentioned in the Koran and *hadiths* (recorded sayings of the Prophet) were the common practices in pre-Islamic Arab society. This is true in many respects but the Koran and *hadiths* cannot be the only sources for reaching a definite conclusion on the issue. Reuben Levy (1992) warns to exercise caution in accepting the evidence of early Muslim scholars as their statements are sometimes made with the deliberate intent of contrasting the blessedness of Islam with what went before.

The notable example of Hazrat Khadija, the first wife of Prophet Muhammad, refutes the view of those writers whose source of evidence is confined to the Koran and *hadiths*. Khadija was a rich Meccan widow and the Prophet Muhammad was managing her business. Impressed by his honesty she sent him a proposal to marry her, which the Prophet Muhammad accepted. This indicates that a woman could own and run a business, had the right to hold and inherit property and was free to enter into a nuptial contract with the person she chose. Leila Ahmad (1992:42) argues that:

> Her [Khadija's] economic independence; her marriage overture, apparently without a male guardian to act as intermediary; her marriage to a man many years younger than herself; and her monogamous marriage all reflect *jahiliya* rather than Islamic practice.

However, this was the case regarding a woman from Mecca, a big commercial city and centre of trade and civilisation. The position of women in Medina, which was rural, agrarian and nomadic, was quite different. 'As at Madina ... the position of woman as regarded property was unfavourable ... Widow ... could not inherit because she was herself ... part of her husband estate' (Smith, 1903:117).

The second group of writers rely for their evidence on the contemporary Arab proverbs, legends and poetry arguing that 'in those days, poetry, rooted in the life of a people, was no luxury for the cultured few, but the sole medium of expression' (Hitti, 1961:72).

> As such, it offers researchers glimpses into many aspects of pre-Islamic society, from tribal relations to the ideals of Arab virtue to the status of women. These poems, however, were not immune from error and corruption, since they were not recorded in writing until two to four hundred

years later, during the second and third centuries of *[h]ijra* (Muslim Women's League, 2002).

Many social vices have not been recorded in these poems and legends. 'To bury a daughter was regarded not only virtuous but a generous deed' (Smith, 1903:293) but these poems and legends mention it seldomly or not at all. 'Even the poetry praising women focused primarily on their physical attributes; seldom was there any appreciation of moral beauty' (Nicholson, 1996:88).

1.2 THE ARAB TRIBAL AND LEGAL SYSTEMS

To find the real place of women in Arab society, it is imperative to understand the organisation of Arab society along tribal lines and the prevailing legal system.

> One cannot fairly address women's position in pre-Islamic Arabia without an understanding of the tribal system. For it was the tribal structure and customs that had the greatest impact on women's rights (Muslim Women's League, 2002).

Arab society consisted of diverse tribal communities and some tribes were living a nomadic and semi-nomadic life. '[The] tribe regarded itself as a group of kindred united by the tie of blood for purposes of offence and defence' (Smith, 1903:73). 'The religion of the Arabic tribes and societies was certainly different in different geographical areas' (Goldziher, 1967:1) but 'generally had little place in the life of Arabs, who were engrossed in worldly interests of fighting, wine, games and love' (Goldziher, 1967:12). In this vastly diverse tribal society, the rights of women, in turn, varied according to the prevailing traditions, customs and religion of the society. The head of the tribe arbitrated disputes within the tribe whose decisions were final and binding. The rule for inter-tribal disputes and feuds was chiefly the primitive rule of 'might is right'. Those who took part in tribal fighting were committed to defending their tribal interests and honour and were regarded as the main source of tribal existence and honour. 'The clan's claim upon its members was strong enough to make a husband give up his wife' (Hitti, 1961:27). It is evident that the 'good warrior, the best for the tribe' approach played a major role in marginalizing the role of women in society and relegating them to subordinate status. It was in this social and tribal backdrop that the theory of 'women's physical inferiority' flourished and passed on to other generations.

The available evidence on the legal system indicates that there was no unified comprehensive legal system as understood today but that Arab tribes had legal systems governing matters such as security of person and property, family and personal affairs, inter-tribal ties, etc. When a member of one group is killed or injured by a member of another group, the first group is in theory entitled to exact an eye for eye, a tooth for tooth, and life for life (Watt, 1969:262). Sometimes an arbiter (a person or group of persons friendly to both parties) would settle the matter by awarding blood money to the aggrieved party. The right hand of a thief was amputated as punishment and the Jews would stone to death those guilty of adultery. Oath-taking played an important role in the settlement of disputes. If the plaintiff failed to produce witnesses and the defendant denied the charge on oath, he was absolved of all liabilities (Rahim, 1911). The system rested on the principle of communal responsibility for crimes. The customs regulating relations between the sexes and the status of the children were uncertain and in transition (Rahim, 1911). The status of the child was determined by marriage and by the kind of sexual relationships. In the case of a woman having sexual relations with several men, she could designate the father of the child. 'Adoption among the Arabs was also in vogue' (Rahim, 1911:11). On the death of an Arab his possessions devolved to his male heirs capable of bearing arms. All females and minors were excluded.

1.3 ISLAMIC REFORMS

Islam introduced changes in all spheres of Arab society but this study is confined to the discussion of reforms related to the rights of women. And within the context of reforms regarding women, only those rights of women will be analysed in depth which are contentious in the Islamic tradition and conflict with international human rights standards. The intention of the Koran was to raise the status of women in Arab society. Mansfield (1990:26) says that: 'Allah's commands in the Koran raised the status of women in seventh-century Arabia' and Muhammad, the Prophet of Islam to whom the Koran was revealed, did his job of reforming the society conscientiously. David Pearl (1979:2-3) asserts that:

> One of Muhammad's major aims was to alleviate the deprived role of the woman, and thus much of the legal material to be found in the Qur'anic

verses concerns the very real attempt to enhance the legal position of the woman.

Esposito and DeLong-Bas (2001) argue that some of the most and fundamental reforms of customary law introduced in the Koran were designed to improve the status of women and strengthen the family in Muslim society.

1.3.1 Marriage Before and After the Koran

Rahim (1911) has mentioned four types of marriage common to Arabs before Islam. First, a form of marriage similar to that sanctioned by Islam; a man would ask another for the hand of his daughter or ward, and then marry her by giving her a certain dower (bride price). Second, a man desiring noble offspring would ask his wife to send for a great chief and have intercourse with him. During the period of such intercourse the husband would stay away, but return to her when her pregnancy was well advanced. Third, a number of men, less than ten, would be invited by a woman to have intercourse with her. If she conceived, and was delivered of child, she had the right to summon all the men and they were bound to come. She would then say, 'O so and so, this is your son'. This established paternity conclusively and the man had no right to disclaim it. Fourth, common prostitutes were well known. They used to have a definite number of visitors and their tents had a special flag as a sign of their calling. If a woman of this class conceived, the men who frequented her house were assembled, and the physiognomists decided to whom the child belonged. Except for the first case, the remainder appear to be a form of sexual relationship rather than marriage in its traditional sense.

Arabs also practised marriage by capture, marriage by purchase, marriage by inheritance and *muta* (temporary) marriage. 'Instances of marriage by capture might be accumulated to an indefinite extent from history and tradition. At the time of Muhammad the practice was universal' (Smith, 1903:89).

> In old warfare the procuring of captives, both male and female, was a main object of every expedition ... Very commonly these captives at once became the wives or mistresses of their captors (Smith, 1903:89).

In marriage by purchase, the woman's family gave her away for a price, also called *mahr*, which usually consisted of camels and horses.

> In all the old stories … it is perfectly plain that the dowry or *mahr* is paid by the husband to the bride's kin … A daughter was welcomed as an addition to a father's wealth, because when he gave her in marriage he would be able to add to his flocks the camels paid to him as her *mahr* (Smith, 1903:96).

Marriage by inheritance 'was widespread custom throughout Arabia, including Medina and Mecca, whereby the heir of the deceased inherited his wife' (Muslim Women's League, 2002). Tabari (as cited in Smith, 1903:105) in his Koranic commentary said that:

> In days of *[j]ahiliya*, when a man's father or brother or son died and left a widow, the dead man's heir, if he came at once and threw his garment over her, had the right to marry her under the dowry (*mahr*) of her lord, or to give her in marriage and take her dowry.

He adds that 'the meaning of this usage is quite transparent; marital rights are rights of property which can be inherited, and which the heir can sell if he pleases' (Smith, 1903:105). The *muta* marriage was a purely personal contract, founded on consent between a man and a woman, without any intervention on the part of the woman's kin. Neither witnesses nor consent of a *wali* (guardian) were required to the contract of marriage. Another comparatively less common practice of marriage was *shighar.* In this marriage 'two men who had marriageable wards gave each his own ward to the other without dowry' (Smith, 1903:112). In *shigar* marriage a woman would get nothing, no dower, no marriage gifts, even her consent was not considered necessary. Men were the only beneficiaries, getting women for themselves losing nothing. 'The exchange took place without offering any *maher*' (Engineer, 1996:24).

The Koran prohibited all forms of sexual union except marital. Sex outside marriage was strictly prohibited and severely punishable (Koran, 24:2). The Koran encouraged people to: 'marry those among you who are single or the virtuous ones among your slaves, male or female …' (24:32). Islamic marriage is regarded 'as a sacred contract or covenant but not a sacrament, legalising intercourse and the procreation of children' (Esposito, 1998:95). The object of marriage, according to Ameer Ali (1969) is the protection of the society, and in order that human beings may guard themselves from foulness and unchastity. In respect of marriage, the Koran points towards a sharing between the two halves of the society, and indicates that its objectives, besides perpetuation of human life, are emotional well-being and spiritual harmony:

> And among his signs is this, that He created for you mates from among yourself, that ye may dwell in tranquillity with them, and He has put love and mercy between your (hearts) … (Koran, 30:21).

According to the Koran, a woman has the right to contract marriage with her free consent: ' … do not prevent them (women) from marrying their husbands, if they mutually agree on equitable terms … ' (Koran, 2:232). The Supreme Court of Pakistan followed this Koranic position in the case of Abdul Waheed (PLD 2004 Supreme Court 219) which is discussed in chapter 7. In a marriage according to the Koran, a woman receives a dower from her husband instead of her father or other male relation:

> And give the women (on marriage) their dower as free gift; but if they, of their own good pleasure, remit any part of it to you, take it and enjoy it with right good cheer' (Koran, 4:4).

The Koran (4:20) also said not to take dower back:

> But if ye decide to take one wife in place of another, even if ye had given the latter a whole treasure for dower, Take not the least bit of it back …

Islam prohibited *muta* and *shigar* marriages. 'From study of *hadith* it would seem that *muta* was a form of legalised prostitution tolerated by the Prophet in the early days of Islam, but later on he prohibited it' (Fyzee, 1999:9). The prohibition of *shigar* marriage was a major Islamic reform converting woman from an exchangeable commodity into a dignified individual. 'The Prophet Muhammad is reported to have said that: 'there is no *shigar* form of marriage in Islam' (Fyzee, 1999:9). Muslim jurists consider *shigar* invalid but some of them (Hanafis, for example) allow it provided this name is not used and *maher mithl* (analogous dower) is paid (Fyzee, 1999).

1.3.2 Prohibited Relations in Marriage

The Koran not only restricted sexual relations to marriage only but it also prohibited marriage with certain blood relations and relations by affinity. However, Asghar Ali Engineer (1996) argues that Arabs also had evolved certain norms in this respect. A father could not marry his daughter nor could a grandfather marry his granddaughter. Similarly, it was not possible for a mother to marry her son. A grandmother could not marry her grandson. Nor could a brother marry his sister. Thus the Arabs prohibited marriage with mothers, daughters, sisters, paternal aunts and maternal aunts (Engineer, 1996). Smith (1903), however, paints a different picture. He argues that in days of *jahiliya*, when a man's father or brother or son died and left a widow, the dead man's heir, if he came at once and threw his garment over her, had the right to marry her under the dowry (*mahr*) of her lord, or to give her in marriage and take her dowry. The Koranic evidence does not support the argument of Engineer as it prohibited marriage with certain relations, which presumably was a common practice before Islam. 'And marry not women whom your father married … ' (Koran, 4:22). The Koran also declares: ' … ye are forbidden to inherit women against their will … ' (4: 19). This verse suggests that the practice of inheriting of widows by sons and to give/sell them in marriage to another was a common Arab practice. Esposito (2001:19) argues that prohibition of marriage based on family relationship is derived from the Koran (4: 23) verse:

> Prohibited to you (for marriage) are – your mothers, daughters, sisters, father's sisters, mother's sisters, brothers daughters, sister's daughters; foster mothers (who give you suck), foster sisters; your wives mothers; your step daughters under your guardianship, born of your wives to whom ye have gone in – no prohibition if ye have not gone in – (those who have been) wives to your sons proceeding from your loins; and two sisters in wedlock at one and the same time …

The Koranic evidence supports the argument that there was no restriction on marriage with blood relatives and relatives by affinity such as foster mothers before Islam and it was the Koran which forbids marriage with these relations. The logic behind this Islamic reform is that it was a common practice among the Arabs to marry near relations to keep the property within the family. These marriages usually took place without women's consent.

> Perhaps the most important trend to be noticed about forbidding degrees is that they attempt to uproot all practices in which the individual is not treated as an independent person (Watt, 1969:281).

1.3.3 Right to Divorce

Arabs were well acquainted with *talaq* (divorce) as they were with the concept of marriage. During *jahiliya* granting divorce was in the hands of men but there were women who could stipulate the conditions at the time of the marriage and ask for divorce but that was not a common practice. It was a privilege of women of high social status.

> If a woman desired to divorce her husband she would change the direction of the entrance to the tent for instance from the west to the east or from the direction of Yemen to that of Syria. When the husband saw this he knew that his wife had divorced him (Engineer, 1996:26).

According to the decontextualised interpretation, the Koran gives a man a unilateral right to divorce his wife whereas a woman does not have such powers. Esposito (2001:32) argues that 'a wife's ability to divorce is very limited, a restriction that mirrors women's dependent role in society'. There are three options available to women to get divorce. First, a wife may ask her husband to delegate her power of divorce (*talaq al-tafwid*). It is a husband-controlled option where a wife is delegated power to divorce herself (Esposito, 2001). This right is based on the Koranic (33:28) verse:

> O Prophet! Say to thy Consorts: "If it be that ye desire the life of this World, and its glitter, then come! I will provide for your enjoyment and set you free in a handsome manner.

The second option is called *khul*, which is based on common consent of husband and wife but the desire to separate comes from wife. In this form of divorce, a wife buys her release by paying back dower to her husband. The Koran (2:229) said:

> ... If ye (judges) do indeed fear that they would be unable to keep the limits ordained by Allah, there is no blame on either of them if *she gives something for her freedom* ... [Emphasis added].

'However, awarding the dower is not absolutely necessary' (Esposito, 2001). The third option is known as *mubarah* when both husband and wife desire and agree on separation.

The Koran prohibited certain forms of divorce prevalent among the Arabs such as *zihar* and *illa*. *Zihar* (meaning back) was an old pagan custom wherein a man would tell his wife that 'thou art to me the back of my mother' (Ali, 1989:1432). This would free a husband from conjugal duties but did not leave the wife free to leave her husband's house or remarry. This custom was degrading to women and the Koran abolished it (Ali, 1989).

> If any men among you divorce their wives by *Zihar* (Calling them mothers), they cannot be their mothers: none can be their mothers except those

who give them birth. And in fact they use words (both) iniquitous and false ... (Koran, 58:2).

In *illa*, a man takes an oath to leave his wife for a period of time during which he abstains from cohabiting as sort of punishment (Engineer, 1996). This was also a pagan custom that will free the husband from conjugal duties but a wife cannot leave her husband (Ali, 1989). The Koran (2:226) abolished this custom:

For those who take an oath for abstention from their wives, a waiting for four months is ordained; if then they return, Allah is Oft-forgiving, Most Merciful.

In pre-Islamic Arabia women had the right to divorce their husbands but it was not the dominant practice. It was confined to a few influential women and to some kinds of marriages such as in a case where a man used to visit a woman. In general practice, men had greater freedom than women in matters of divorce. What Islam did was to provide rules empowering a woman to ask for delegating power of divorce before contracting marriage (*talaq-al-tafwid*), or she may buy her release through *khul* or both husband and wife may agree on separation (*mubarah*). The Koran does give a woman the right to divorce but whether it is an equal right is discussed in chapter 2?

1.3.4 The Right to Remarriage and Iddat

The Koran encourages remarriage after waiting for a fixed period known as *iddat* (waiting period) in Islamic family law. There is controversy among the researchers whether or not there was 'waiting period' after divorce or a husband's death in pre-Islamic Arabia. However, the Koran has fixed different waiting periods for widows and pregnant and normal divorcees and thereafter women are free to remarry. The Koran (2:234) fixed four months and ten days for widows:

If any of you die and leave widows behind, they shall wait concerning themselves four months and ten days: When they have fulfilled their term, there is no blame on you if they dispose of themselves in a just and reasonable manner ...

For normal divorcees the waiting period is three menstrual periods:

Divorced women shall wait concerning themselves for three monthly periods. Nor is it lawful for them to hide what Allah hath created in their wombs ... (Koran, 2:228).

For pregnant divorcees, the waiting period is until delivery, 'for those who carry (life within their wombs) their period is until they deliver their burdens' (Koran, 65:4). The Koran seems to discourage the extended bereavment period and fosters the notion that widows and divorcees are free to remarry and worthy to be married.

1.3.5 Right to Maintenance

During *jahiliya* divorcees and widows were given nothing by way of maintenance. They were not entitled to a house or anything else in the case of divorce. But the Koran provided for maintenance to widows and divorcees. Regarding widows, the Koran (2:240) said:

> Those of you who die and leave widows should bequeath for their widows a year's maintenance and residence; but if they leave (The residence), there is no blame on you for what they do with themselves, provided it is reasonable.

In the case of a pregnant divorcee, she must be helped economically and otherwise until delivery and had nursed the infant to the point where the husband's family could care for the child (Minai, 1981). Regarding normal divorcees, the Koran (2:241) said: 'for divorced women maintenance (should be provided) on a reasonable scale. This is a duty on the righteous'. Providing maintenance to a divorcee was a real improvement, releasing women from economic hardship during *iddat*; thereafter they were free to do whatever they wanted reasonably. However, those women who either did not marry or could not remarry were left to rely on themselves or their relations for maintenance, putting many women in a precarious financial situation. Whether the Koran allows maintenance beyond *iddat* is discussed in chapter 7.

1.3.6 Polygamy

Polygamy is a much-criticised aspect of Islamic law but this was a pre-Islamic Arab custom, which the Koran allowed under exceptional circumstances by reducing the number of wives to four only and that too when injustice to orphans was feared. The tribal chiefs and leaders used to acquire many wives in order to build relationships with other tribes and families, strengthening their tribal power. A person belonging to the tribe of Quraysh (the tribe wherein the Prophet Muhammad was born) on average had ten wives (Engineer, 1996). Islam drastically reduced the number of wives:

strictly no more than four and encouragement to have only one in the event there was fear of doing injustice among wives. Esposito (2001:35) explains that:

> Polygamy (or more precisely, polygyny) is most often identified with Islam in the minds of Westerners. In fact, the Quran and Islamic law sought to control and regulate the number of wives rather than grant men free license to marry. In a society where no limitations existed, Muslims were not told to marry four wives but instead no more than four.

No doubt it was an improvement but whether and when polygamy is allowed is discussed in detail in chapter 2.

1.3.7 Right to Inheritance

Before Islam, women had no rights of inheritance generally. Rather they themselves were the part of a husband's estate to be inherited. Arab society was tribal and patriarchal and so was the custom of inheritance. 'None should inherit save warriors' (Smith, 1903:117). Robert Roberts (1980:62-63) argues:

> The chief object kept in view by the pagan Arabs in the succession of property was that of retaining it in the family. And in order to secure this object the right to succeed was confined exclusively to male relations, and even among them to those who were capable of bearing arms, and of defending their possessions. Consequently, all female relations as well as all male minors were excluded from the right to succeed. Widows were excluded because they were regarded as the part of the estate, and as such passed ordinarily into the hands of their husband's heirs; the daughters were excluded because upon marriage they ceased to be members of their natural families; finally, male minors were excluded because as yet they were not able to bear arms, and so to defend the tribal property, rights, and privileges.

Women who were dependent for their survival on males had no property rights except in the privileged class of society and in big commercial cities. The tribal chief used to take all the decisions on behalf of the tribe and women had no political or decision-making influence in day-to-day life.

The Koran changed the situation of women in terms of inheritance. First, it prohibited women from being inherited: 'ye are forbidden to inherit women against their will' (Koran, 4:19) and then endowed them with the right to inherit:

> From what is left by parents and those nearest related, there is a share for men and a share women, whether the property be small or large—a determinate share (Koran, 4:7).

This was a substantial Islamic reform towards women's economic independence and a complete deviation from Arab custom. However, a man was allowed to receive a double share in certain situations: 'Allah (thus) directs you as regards your Children's (Inheritance): to the male, a portion equal to that of two females ... ' (Koran, 4:11). Whether a man was given 'portion of two females' because of his gender or his economic responsibility in the family system and the questions whether it should change now or should women making an equal economic contribution to the family get an equal inheritance are discussed in details in chapter 2.

1.3.8 Banning Infanticide

As stated above, infanticide was not only common but considered a virtuous deed. The Koran strictly prohibited female child murder, endowing her with the right to life. The Koran said:

> 'When news is brought to one of them, of (the birth of) a female (child), his face darkens, and he is filled with inward grief!' (16:58).

> 'With shame does he hide himself from his people, because of the bad news he has had! Shall he retain it on (sufferance and) contempt, or bury it in the dust? Ah! what an evil (choice) they decide on?' (16:59).

The Koranic prohibition on infanticide is an unequivocal evidence of not only of the right to life but also for the claim that the position of woman was dramatically improved after the advent of Islam (Mirza, 2000).

1.4 THE KORANIC METHODOLOGY OF REFORMATION

As the above account demonstrates, Islam brought about substantial reforms in Arab society. The approach followed in the process of reformation was gradual and pragmatic which is discussed under the following two subsections.

1.4.1 Pragmatism

The Koran was not revealed as a book as we see it today; rather the legislation was revealed piecemeal to meet the requirements (spiritual as well as temporal) of the nascent Islamic society. 'Legal precepts were revealed to Muhammad to meet certain contingencies in a pragmatic and empirical fashion' and 'the legislation contained in the Quran, therefore, is piecemeal' (Pearl, 1979:1-2). To substantiate this point, two illustrations from the Koran follow. One day Aisha, the wife of Prophet Muhammad, was left behind from Prophet Muhammad's caravan. A man younger than her middle-aged husband brought her to the caravan the following day. This event engendered doubts about Aisha's faithfulness towards her husband. The Prophet Muhammad's faith in his wife was also severely shaken. It was at this stage that the Prophet Muhammad received the following revelation:

> And those who launch a charge against chaste women, and produce not four witnesses (to support their allegation) – flog them with eighty strips; and reject their evidence ever after … (Koran, 24:4).

In another case the widow of Saad bin Rabeegh complained to Prophet Muhammad that her husband died in the war of *Uhud* and his brothers had taken away all the property leaving nothing for her daughters to live on (Maududi, 1987). The Prophet Muhammad received the following revelation:

> From what is left by parents and those nearest related, there is a share for men and a share for women, whether the property be small or large – a determinate share (Koran, 4:7).

1.4.2 Gradualism

'Gradualism is a method of interpretation that proceeds by degrees, over time, advancing slowly but regularly' (Sayeh and Morse, 1996). Two distinct levels of gradualism are visible in the Koranic way of reformation and teachings. First, the Koran tried to eradicate the deeply rooted harmful social and cultural traditions gradually. Second, some verses of the Koran contain strong seeds of gradualism. However, the Koran resorted to radicalism where the customs and traditions were baneful and demanded complete eradication. For example, the Koran put an outright stop to the cruel and inhumane tradition of infanticide (16:58, 59).

Two notable instances of gradualism inherent in the Koranic teachings are the method of banning consumption of alcohol and polygamy. The Arabs were accustomed to drinking alcohol and gambling for generations. The Koran followed three stages to prepare the Arabs for final abandonment. First, drinking was declared 'sinful': 'in them [wine and gambling] is a great sin, and some profit, for men; but the sin is greater than the profit' (2:219). Second, drinking was prohibited during the time of prayers: ' ... approach not prayers with a mind befogged ... ' (4:43). The final stage was the total prohibition: ' ... intoxicant and gambling ... are an abomination, - of Satan's handiwork; eschew such (abomination) ... ' (5:90).[1] Regarding polygamy, Sayeh and Morse (1996:328) call the verse dealing with polygamy a 'microcosm of the gradualism inherent in Islam'. This claim is warranted to the extent that it has great potential for gradual interpretation leading to reformulation of the law prohibiting polygamy. The relevant verse is:

> If ye fear that ye shall not
> Be able to deal justly
> With the orphans,
> Marry women of your choice,
> Two, or three, or four
> But if ye fear that ye shall not
> Be able to deal justly (with them)
> Then only one, or (a captive)
> That your right hand possess,
> That will be more suitable,
> From doing injustice (Koran, 4:3)[2]

The verse first allows polygamy conditionally, if there is fear that orphans will not be treated justly, then marrying up to four wives is permitted only, not obligatory. Second, this permission is further contingent upon 'just dealing' among wives. If there is fear of unjust dealing among wives, then

---

[1] Gordon Anthony (Senior Lecturer, School of Law, the Queen's University Belfast) argues that it is a negative right taking away individual's liberty. First, it is a negative right in the Western scheme of human rights and the rest of the world cannot be measured by this standard. Second, the Koran (2:219) said that there is some benefit in it but its harm is greater. The Koranic approach seems to be more practical and plausible in general but more so in the Western context. For instance, UK has units limit for alcohol consumption per week. Other disadvantages are high level of teens' pregnancies, rapes, violence by intimate partners, dangerous driving and the state of insecurity and disorder at weekends. To control drinking and problems attached to it cost the taxpayers dearly.

[2] The Koran did not abolish the practice of keeping women captured during wars as concubines. However, like slavery, it is no longer practised despite its Koranic approval.

there should be only one wife. Next the Koran states: 'ye are never able to be fair and just as between women, even if it is your ardent desire ... ' (4:129). In the first stage, the Koran allows polygamy conditionally, just dealing among wives. In the second stage, it declares the condition of 'just dealing' an impossibility, thus making monogamy a norm. This argument is further elaborated in chapter 2. The Koranic evidence suggests that the Koran was revealed gradually and in stages:

> (It is) a Qur'an which We have divided (into parts from time to time), in order that thou mightest recite it to men at intervals: We have revealed it by stages (Koran, 17:106).
>
> Those who reject Faith say: "Why is not the Qur'an revealed to him all at once? Thus (is it revealed), that We may strengthen thy heart thereby, and We have rehearsed it to thee in slow, well-arranged stages, gradually (Koran, 25:32).
>
> It is We Who have sent down the Qur'an to thee by stages (Koran, 76:23).

1.5 CONCLUSION

The position of women in Arab society before the emergence of Islam was not as deplorable as some Muslim scholars describe but was not as good as some Western writers would make us believe. It was worse for women belonging to a lower social stratum and to nomadic tribes. Women of high social class were able to choose their spouses on an equal basis and to own and run their businesses in contrast to women from lower strata and nomadic tribes. The position of women also varied from tribe to tribe and region to region. The Koran eliminated all these distinctions and introduced egalitarianism for all segments of society, specifically women. Some harmful traditions were abolished outright, such as infanticide, while others were approved after some modification. Some were endorsed fully, such as arbitration in some cases, whereas the deeply ingrained ones were eradicated gradually, such as the consumption of alcohol and gambling. These reforms demonstrate pragmatism and gradualism running throughout the process of reformation and teachings of the Koran. The process of reformation also reflects the intention of the Koran *inter alia* to liberate and uplift the status of women in society. Whether women were given equal status in all spheres of life is discussed in the following chapter.

REFERENCES

Ahmad, L. (1992) *Women and Gender in Islam: Historical Roots of a Modern Debate.* New Haven: Yale University Press.

Abdul Waheed: *All Pakistan Legal Decisions* 2004 Supreme Court 219.

Ali, A. (1969) *The Spirit of Islam.* Pakistan.

Ali, Y. (1989) *The Meaning of the Holy Qur'an.* Maryland: Amana Corporation.

Engineer, A. A. (1996) *The Rights of Women in Islam.* Islamabad: Vanguard Books Limited.

Esposito, J. L. (1998) *Islam: The Straight Path.* New York: Oxford University Press.

Esposito, J. and DeLong-Bas. (2001) *Women in Muslim Family Law.* 2nd ed. Syracuse: Syracuse University Press.

Fyzee, A. A. (1999) *Outlines of Mohammedan Law.* 4th ed. Oxford University Press.

Goldziher, I. (1967) *Muslim Studies.* Stern (eds.) Barber and Stern (trans.), George Allen & Unwin Ltd. Volume I.

Hitti, P. (1961) *History of the Arabs.* London: McMillan.

Levy, R. (1979) *The Social Structure of Islam.* Cambridge: Cambridge University Press.

Mansfield, A. (1990) *The Arabs.* Penguin Books.

Maududi, S. A. (1987) *Tafeheem-ul-Quran.* 6th ed. Lahore: Adara Turjuman-nul-Quran.

Minai, N. (1981) *Women in Islam: Tradition and Transition in the Middle East.* New York: Seaview Books.

Mirza, Q. (2000) 'Islamic Feminism and the Exemplary Past' In: Richardson (eds.) *Feminist Perspectives on Law and Theory.* Cavendish Publishing Limited.

Muslim Women's League (2002) 'Women in Pre-Islamic Arabia' available at http.islamfortoday.org. [Accessed Nov. 2002].

Nicholson, R. A. (1996) *A Literary History of the Arabs.* Cambridge University Press.

Pearl, P. (1979) *A Textbook on Muslim Law.* London: Croom Helm.

Rahim, A. (1911) *Muhammadan Jurisprudence.* Lahore: PLD Publishers.

Roberts, R. (1980) *The Social Laws of Koran.* 5th ed. London: Curzon Press.

Sayeh, and Morse (1996) 'Islam and the Treatment of Women: An Incomplete Understanding of Gradualism' *Texas International Law Journal.* 30 (2) pp.311-334.

Smith, W. R. (1903) *Kinship and Marriage in Early Arabia.* Cook (eds.) London: Adam and Charles Black.

Watt, W. M. (1969) *Muhammad at Median.* Karachi: Oxford University Press.

CHAPTER 2

The Equality of Men and Women in the Koran

This chapter is focused on whether or not women are treated equally in the Koran. To establish the facts an analysis of the relevant (mainly controversial) verses of the Koran is made to see whether it is the Koran or the interpretation of the Koran that discriminates against women. The main areas of discussion are polygamy, divorce, evidence and inheritance. The Koranic verse (4:34) that 'men are in charge of women' is not strictly legal in its purport but it is discussed here since its interpretation has led to the perception that women are inferior and men are their rulers. It has also been used as a guide/standard for interpreting other verses to reinforce the theory of 'women's inferiority'. Whether the Islamic concept of gender equality is different from the one as understood in human rights scholarship will be discussed in Chapter 10.

It is argued that to understand the Koranic concept of gender equality properly, it is essential to look holistically at all the verses of the Koran dealing with women's rights and interpret them in their proper social and historical context. If these verses are interpreted in isolation and out of their proper context, the result would be misinterpretation of women's position in the Koran and a misunderstanding of the Koranic universal goal: a just society based on human equality. This type of misinterpretation fosters the theory of women's physical and intellectual inferiority culminating in women's legal and social subordination. Riffat Hassan (2003)[1] argues that this is the trap into which the conservative Islamic scholars have fallen. They have taken Koranic verses out of context and read them literally, ignoring the fact that the Koran often uses symbolic language to portray deep truths. Another significantly important point to keep in view while interpreting these verses is the liberating thrust of the Koran: liberating human beings from tribalism, traditionalism, sexism, racism, etc. The focus of the Koran is more on women than on men for much Koranic legislation is designed to ensure

---

[1] There is no date available for this article on the website, so I am using the date I accessed the website.

that women are treated with justice in the home and in society (Hassan, 2003). But, again, the male and conservative interpreters of the Koran ignore this fact. Fatima Mernissi (1985:18) calls this 'Islam as interpreted in official policy' since most of the laws of Muslim states are based on this kind of interpretation.

There are several reasons for privileging this type of interpretation and incorporating it into official policies. Only two will be mentioned here, however. First, this type of Koranic interpretation represents the patriarchal and masculine bias of the interpreters. Society and the lay followers of Islam are made to believe that women belong solely in the home with responsibility for child-bearing and rearing and household chores. Second, governments always seek popular support for their policies on issues of national concern and take into consideration the religious feelings and perceptions of the public. As many people believe or are made to believe in the conservative interpretation of the Koran, the government incorporates it into official policy. Another political dimension of the incorporation of the conservative interpretation into the policies of states is that politico-religious organisations usually mount strong resistance to any governmental drive to move away from the traditional religious thinking. The resistance of the religious political parties in Pakistan to the decision of the Federal Shariat Court, in the case of *Hazoor Bakhash* (PLD 1981 FSC 145) is a notable example (see Chapter 6.2.1). In this case the punishment of stoning to death for adultery was declared extra Koranic, but the Supreme Court reversed it after street demonstrations organised by different religious political factions.

2.1 THE RIGHTS OF MEN AND WOMEN IN THE KORAN

The Koran strongly guarantees fundamental rights without reserving them to men alone. These rights are so deeply rooted in our human nature that their denial or violation is tantamount to a negation or degradation of that which make us human (Hassan, 2003). The Koran (49:13) does not make any distinction on the basis of sex and believes in human equality:

> O Mankind! We created you from a single (pair) of a male and a female, and made you into nations and tribes, that ye may know each other (not that ye may despise each other).

The Koran (46:19) also lays down that men and women are equally responsible for their actions: 'every soul will be held in pledge for its deeds'

(74:38). The Koran uses the non-sexist word 'soul' reflecting complete gender neutrality. The Koran specifies only one criterion for distinction between human beings, namely righteousness:

> And to all are (assigned) degrees according to the deeds which they (have done), and in order that (Allah) may recompense their deeds, and no injustice be done to them.

The Koran (6:151) upholds the right to life and considers it sacred and no life can be taken without law: 'take not life, which Allah hath made sacred, except by way of justice and law'. Al-Hibri (1982:212) argues that the life of a woman has the same value as that of a man: 'Islam made killing women a crime equal to that of killing men'. The Koran (17:70) considers all human beings worthy of equal esteem: 'we have honoured the sons of Adam …' and 'we have indeed created man in the best of moulds' (95:4). The Koran (24:27) recognises the need for privacy as a right and lays down rules for protecting an individual's life in the home from undue intrusion: 'enter not houses other than your own, until ye have asked permission and saluted those in them: that is best for you … ' (see Alsech, 2004). The Koran (4:7) also recognises women's right to property in general terms and forbids its improper acquisition: 'from what is left by parents and those nearest related there is *a share for men and a share for women*, whether the property be small or large, a determinate share' [emphasis added]. In another place, the Koran (2:188) proscribed taking each other's properties:

> And do not eat up your property among yourself for vanities, nor use it as bait for the judges, with intent that ye may eat up wrongfully and knowingly a little of (other) people's property.

The Koran (62:10) enjoins believers to pray and then spread on earth in pursuit of an honest livelihood: 'And when the Prayer is finished, then may ye disperse through the land, and seek of the Bounty of Allah … ' The fruits of the work belong to the person who has worked: ' … to men are allotted what they earn, and to women what they earn … ' (Koran, 4:32). The earning of a woman belongs to her, not to her husband or parents.

Khalid Ishaque (1974) argues that modern constitutions guarantee a number of different freedoms whereas the Koran (3:79) makes one comprehensive declaration: 'it is not (possible) that a man, to whom is given the Book, and Wisdom, and the prophetic office, should say to people: "Be ye my worshippers rather than Allah's"'. This verse reflects the Koranic emphasis on manifold facets of personal freedom, not to be a slave-like follower of any other person even if he is the Prophet. Everyone has to follow God, not human beings. The Koran stresses justice without distinction between men and women: 'Stand out firmly for Allah, as witness to fair dealing, and let not the hatred of others to you make you swerve to wrong and depart from justice' (5:8). Everyone is equal before the law according to the Koran (4:135): 'Stand out firmly for justice, as witness to Allah, even as against yourselves, or your parents, or your kin, and whether it be against rich or poor'. The Koran puts the highest emphasis on the acquisition of knowledge (right to education) and considers it the prerequisite for a just and peaceful world:

> Read in the name of thy Lord and Cherisher (96.1).
> He who taught (The use of) the Pen (96.4).
> Taught man that which knew not (96:5).

According to the Koran, establishment of authority in this world is a grace of God in favour of the whole community: ' ... who (conduct) their affairs by mutual Consultation ... ' (42:38), and ' ... and consult them in affairs (administration) ... ' (3:159). These two verses indicate that everyone has the right to participate in the administration of the state and take part in the decision-making process (Ishaque, 1974). The Koran (2:256) recognises the right to freedom of religion: 'Let there be no compulsion in religion'. The Koran enjoins the Prophet to communicate the message of God to people in ' ... ways that are best and most gracious ... ' (16:125), and: ' ... let him who will believe, and let him who will reject (it) ... ' (18:29). It is God who will punish the wrongdoers. God warns the Prophet Muhammad: 'we know best what they say; and thou art not one to overawe them by force. So admonish with the Qur'an such as fear My Warning!' (Koran, 50:45). Both men and women can enjoy all these rights since the Koran does not specify either sex leaving out the other.

2.2 RELEVANT KORANIC VERSES AND ALTERNATIVE INTERPRETATIONS

As demonstrated above in general terms, the Koran guarantees equal rights to men and women. However, certain verses of the Koran have been interpreted in a way which goes against women's equal rights, reducing them to a disadvantaged group. Gender-biased laws in many Islamic jurisdictions are based on this kind of interpretation. Pakistan, as discussed in

Part II, is a case in point. These verses are discussed below in some detail to clarify their contextual meanings: when and why a verse was revealed, keeping in view the overall spirit and intent of the Koran, a just society based on human equality.

2.3 THE INSTITUTION OF POLYGAMY

Many Islamic legal codes allow a man to marry up to four wives simultaneously. This principle of law is justified on an out of context interpretation of the verse below:

> If ye fear that ye shall not be able to deal justly with the orphans, marry women of your choice, two or three or four, but if ye fear that ye shall not be able to deal (with them equitably), then only one, or (a captive) that your right hand possess. That will be more suitable and, to prevent you from doing injustice (Koran, 4:3).

The plain wording of the verse demonstrates that the subject of the verse is doing justice to orphans, not polygamy *per se* (Wadud, 1999). Polygamy is only permitted (not obligatory) conditionally in order to do justice to orphans and war captives. These conditions are (1) if there is fear that orphans will not be treated justly, then marrying up to four wives is permitted, and (2) this permission is further contingent upon 'just dealing' among wives. If there is fear of unjust dealing among wives then there should be one wife. Yusuf Ali (1989) goes into the reasons why the permission was granted in order to prevent injustice to orphans, widows and war captives. In the battle of *Uhud* many men died and the Muslim community was left with many orphans, widows and captives of war. So the Koran allowed marrying them if one is sure to do perfect justice and protect their rights and property in this way or make other arrangement for the orphans. Looking into the reasons for and the context of revelation it seems that the Koran intended to protect the rights of women for two reasons. First, women outnumbered men after the battle of *Uhud* and were left unprotected. It should be recalled that the Koran was revealed in a patriarchal society. Orphans and women captured in war were usually exploited in that society, so the Koran allowed polygamy so that every woman could enjoy her right to marriage rather than remain a concubine for good. Second, it was an indirect restriction on an unlimited number of wives, which was common practice in that society. The aim of the Koran (4:3) was to 'prevent ... doing injustice' not to give men control over women using them for the gratification of their lust. Muhammad Abduh (cited in Stowassar, 1994) argues that polygamy was sound practice among the early righteous believers, but it later developed into a corrupt practice of unbridled lust, without justice and equity.

Murtaza Mutahhery (1982:240) maintains that: 'the system of polygamy has been laid down by Islam with a view to safeguarding the interests of women'. In case of numerical superiority of women over men, polygamy becomes a woman's right which society and man must discharge. Monogamy becomes repugnant to the basic human rights of women in the case of the existence of a larger number of women of marriageable age than available men. Mutahhery (1982) cites the example of Germany when many men died in World War II; the German government approached Al-Azher University in Egypt to provide it with a formula for polygamy. Parveen Shaukat Ali (1975:23) makes a similar argument that one of the major reasons for granting permission for a plurality of wives was a rapid decrease in male population due to wars. This would leave countless widows and innumerable orphans completely unattended and shelterless. After explaining when and why polygamy is allowed, the Koran (4:129) adds: 'Ye are never able to do justice between wives even if it is your ardent desire ... ' This is general Koranic comment on a man's nature, implying that a man would never be able to do justice among his wives and thereby implying that a man should stay with one wife. This has led many scholars to believe that the Koran intended polygamy to protect women's rights when needed and that monogamy should be the norm. Al-Hibri (1982) noted the combined implication of the two verses: 4:3 and 4:129. First, if you can be just and fair among orphans, then you can marry up to four wives. Second, if you cannot be just and fair among women, then you may marry only one. Third, you cannot be just and fair among women, hence marry one. Raga' El-Nimr (1997:15) says that permission for polygamy is 'an exception to the ordinary course'. Many scholars consider verse 4:129 as a legal condition attached to polygamy. Since impartial treatment is almost impossible, one must restrict oneself to monogamy. Two points need to be highlighted here. First, nowadays the circumstances are different than those which existed in 7th century Arab society when polygamy was allowed, so polygamy is not required. Second, as the Koran indicated that one cannot be just among wives, this makes polygamy an impossible exception.

It seems that the intention of the Koran was to protect women's rights so polygamy was allowed conditionally and in certain circumstances. It was also an indirect restriction on the unlimited polygamy common in that society. The Koran has, however, indicated that a man will never be able to deal with his wives justly, thus laying down the foundation of monogamous life. Verses such as these have general normative value in contrast to specific and conditional ones.

2.4 RIGHT TO DIVORCE (*TALAQ*)

According to the conservative interpretation of the Koran, a man has unilateral power to divorce his wife without giving any reason. It 'is the husband's right to divorce his wife by making a pronouncement that the marriage is dissolved' (Esposito and DeLong-Bas, 2001:29). According to this view, the Koran gives both men and women the right to divorce but the options and procedures to exercise it are different for men and women. Women's power to divorce is limited and in some cases dependent on the will of men. Divorce is the subject of so many verses but Fatima Mernissi (1985) argues that the following legally significant one reveals the basic capriciousness of the male decision to sever the marital bond: 'But if ye decide to take one wife in place of another, even if ye had given the latter a whole treasure for dower, take not the least bit of it back ... ' (Koran, 4:20). Mernissi's translation is slightly different than the above: 'And if ye wish to exchange one wife for another and ye have given unto one of them a sum of money (however great) take nothing from it ... ' (Koran, 4:20). Mernissi (1985) stresses that the words 'wish' and 'exchange' are the key elements in the Muslim institution of verbal repudiation, whose characteristic is the unconditional right of the male to break the marriage bond without any justification, and without having his decisions reviewed by a court or a judge. However, a woman has either to resort to *mubarah* (mutual release) or *khul*. In the case of *mubarah*, the husband has leverage and may not consent to mutual release, especially in a society such as Pakistan where divorce is considered socially unfavourable. Not surprisingly, this remedy is rarely practiced in such societies. The second course open to a wife is that of *khul*: to buy her release by returning her dower. The main difference between *khul* and *mubarah* is that in the former the wife is bound to give a consideration to a husband to end the marital tie whereas in the latter both agree to terminate the marriage contract (Balchin, 1994).

The third option available to a wife is known as *talaq al-tafwid* (delegated power of divorce). Mernissi (1985) describes it as *tamlik* and argues that it confers upon a wife the right to divorce her husband if he delegates such power to her. The right to delegate power of divorce to a wife is based on the Koranic (33:28) verse:

> O Prophet! Say to thy Consorts: "If it be that ye desire the life of this World, and its glitter, then come! I will provide for your enjoyment and set you free in a handsome manner".

Abdul Rahim (1911) contends that a man has the power to dissolve marriage but as marriage is founded on contract and a husband's right to divorce arises by implication of such contract, it is open to a woman at the time of marriage to stipulate the curtailment of this right or establish a similar right for herself, such as the right to dissolve the marriage. Al-Hibri (1982) also emphasises the contractual nature of Islamic marriage: it is exactly like other contracts made between people in that either side may include any condition. One such condition could be that if the groom marries another woman later, the bride will be automatically divorced; or that the woman has the right to divorce her husband at will. However, in practice this power is never or rarely delegated to a wife because of social perceptions (particularly in Pakistan) such as that a husband and wife cannot be equal. When man's absolute power to divorce is compared with the three options available to women, we reach the conclusion that women do not have equal power to divorce.

When man's right to divorce is analysed in its proper Koranic context, we reach the conclusion that men's right to divorce is not absolute nor that the Koran bars women from divorcing husbands. Esposito and DeLong-Bas (2001:29) said:

> That men were recognised as enjoying more extensive rights than women is most clearly illustrated in the Muslim male's essentially blanket right of divorce. Many Quranic verses make clear the undesirability of divorce and the punishments awaiting those who exceed the limits set by God [65:1]. However, the law did not translate these teachings and values of the Quran into specific legal restrictions on the husband's right to divorce to guard against abuses.

Amina Wadud (1999) has made two valid arguments after looking into the issue of divorce in its proper context. First, the Koran has not made a rule that a man should have uncontrolled power of repudiation. It has placed certain restrictions on man's power to divorce before it becomes irrevocable. The Koran (4:128) stipulates equitable separation:

> If a wife fears cruelty or desertion on her husband's part, there is no blame on them if they arrange an amicable settlement between themselves; and such settlement is best; even though men's souls are swayed by greed. But if ye do good and practise self-restraint, Allah is well-acquainted with all that ye do.

The Koran wants reconciliation between the spouses before getting divorced:

> Divorced women shall wait concerning themselves for three monthly periods. Nor is it lawful for them to hide what Allah hath created in their wombs, if they have faith in Allah and the Last Day. And their husbands have the better right to take them back in that period, *if they wish for reconciliation*. And women shall have rights similar to the rights against them, according to what is equitable; but men have a degree (of advantage) over them (2:228).
>
> A divorce is only permissible twice: after that, the parties should either hold together on *equitable terms*, or separate with kindness ... (2:229).
>
> When ye divorce women, and they fulfil the term of their (*Iddat*), either take them back on equitable terms or set them *free on equitable terms*; but do not take them back to injure them, (or) to take undue advantage; if any one does that; He wrongs his own soul ... (2:231).
>
> Thus when they fulfil their term appointed, either take them back on equitable terms or p*art with them on equitable terms* ... (65:2) [emphasis added in all verses].

The Koran (4:129) also enjoined:

> ... Turn not away (from a woman) altogether, so as to leave her (as it were) hanging (in the air). If ye come to a friendly understanding, and practise self-restraint ...

The verses mentioned above show the following. First, the Koran places conditions on a man's right to divorce and encourages reconciliation in case of dispute. Second, it asks for equitable separation when all efforts of reconciliation have failed. Finally, the Koran says that one should not turn away from women leaving them in the air and it urges self-restraint. However, all these Koranic conditions are not reflected in the Islamic statutory laws of the majority of Muslim states.

Wadud's second argument is that the Koran does empower men to divorce under certain conditions but makes no reference to women repudiating their husbands. This has been used to conclude that they cannot. This is in contrast to pre-Islamic custom where a woman would turn the entrance of her tent in another direction indicating the end of conjugal relations. There is no indication in the Koran that all power of repudiation should be removed from a wife (Wadud, 1999). If women had power of repudiating marriage in pre-Islamic Arab society and the Koran has not explicitly taken away that power or is silent on it, then there is no bar on empowering women to do so. In the case of *Abdul Majid* (PLD 2004 Federal Shariat Court 1) the Federal Shariat Court of Pakistan said that in matters where specific guidance is not available from the Koran or the *Sunnah*, 'the principle governing such situations is that whatever has not been disallowed is allowed'.

2.5 RIGHT TO INHERITANCE

According to the Islamic law of inheritance, a man is allowed double shares on the basis of the following verses:

> Allah (thus) directs you as regards your Children's (Inheritance): *to the male, a portion equal to that of two females*: if only daughters, two or more, their share is two-thirds of the inheritance; if only one, her share is a half. For parents, a sixth share of the inheritance to each, if the deceased left children; if no children, and the parents are the (only) heirs, the mother has a third; if the deceased left brothers (or sisters) the mother has a sixth. (The distribution in all cases is) after the payment of legacies and debts. Ye know not whether your parents or your children are nearest to you in benefit. These are settled portions ordained by Allah; and Allah is All-knowing, All-wise (Koran, 4:11). [Emphasis added].

> In what your wives leave, your share is a half, if they leave no child; but if they leave a child, ye get a fourth; after payment of legacies and debts. In what ye leave, their share is a fourth, if ye leave no child; but if ye leave a child, they get an eighth; after payment of legacies and debts. If the man or woman whose inheritance is in question, has left neither ascendants nor descendants, but has left a brother or a sister, each one of the two gets a sixth; but if more than two, they share in a third; after payment of legacies

and debts; so that no loss is caused (to any one). Thus is it ordained by Allah; and Allah is All-knowing, Most Forbearing (Koran, 4:12).

Many Islamic scholars justify the double shares for a man on the basis of their greater economic responsibility in the family system of Islam. Muhammad Qutab (1964) argues that it is a man who is burdened with spending on his wife, children and other relatives (sisters, widows etc). A woman is under no obligation to spend money on her family. She gets less than a man to be spent on herself and also may keep her own property without spending it on her household. Raga El-Nimr (1997) argues that this was not determined because of any inferiority on her part, but in view of her economic situation, and the place she occupies in the social structure of which she is part and parcel. Islam places greater economic responsibility on men while women's role is economically much lighter. Abul Aala Maududi (1987) also justifies men's double share on the basis of men's greater economic responsibility in the family system of Islam. This argument is valid to the extent that man's double share in inheritance is not based on gender; it is rather based on the different economic roles of men and women in the family. It supports the argument of this study together with other Muslim feminists. The argument of this study, however, differs in that if men do not discharge their economic responsibility, or women contribute equally to family income, then women must get an equal share in inheritance. Men are not allowed double shares in all circumstances irrespective of their economic role and contribution to the family. Wadud (1999) argues that the two-to-one formula is an oversimplification of verse 4:11 and if we look at the complete verse it enumerates a variety of proportional distribution between males and females. In fact if there is one female child, her share is half of the inheritance. In addition, the consideration of parents, siblings, distant relatives, as well as offspring is discussed in a variety of different combinations to indicate that the proportion for the female of one-half the proportion for the male is not the sole mode of property division but one of several proportional arrangements possible.

Zainab Chaudhry (1997) has meticulously dispelled the perceived myth of misogyny in the Koranic system of inheritance. The Koran specifies three classes of heirs: the Koranic heirs (sharers), agnatic heirs (residuaries) and uterine heirs (distant kindred). Not all heirs always inherit; some classes may exclude other classes whereas in one class some heirs may exclude others. However, the spouse, parents, and children of the deceased may not be excluded although their share may be decreased by the existence of more heirs. To substantiate her point, she has given four examples where men and women get different shares. Two are reproduced here. First, a woman dies leaving no children or grandchildren and her only survivors are her husband and her full sister. Her estate is distributed so that her husband gets one-half and her sister gets another half. Here is a situation where both male and female get an equal share. Second, a woman dies leaving her husband, one daughter and one full brother. The husband receives one-fourth of her estate whereas the daughter receives one-half and the remaining one-fourth goes to the full brother. In this case a female has taken twice the share of her father and uncle (see Hamid Khan, 1980). The Supreme Court of Pakistan held that:

> In absence of son, two daughters, under Islamic law could not inherit whole property and both of them could inherit 2/3rd share devolved on them. Remaining 1/3rd share had devolved on the collaterals of the deceased ... (2004 Supreme Court Monthly Review 432).

The issue here is that the question of gender is irrelevant in the inheritance law of the Koran as in this case women get a bigger share than other male and female kin.

The verse 4:11 is often misinterpreted suggesting some inherent superiority of men over women but as explained above, that is not the case. However, in some cases a man does get a greater share because of economic responsibility, which can be rationalised in different circumstances. For example, in a family of a son and two daughters in which a widowed mother is cared for and supported by one of the daughters, why should the son receive a larger share? Wadud contends that the Koran does not elaborate all the possibilities and many combinations can and do exist which must be considered for the equitable distribution of inheritance (Wadud, 1999). One such case is that the Koran allows one-third of the wealth to be bequeathed without restriction on the beneficiary. Such bequests should be made in favour of women where economic hardship or injustice is feared. The Koran declares:

> It is prescribed, when death approaches any of you, if he leave any goods that he make a bequest to parents and next of kin, according to reasonable usage; this is due from the Allah-fearing (2:180).

This verse has been invariably used for the benefits of women. The case of *Riaz Ullah Khan* (2004 Supreme Court Monthly Review 1701) from the Supreme Court of Pakistan is a notable instance where a husband gifted his property to his wife before his death. The legal heirs of the donee challenged the validity of the gift and claimed their Islamic shares in the property of their uncle. The Supreme Court held that the gift made in favour of the wife was valid. It seems that women are allowed a smaller share in inheritance not because of gender but because of their economic role and contribution to the family. If women contribute equally to family expenses, or men do not discharge their economic responsibility, women are entitled to an equal share in all inherited estates. The Koran also allows for bequests and this permission may be used in favour of deserving women in order to prevent economic injustice.

2.6 ARE WOMEN EQUAL WITNESSES?

The statutory Islamic laws of majority Muslim countries treat the evidence of a woman as inadequate in financial transactions involving future obligations and inadmissible in cases of *hadd* (cases where the Koran has fixed the punishment), such as adultery and fornication, *qisas* (retribution) and *diyat* (blood money), etc. Pakistan is a case in point, which is the subject of discussion in Part II. For the sake of analysis, these cases are divided into two categories: financial transactions and *hadd* cases.

2.6.1 Financial Transactions

The legal norm that the testimony of a woman is not adequate in financial matters is based on the following Koranic (2:228) verse:

> *O ye who believe*! When ye deal with each other, in transactions involving *future obligations* in a fixed period of time, reduce them to writing. Let a scribe write down faithfully as between the parties: let not the scribe refuse to write: as Allah Has taught him, so let him write. Let him who incurs the liability dictate, but let him fear His Lord Allah, and not diminish aught of what he owes. *If the party liable is mentally deficient*, or weak, or unable Himself to dictate, Let his guardian dictate faithfully, and get two witnesses, out of your own men, and if there are not two men, then *a man and two women*, such as ye choose, for witnesses, *so that if one of them errs, the other can remind her*. The witnesses should not refuse when they

> are called on (For evidence). Disdain not to reduce to writing (your contract) for a future period, whether it be small or big: *it is juster in the sight of Allah*, More suitable as evidence, and more convenient to prevent doubts among yourselves but if it be a transaction which ye carry out on the spot among yourselves, there is no blame on you if ye reduce it not to writing. *But take witness whenever ye make a commercial contract*; and let neither scribe nor witness suffer harm. If ye do (such harm), it would be wickedness in you. So fear Allah; For it is Good that teaches you. And Allah is well acquainted with all things (2:282) [emphasis added].

Four express points can be gleaned from the reading of this verse. First, that the order of the verse is confined to Muslims and all others are excluded as witnesses. Second, it is related to commercial transactions involving future obligations which require writing down and witnesses. Third, the aim is the prevention of doubt and doing justice, not dealing with the competency of witnesses. Fourth, the verse provides that a guardian should conduct the transaction for those who are mentally deficient or weak, but women are not put into that category.

The conservative scholars have interpreted this verse out of its proper context. First, they have extended the rule of requiring 'two women' witnesses to every case instead of confining it to commercial transactions involving future obligations. Second, they ignored the fact that the role of a second female witness is 'to remind', not 'to testify'. Instead they interpret the verse as if the testimony of the second female witness is obligatory, reinforcing the theory that women are intellectually inferior and therefore testimony of one female is insufficient. This interpretation is wrong for two reasons. First, the verse does provide for mentally deficient and weak people in that their guardian may conduct transactions for them. The verse does not consider women to be mentally deficient or weak which is why they are allowed to be witnesses. If a person is mentally deficient he/she can neither conduct transactions nor can be a witness. Second, as Nazirah Zein Ed-Din (1982) argues, if women's testimony is considered worth half that of men's because of mental inferiority then all non-Muslim males as well as females are mentally inferior as their evidence is also not acceptable for or against Muslims.

Justice Aftab Hussian (1987) argues that the verse does not lay down the rule that the evidence of two women is equal to one man:

> The scope of the verse is confined to the law about reducing to writing the contracts of debt or of sale and purchase. The witnesses required are for the attestation of documents. The only reference to any future contin-

> gency is in the reasons of the execution of the document or for having two women as attesting witnesses. The reason for execution of the document is that it avoids doubt and becomes testimony or evidence of transaction while the reason for having two women is that if one forgets in future the other may remind her. It does not necessarily follow from this that the need to remind must arise in court proceedings only. Assuming that the need arises in court proceedings only, the verse nowhere says that a matter cannot be proved there except by the testimony of two male witnesses or one male and two female witnesses. On the plain reading of the verse it appears that it does not formulate or prescribe the method of proof of the document. In case of denial of execution of the document by the debtor, the only proof required would be whether or not he executed it. This may be established by the evidence of one man, of the scribe only, of the expert of questioned documents who compared the signature or thumb-impression of the executant with the signature or thump-impression on the document. Even the evidence of one woman may be sufficient for that purpose. The object is that if one of the two women forgets the other may remind her. What is therefore, visualised by the verse is the evidence of one woman only. *The presence of the other is required only when the woman witness forgets or errs in her testimony on account of forgetfulness. The only role that the Quran mentions of that other woman is that she may remind the female witness.*

The jurists differ whether at the time of examination in court both women should be present before the judge or the other should stay out until summoned for her own evidence. If both women are appearing simultaneously in court, obviously the role of one is to remind the other and the only witness is the one who is reminded to correct herself. If on the other hand one of them is to stay out, to be summoned when the other woman errs on account of forgetfulness, and she merely discharges the functions of the one who reminds, in that case too the evidence would be of the woman who had erred. If in either of the two cases the independent evidence of the two women is recorded, one of whom erred and the other made a correct statement, then the *qazi* would in effect be relying upon the evidence of one woman and not two (Hussain, 1987). Wadud (1999) argues that in the verse both women are not called as witnesses. One woman is designated to 'remind' the other: she acts as corroborator. Although there are two women, they each function differently.

The question that comes to mind is why a woman is supposed to forget as opposed to a man. Some interpreters explained the fact that women are more prone to error than men because of their 'nature'. Fakher al-Din Al-Razi (d.1210) (cited in Fadel, 1997) explained that the woman's different biological nature made women more prone to forget than a man. The 20th century writer, Qutab (cited in Fadel, 1997)[2] argues that it is the woman's psychology – especially her motherly instincts – that prevents her from possessing the objectivity necessary for a witness. Abduh (cited in Fadel, 1997) was the first reformer who denied that the requirement of two female witnesses was based on the different natures of men and women. He argued instead that both men and women have the same capacity for remembering and forgetting and the sole difference being that the different economic roles of men and women in society made each vulnerable to forgetting those things which were not part of his or her daily experience. Thus a woman was more prone than a man to make a mistake regarding a commercial transaction, she would be more likely to be correct concerning a household matter. The position of writers such as Qutb, suggesting inherent weakness in women, conflicts with the Koranic concept of human creation: 'we have indeed created man in the best of moulds' (95:4). Yusuf Ali (1989) uses words such as nature, symmetry, and constitution simultaneously with the word 'mould'. He argues that there is 'no fault in Allah's creation'.

Wadud (1989), like Zein Ed-Din, says that this verse is concerned with particular circumstances. First, in 7th century Arab society commercial transactions were considered the domain of men, and women had little or no experience and so were less equipped for testimony in comparison to men in commercial transactions. Second, women could be coerced in that society; if one witness was female she would be easy prey for some male who wanted to force her to disclaim her testimony. Women's lack of involvement in financial matters and the practice of coercing women seem to be the probable reasons. Fazlur Rahman (1982) argues that since the lesser value of woman's testimony was dependent on her weak memory [due to lack of experience] in financial matters, when women become conversant with such matters, their evidence can equal that of men. In today's circumstances where men and women in many Muslim societies are better educated and have access to information directly and indirectly, their evidence should have equal weight.

---

[2] Most of the authorities cited in Fadel and Stowassar are in Arabic so the translations of these authors are used.

2.6.2 *HADD* CASES

It is also unwarranted to interpret the Koran in a way that makes women's testimony inadmissible in *hadd* cases. The Koran does not bar a woman's testimony in *hadd* cases. Rather it furnishes examples of sexual offences where the evidence of men and women are given equal weight. The two Koranic illustrations given below are related to *lian* and the incident of Yousaf's alleged seduction of a woman called Zulakha.

Lian is a Koranic procedure, which is resorted to in the absence of any other evidence for dissolving marriage when a husband launches charges of unfaithfulness against his wife. The Koran says:

> And for those who launch a charge against their spouses, and have (in support) no evidence but their own – their solitary evidence (can be received) if they bear witness four times (with an oath) by Allah that they were solemnly telling the truth (24:6).
>
> And the fifth oath (should be) that they solemnly invoke the curse of Allah on themselves if they tell a lie (24:7).
>
> But it would avert the punishment from the wife if she bear witness four times (with an oath) by Allah that (her husband) is telling a lie (24:8).
>
> And the fifth (oath) should be that she solemnly invokes the wrath of Allah on herself if (her accuser) is telling the truth (24:9).

The subject of this verse is unfaithfulness on the part of a wife that clearly falls in the category of *hadd*. But the verse explicitly states that solitary evidence of each spouse is acceptable. Testimonies of both spouses carry equal weight in the process of *lian*. 'The four oaths of the man are frustrated by the four oaths of the wife. Thus the testimony of a woman is not unequal to that of man' (Hussain, 1987:282).

The second example is the incident of the Prophet Yousaf wherein he was accused of seducing Zulakha, the wife of the king in whose kingdom Yousaf was staying. She accused Yousaf of seducing her and asked her husband to punish him severely. Yousaf refuted the charge and the king chose, giving equal weight to the testimony of both sides, to settle the case on the basis of circumstantial evidence. It was decided if the shirt of Yousaf is torn from the front, he is guilty and if the shirt is torn from the back Zulakha would be guilty. The shirt was found torn from the back and Yousaf was absolved from the allegation (Koran, 12:25-29). This example demonstrates that the testimony of a man and a woman was given equal weight and the case was decided on the basis of circumstantial evidence. If the Koran considered testimony of a woman to be of lesser value, it would have said so clearly and this case would have been decided differently.

These are two notable examples from the Koran dealing with *hadd* cases where the question of gender never arose. Justice Hussian (1987:289) has analysed seven Koranic verses (5:106, 65:2, 4:15, 4:6, 24:4, 24:6-9, 2:282) related to evidence and concluded that 'the theory that women are weak in memory is proved erroneous by the Koran which does not make any distinction in matters of evidence between man and woman'. Out of these seven verses, however, one verse does mention the gender 'call to witness two just men among you' (65:2) but Hussain (1987:280) argues that 'there is nothing to suggest that the principle of interpretation that the male includes female is not applicable to the word *minkum* (from among you)'. Rafi Ullah Shahab (1984) argues that almost all the Koranic injunctions are addressed to men but these injunctions equally apply to women. For example, the verse dealing with fasting is addressed to men only. It cannot be argued that women are exempted from fasting as they have not been addressed in this verse. If such arguments were ever accepted, then the Muslim women would stand exempted from almost all Islamic injunctions.

The historical and contextual interpretation of these verses is in congruity with the overall aim of the Koran: to establish a just society where human beings are equal. The Koran (4:135) said:

> O ye who believe! Stand out firmly for justice, as witnesses to Allah, even as against yourselves, or your parents, or your kin, and whether it be (against) rich or poor.

The Koran (2:42) adds: 'cover not truth with falsehood, nor conceal the Truth when ye know (what it is)'. The concern of the Koran is to find out the truth in order to prevent injustice and that could be done either by the evidence of a man or a woman or by circumstantial evidence as demonstrated in the case of Yousaf. The Koran also says everyone is responsible for what he/she does. So if a woman knows the truth, e.g. witnessing a rape incident, and does not reveal/report it or is prevented from doing so, it is a breach of the Koranic command.

2.7 ARE 'MEN A DEGREE ABOVE WOMEN'?

A belief exists among some Muslims that women are 'inferior intellectually and physically' as compared to men. This emanates from the 'out of context' and patriarchal interpretation of the following Koranic verse:

> Men are the [*qawwamun*] protectors and maintainers of women, because Allah has given the one more (strength) than the other, and because they support them from their means ... '(4:34).

This verse as a whole and more specifically the word '*qawwamun*' is interpreted differently. Some scholars translate '*qawwamun*' as 'ruler' and 'in charge' while others translate it as 'protector' and 'maintainer' as in the above citation. Baydawi (cited in Stowassar, 1998:33) compares men's 'guardianship of' or 'superiority over' women to that of 'ruler over subjects'. Tabri (cited in Stowassar, 1998:33) says that the verse is primarily concerned with the:

> Domestic relations between husband and wife legislating men's authority over their women ... The system is deemed equitable in that it sets out men's obligation to pay the dower for women, spend their wealth on them, and provide for them. Female obedience consists of marital fidelity, friendly behaviour towards the husband and his family, and good household management ...

Stowasser (1994:38) has succinctly summed up the theses of the conservative scholars:

> The equity of this system lies in the fact that God both favoured the man with the necessary qualities and skills for the 'guardianship' and also charged him with the duty to provide for the structure's upkeep. In any human organisation, power and organisation belong to the most qualified candidate – how much more so here. Both men and women are God's creatures, and neither is to be oppressed. However, each was fashioned for a special task – the woman to bear and raise the children and the man to provide for her necessities and protection – so that she devote herself to her important task without worry about 'work' or her safety and that of her child.

The view of those scholars who understand the verse in its proper context and follow a holistic view of the Koran regarding women's rights is different. Ali (1989:195) translates '*qawwamun*' as:

> One who stands firm in another's business, protect his interests, and looks after his affairs; or it may be, standing firm in his own business, managing affairs, with steady purpose.

Abduh (cited in Stowassar, 1998) argues that the husband's '*qiwama*' over his wife consists not in acts of tyranny but of guidance towards righteous behaviour, education, domestic efficiency, houseboundness, and fiscal responsibility to his budgetary guidelines. Then the woman can keep her house in safety, order and bear and raise the children. Al-Hibri (1982:217) believes that the basic notion involved here is one of 'moral guidance and caring'. God has not 'preferred' men over women. Wives can even surpass their husbands in knowledge, work, bodily strength, and earning power. The verse addresses the biological and social functions of the sexes in the family as a whole. Engineer (1996:45) holds a similar view:

> When the Quran gives man a slight edge over woman it clarifies that it is not due to any inherent weakness of the female sex, but to the social context ... it is due to the social functions that were then performed by the two sexes. Since man earns and spends his wealth on women, he by virtue of this fact, acquires functional superiority over women.

Parveen Shaukat Ali (1975:17) asserts that: 'the correct explanation of the verse is that men are the sustainers and supporters of women in an economic sense'.

Al-Hibri (1982) contends that there are two conditions for being '*qawwamun*'. First, that a man is someone whom God gave more in the matter at hand than woman, and second, that he be her provider. If either of the conditions fails, then the man is not '*qawwamun*'. If both obtain, then all that entitles him to is caring for her and providing her with moral guidance. Riffat Hassan (1988) argues that '*qawwamun*' is a reciprocal form of a word, which is generally translated as lord, master, ruler, governor, and manager. Once you make the man the ruler obviously you make the woman the ruled. You have established a hierarchical relationship. In fact this word doesn't mean ruler at all. It means 'breadwinner' and it is an economic term. If we translate that word as breadwinner the interpretation of the entire verse changes. It is talking about the division of functions that, while women have the primary responsibility of being childbearers, during that time when they are undergoing the process of childbearing they should not have the obligation of being breadwinners, and therefore men should be breadwinners during this period. This verse is addressed to the Islamic community in general, not to the husbands. Ismail Ragi al-Faruqi (cited in Stowassar, 1994) states that in the twentieth century socio-economic conditions women are no longer dependent on their husbands and the husband's economic superiority is subject to change. Al-Hibri (1982) stresses the point that nowhere in the said passage is a reference made to man's physical or intellectual superiority. Men are '*qawwamun*' in matters where God gave '*some*' of the men more than '*some*' of the women, and in what the men spend of their money, then clearly *men as class* are not '*qawwamun*' over *women as class*. Wadud (1999) has looked at the verse from the grammatical perspective. She states that the verse cannot be read in that way. It does not say:

> They (masculine plural) are preferred over them (feminine plural). All men do not excel all women in all manners. Some men excel over some women in some manner and vice versa (Wadud, 1999:71).

To interpret this verse that men are in charge of women conflicts with what the Koran (9:71) said elsewhere: 'the believers, men and women, are "*awliya*" of one another'. The Arabic word '*awliya*' has different meanings: 'protectors', 'in charge' and 'guides'. It is quite similar to '*qawwamun*'. How can a woman be '*awliya*' of a man if men are physically and intellectually superior and in charge of women? The interpretation that men are in charge of women is a misinterpretation because it conflicts with the Koran and the Koran itself is free from contradictions:

> Do they not consider the Qur'an (with care)? Had it been from other Than Allah, they would surely have found therein much discrepancy (4:82).

2.8 CONCLUSION

The Koran has given women equal rights in all spheres of life. Nonetheless, some verses of the Koran have been interpreted out of their proper Koranic and social contexts. Many Islamic statutory laws of Muslim states are based on this type of interpretation and are expressly discriminatory towards women. When these verses are interpreted in their proper Koranic and social contexts, the conclusion is that the Koran never discriminates on the basis of gender. It is the interpretation of the Koran, reflecting the masculine and patriarchal prejudices of the interpreters, that is discriminatory. Shakespeare (1983: 1.2.135) said: 'The fault ... is not in our stars, But in ourselves ...'. The fault lies in the interpreters of the Koran, not in the Koran. How Islamic law evolved over the ages and whether there is room for reform is discussed in the following chapter.

REFERENCES

Abdul Majid (2004) *All Pakistan Legal Decisions* 2004 Federal Shariat Court 1.

Al-Hibri, A. (1982) 'A Study of Islamic Herstory: or How did We Ever Get into this Mess' In: Al-Hibri (eds.) *Women and Islam*. Oxford: Pergamon Press.

Ali, P. S. (1975) *Status of Women in the Muslim World*. Lahore: Aziz Publishers.

Ali, Y. (1989) *The Meaning of the Holy Qur'an*. Maryland: Amana Corporation.

Alshech, E. (2004) 'Do Not Enter Houses Other Than Your Own': the Evolution of the Notion of a Private Domestic Sphere in Early Sunni Islamic Thought' *Islamic Law and Society*. 11 (3) p.291-332.

Balchin (eds.) (1994) *A Handbook on Family Law in Pakistan*. Lahore: Shirkat Gah.

Chaudhry, Z. (1997) 'The Myth of Misogyny: A Reanalysis of Women's Inheritance in Islamic Law' *Albany Law Review*. 61 pp. 511-555.

El-Nimr, R. (1997) 'Women in Islamic Law' In: Yamani (eds.) *Feminism and Islam: Legal and Literary Perspectives*. University of London: Ittaca Press.

Engineer, A. A. (1996) *The Rights of Women in Islam*. Islamabad: Vanguard Books Limited.

Fadel, M. (1997) 'Two Women, One Man: Knowledge, Power, and Gender in Medieval Sunni Legal Thought' *International Journal of Middle East Studies*. 29 (2) pp.185-204.

Hassan, R. (1988) *Feminist Theology and Women in the Muslim World*. Interviewed by Mistead, B. 1988. Available at 'Women Living Under Muslim Laws' (Dossier 4, 1988): http://www.wluml.org/english/pubsfulltxt.shtml?cmd[87]=i-87-2595. [Accessed Feb. 2005].

Hassan, R. (2003) Members, One of Another: Gender Equality and Justice in Islam. Available at http://www.religiousconsultation.org/hassan.htm. [Accessed in Nov. 2003].

Hazoor Bakhash (1981) *All Pakistan Legal Decisions* 1981 Federal Shariat Court 145.

Hussian, A. (1987) *Status of Women in Islam*. Lahore: Law Publisher Company.

Ishaque, K. (1974) 'Human Rights in Islamic Law' *Review of the International Commission of Jurists*. 12 pp.30-39.

Khan, H. (1980) *Islamic Law of Inheritance: A Comparative Study with Emphasis on Contemporary Problem*. Lahore: Pakistan Times Law Publication.

Maududi, S. A. (1987) *Tafeheem-ul-Quran*. 6th ed. Lahore: Adara Turjuman-nul-Quran.

Mernissi, F. (1985) *Beyond the Veil: Male-Female Dynamics in the Modern Muslim Society*. Indiana University Press.

Mutahhery, M. (1982) *Women and Her Rights*. Karachi: Islamic Seminary.

Qutb, M. (1964) *Islam the Misunderstood Religion*. Kuwait: Darul Bayan Bookshop.

Rahim, A. (1911) *Muhammadan Jurisprudence*. Lahore: PLD Publishers.

Riaz Ullah Khan (2004) *Supreme Court Monthly Review* 1701.

Shakespeare, W. (1983) *Julius Caesar*. Penguin Classics.

Stowasser, B. (1994) *Women in the Quran, Traditions and Interpretation*. Oxford University Press.

Stowasser, B. (1998) 'Gender Issues and Contemporary Quran Interpretation' In: Haddad (eds.) *Islam, Gender and Social Change*. Oxford University Press.

Wadud, A. (1999) *Quran and Woman: Rereading the Sacred Text from the Woman Perspective*. New York: Oxford University Press.

Zein En-Din, N. (1982) 'Removing the Veil and Veiling' In: Al-Hibri (eds.) *Women's Studies International Forum*. Pergamon Press.

CHAPTER 3

The Evolution of Islamic Law and Ijtihad

There is a strong belief among orthodox Muslims and some ill-informed and misinformed non-Muslims that Islamic law is a monolithic whole and immutable. They believe it cannot be changed and it is its followers who have to conform to the rules of Islamic law. This chapter attempts to show how the myth of the immutability of Islamic law can be dismantled. It is argued that Islamic law consists of various schools and sources, both divine and human, and that foreign/un-Islamic elements have influenced the evolution of Islamic law over the centuries. The argument of conservative Islamic scholars that Islamic law has achieved finality and the process of *ijtihad* (individual independent reasoning) has come to an end is challenged and it is demonstrated that *ijtihad* is a continuous process and courts in Muslim states, for instance the Federal Shariat Court of Pakistan, are competent to be engaged in the process of *ijtihad* known as 'judicial *ijtihad*'. The treatment of the private domain by Islamic law is analysed in order to find out whether and how it protects or undermines women's rights.

The followers of Islam are divided into two groups: Sunnis and Shias, and so are their laws. The Sunni, the majority school, is further divided into four sub-schools (also called *mudhabs*): Hanafi, Maliki, Shafii and Hambali. The Shai sect is divided into Ithna Ashari (Twelvers) and the Ismaili (Seveners) (Fyzee, 1955). The political conceptions of Sunnis and Shias differ widely but the criminal laws and laws of personal status vary only in their details. The four sub-schools of the Sunnite doctrine have disagreements but share a common vision of law, its sources and the methods of its elaboration (Weiss, 1998). In the same fashion, Shia sub-schools differ in details from each other but are in agreement on the general rules among themselves and share a consensus with other Sunni schools (Schacht, 1955). However, despite their differences, all the schools and sources of Islamic law are considered valid and Muslims are free to follow whichever school they want. The Koran (39:55) said: 'and follow the best of (the courses) revealed to you from your Lord ...'

3.1 THE SOURCES OF ISLAMIC LAW

There are four major sources of Islamic law: the Koran, the *Sunnah* (the model behaviour of the Prophet Muhammad), *ijma* (consensus of opinion) and *qiyas* (analogical deduction) (Esposito and DeLong-Bas, 2001).[1] Hashim Kamali (2000) has divided these sources into two types: revealed and non-revealed. The revealed sources are the Koran and the *Sunnah* forming the *nass* (nucleus/core) of the *Sharia* whereas *qiyas* and *ijma* are the non-revealed sources and are employed to derive law from the *nass* (plural, *nusus*) through the use of human reason and endeavour called *ijtihad*. 'Literally *nass* means "something clear" but technically it signifies a clear injunction which is textually evidenced with regard to a certain point in the Quran and or *hadith* [recorded sayings of the Prophet]' (Hassan, 1970:122). The specific rules of the Koran and the *Sunnah*, which are relatively small in number, are collectively known as *nusus* (Kamali, 2000:108; Weiss, 1998:200). It is from the *nass* that the law is to be derived.

3.1.1 The Koran

The word Koran means 'recitation' and Muslims consider it 'the word of God' (Rahman, 1966:30). The Koran (26:192) said 'verily this is a Revelation from the Lord of the Worlds' and 'this Qur'an is not such as can be produced by other than Allah ...' (10:37). It was revealed to the Prophet Muhammad through the angel Gabriel. The words of the Koran (God) are eternal and ' ... none can change His words ... ' (18:27). It is regarded as the final authority in terms of law and other issues. It is the constitution of the state and of society, the categorical imperative of personal ethic and the sublime expression of the *summum bonum* of the highest aspiration (Al-Faruqi, 1962). The Koran is 'primarily a book of religious and moral principles and exhortation, and is not a legal document. But it does embody some important legal enunciations ...' (Rahman, 1966:37) and 'also contains general injunctions, which have formed the basis of important juristic inferences' (Rahim, 1911:71). Kamali (2000:119) claims that 'less than three percent of the text deals with

[1] There are other sources called minor sources as well but disagreement exists among the jurists whether or not they should be considered as independent sources. They are: *Istihsan* (juristic preference), *istislah* (human welfare) and *maslaha* (public interest). See, *All Pakistan Legal Decisions* 2000 Federal Shariat Court 1. These minor sources are all considered as forms of *ijtihad*.

legal matters' whereas Fitzgerald (1955:120) says that 'there are 500 such texts'. Some of the earlier verses of the Koran were abrogated (repealed) and God revealed new ones (to the Prophet Muhammad) when new circumstances demanded (Kamali, 2000). Reuben Levy (1957:163) argues that the 'reason for [this] is that laws are formulated and verses revealed as they are required, to suit the good of mankind'.

3.1.2 The Sunnah *(Model Behaviour of the Prophet)*

The scholars of Islamic law unanimously believe that the *Sunnah* of the Prophet Muhammad is the second source of Islamic law. They are the rulings of the Prophet on what is lawful and unlawful and stand on an equal footing with the Koran (Kamali, 2000). The Koran (53:3) says that the words of the Prophet are divinely inspired, 'nor does he [the Prophet] say (aught) of (his own) Desire', and obedience to them is considered obedience to God, 'he who obeys the Messenger, obeys Allah' (Koran, 4:80). The *Sunnah* either corroborates the Koran or clarifies its ambiguous parts by qualifying and specifying its general rulings. The *Sunnah* may also consist of rulings on which the Koran is silent in which case it becomes an independent source known as the 'founding Sunnah' (Kamali, 2000). Fitzgerald (1955:93; see Schacht, 1950) maintains the fact that 'there has been wholesale fabrication of traditions [*hadiths*] is universally admitted by Muslim and Western scholars alike'. The *Sunnah* of the Prophet was recorded two centuries after his death. There are many sayings attributed to the Prophet and therefore authentic *Sunnah* must be sifted from the unauthentic.

3.1.3 Ijma *(Consensus of Opinion)*

Ijma is defined as an agreement of the jurists among the followers of Muhammad in a particular age on a question of law (Rahim, 1911) when a solution to an issue was not provided either in the Koran or the *Sunnah*. *Ijma* is of two kinds: consensus of the whole community and consensus of the jurists. The authority of *ijma* as a source of law is based on the Koran, and notably the Prophetic sayings: 'whatever the Muslims hold to be good is good before God', and 'my followers will never agree upon what is wrong', and the practice of the Companions of the Prophet Muhammad (Rahim, 1911:115-16). The Shia outlook is different in that the *imam* (ruler) must approve the consensus of opinion (Kamali, 2000). 'According to the accepted opinion of all four Sunni Schools, *ijma* is not confined to any particular age or country' (Kamali, 2000:122) and the learned people of any age can agree on a point of law. The *ijma* of one generation does not bind future generations. Esposito and DeLong-Bas (2001) argue that *ijma* contributed significantly to the corpus of law. If questions arose about a Qura'nic text or tradition, or a problem for which no *Sunnah* existed, the jurists applied their own reasoning (*ijtihad*) to arrive at an interpretation.

3.1.4 QIYAS *(ANALOGY)*

The root meaning of *qiyas* is 'measuring', 'accord', and 'equality'. As a source of law, *qiyas* is the process of deduction by which the law of a text is applied to cases which, though not covered by the language of the text, are governed by its reason (Esposito and DeLong-Bas, 2001). It is a source of 'less authority' as compared to the former three authorities but may be older than *ijma* (Fitzgerald, 1955). Rahman (1966) argues that it was present in its rudimentary form from the very beginning. However, generally it is associated with the name of Abu Hanifa, the founder of the Hanafi School (Levy, 1957). His method was not to look for verbal resemblance between the Koran and what he wanted to evolve; rather he penetrated behind the wording of the text to find the *illa* (cause) or motive and in any new application there must be the same *illa* or motive. For instance, an analogy was established between the loss of virginity following marriage and the Qura'nic penalty for theft, the amputation of the hand. The sum of the minimum dower given to a bride in Kufa and in Medina was equivalent to the established values of stolen goods (Coulson, 1964).

3.2 FOREIGN ELEMENTS IN ISLAMIC LAW

'At first sight it might seem surprising that one should look for foreign influences in a legal system that unmistakably bears the stamp of uniqueness' but the fact is that 'many prominent features of Islamic civilisation, notwithstanding a deceptive Arab appearance, turn out to be borrowings [*inter alia*] from the Hellenistic and Iranian world ...' (Schacht, 1950:10). 'These foreign elements have been so thoroughly assimilated and Islamised that, taken in their ordinary Islamic setting, they hardly seem to reveal a trace of their foreign origin' (Schacht, 1950:10). 'Muhammad's thought was always occupied ... with the immediate condition of his moment and 'the institutions he had created could in no sense provide for the vastly enlarged circumstances that triumphant Islam was very soon to face' (Schacht, 1950:10). 'In the conquered provinces and at home, every day fresh circumstances required regulation' (Schacht, 1950:10) and Muslim jurists/rulers laid their hands on any law, custom or legal notion that did not conflict with Islam and could serve the community. Goldziher (1981:33) maintains that 'in Islam legal development commensurate with public need began immediately after the Prophet's death'.

> The evidence allows us to say that on the whole the religious leaders of Islam ... did not always stubbornly ignore changing needs and new circumstances that arose with the passage of time (Goldziher, 1981:233).

The point here is not to probe the processes of how these elements entered into the Islamic legal system; rather it is to illustrate that Islamic law did borrow elements directly as well as indirectly from other legal systems and assimilated local institutions and customs when needed.

> There are four legal schools whose influence on nascent Muhammadan law and jurisprudence is at least possible: Persian Sassanian law, Roman Byzantine (including Roman provincial) law, the canon law of the Eastern Churches and Talmudic law (Goldziher, 1981:10).

Schacht (1950:14) argues that the influences of Talmudic law are frequently pointed out and are easy to account for. One such instance is '*[q]iyas*, which is the technical term for analogy, systematic reasoning, must for linguistic reasons have been borrowed from Rabbinic *heqqesh* ...'. Libson (1997:135) also holds that '*qiyas* is similar to Jewish methods of halakhic exegesis'.

Regarding Roman law influence, Libson (1997:135) says that 'a number of parallels have been established which are too numerous and too striking to be coincidences'. The parallels between Roman and Islamic law are not confined to rules and institutions of positive law only; they can be found in the legal concepts and principles and fundamental ideas of legal science (Schacht, 1950:11). 'Outstanding examples are the treatment of tolerated religions, the methods of taxation, and the institutions of emphyteusis and of pious endowment' (Schacht, 1955:35). Goldziher (1981) has also pointed out the resemblance between the rite attached to the name of Malik ibn Anas (the founder of Maliki School) *maslaha* (public good) and Roman *utilitas publica* (that which is required for the benefit of the community). Fitzgerald (1951:97) has, however, challenged this view:

> '*Utilitas publica*' was never an avowed principle in the development of Roman law; its first appearance as the name of a principle ... is among the schoolmen of middle ages. But it was a prominent principle of Jewish law, e.g. Mishna, Gittin 4 and 5.4, in which the words 'as a precaution for the general good' occur no less than twelve times.

Similarly Goldziher (1981) likens the Muslim doctrine of *ijma* to that of the Christian church. Fitzgerald (1951), challenging it, argues that likeness does not mean dependence on Roman law. Agreement of the learned was never the formal source of Roman law since Diocletian; however, it was the regular source of rabbinical law, and the phrase 'all our Rabbis hold' was common in the Talmud. Gamal Moursi Badr (1978) also holds the view that Roman and Talmudic law have no influence on Islamic law. He said no good case is made of borrowing from Roman law. Some of the parallels are no more than coincidences and similar treatment of identical problems. Agreeing with Goldziher on the Jewish borrowings, however, Fitzgerald (1951) holds that the descendants of those Greek philosophers who had been exiled by Justinian from Athens and found a refuge in the Sassanian Empire have also informed Islamic law. For example, the word *fasid* in terms of 'essence' and 'accident' is reminiscent of Aristotelian logic, though the idea involved is purely Islamic in origin. He also seems to believe that the word '*qanun*' which means administrative regulation (or sometimes custom) rather than law might be borrowed from Latin or Greek (Fitzgerald, 1951). He also supports the view of Goldziher and Schacht that very little is known of Sassanian influence on Islamic law.

> It has been suggested that the office of Chief Qadi [chief justice] ... is of Persian origin and the translation, into an Islamic context, of the Zoroastrain *Mobedan Mobed*. Its introduction by the early Abbasids certainly coincides with the official adoption of many features of Sassanian administration ... '(Schacht, 1950:10).

3.3 CUSTOM AS SOURCE OF ISLAMIC LAW

The status of custom as a source of law is disputed. Lisbon (1997) argues that the role of custom in law-making is impossible because law in Islam is a superhuman system. However, 'whatever little authentic evidence is available shows that the ancient Arab system of arbitration, and Arab customary law in general, continued under the first successors of the

Prophet …' (Rahman, 1966:V). The early lawyers of Islam, at the beginning of the second century of the *Hegra* [the date when the Prophet Muhammad migrated from Mecca to Medina wherefrom the Islamic calendar begins], took the popular and administrative practices of their time as their raw material and endorsed, modified or rejected them, thereby creating Muhammadan law (Schacht, 1955:13). Modern Muslim scholars treat custom as a fully-fledged source of law, an approach that was rejected in the classical period (Schacht, 1955:13). Coulson (1964:143,155) argues that 'custom *per se* had no binding force in Islamic legal theory' but 'operated as a principle of subsidiary value'. However, he concedes that 'on none but the highest theoretical plane can it be defined that custom is an important source of law in the world of Islam'. Abdulaziz Sachedina (1999:22) holds that 'the role of custom and usage (*urf*) in the formulation of legal principles of every type is acknowledged by all Muslim jurists'. Rahim (1911:136), citing *Hedaya* (Hamilton, 1989), holds that 'custom holds the same rank as Ijma' and is 'the arbiter of analogy'.

3.4 THE PUBLIC/PRIVATE DICHOTOMY IN ISLAMIC LAW

As this study is focused on women's rights in all spheres, the picture would be incomplete if the reach of Islamic law into the private domain is not analysed. 'The public/private divide as drawn by modern liberalism affects everything from how power is attained and exercised to how women are treated' (Cole, 2003:771). Legal feminists consider the private sphere as a place where women live out their lives and assert that it is in this area where most of women's rights violations take place. The argument of the feminists is equally applicable to the Islamic tradition particularly where the private sphere is assumed to belong to women and social and cultural mores do not allow law to interfere with what happens in the private domain: keeping it out of the business of law.

Mohsen Kadivar (2003:660-61) argues that 'the terms "private" and "public" are not rooted in the heart of Islamic doctrine. The two terms occur neither in the Qur'an nor in the traditions conveyed from the Prophet and the *Imams* but 'the basic distinction between that which is private and that which is not can be visibly discerned in the fields of Islamic ethics, law, and jurisprudence'. Kadivar first explores the general meaning of 'private' and 'public' and then attempts to find out the equivalent notions in the Islamic tradition. The three distinct but related meanings of 'private' are: 'first, that which is personal or exclusive to the individual; second, that which one would rather keep concealed and protected from others; third, that over which the individual should exercise exclusive authority and control' (Kadivar, 2003:661). In contrast, in the 'public' sphere, nothing is kept secret from or rendered by the citizens: management, improvement, and alteration of the public sphere are the prerogative of the citizenry. The public domain is the sphere of influence for governmental authority. This domain is jointly owned by all citizens and is transparent; it is in everyone's plain view (unless some defence and security issues are not made public) (Kadivar, 2003). An-Nai'm (1996) argues that although early jurists of Islamic jurisprudence do not make a distinction between public and private, the *Sharia* regulates both spheres. He considers constitutional order, criminal justice, international relations, and human rights to be matters in the public domain whereas matters related to religious practices, private and personal law falls within the private sphere. However, the distinction is not absolute, as some overlapping exists between the two spheres. Family matters and inheritance law have clear public law implications.

Islamic jurisprudence, in accordance with the two criteria given above, fully acknowledges the sanctity of the private domain. God admonishes the faithful to refrain from suspicion and scepticism of others, and to refrain from prying into the personal affairs of others: 'O ye who believe! Avoid suspicion as much (as possible): for suspicion in some cases is a sin: And spy not on each other behind their backs …' (Koran, 49:12). The Koran (24:19) not only admonishes against prying into each other's personal spheres, but also forbids dissemination of such information: 'Those who love (to see) scandal published broadcast among the believers will have a grievous Penalty in this life and in the Hereafter …'. The clear implication of these two verses is the full religious guarantee of the individual's sphere of privacy.

> The individual, in his or her private space-which we call home-is on his own, and away from the public eye. There, he or she would be free to act, even though it may be a sin. There is only one condition to this freedom, which is that it cannot harm anyone else (Kadivar, 2003:669).

The condition of not harming anyone in the private domain is important for women as many rights of women are breached in the sphere of 'family and home'. Thus, in Islam the private sphere is not immune from law. If someone is harmed, for example if spousal violence takes place behind closed doors, the hands of law will reach there.

3.4.1 The Private Sphere and Ordering Good and Preventing Evil

Despite the strong protection of individual privacy available under Islamic law, the privacy of the individual (women in particular) is invaded under another principle of Islamic law: 'ordering good and forbidding evil'. According to this principle, it is incumbent upon the ruler of an Islamic country as well as every Muslim to 'order good and forbid evil'; it is a command that covers every individual, party, or government (ruler, sovereign, etc) (Kadivar, 2003). Ibn Khaldun (1398) holds that the inspection authority is among the institutions of Islamic government that actively enforce the principle of 'commending good and forbidding evil' in society. The inspection authority, known as *muhtasib* (administrator/market inspector etc), encompasses the entire public sphere, including transactions in the field of trade and commerce, and also extends to the realm of religious rituals. He recognizes not only individuals' rights toward one another and those between the people and the divine, but the observance of religious duties in the public domain is also required. He also does not permit any repugnance to persist in the public sphere, and sees that every commandment is followed and fulfilled (Kadivar, 2003). Two instances will suffice here to show how this principle is subverted by fundamentalist regimes to the detriment of women.

Mehrangiz Kar (2003) alleges that the Islamic regime of Iran constantly violates the private domain of the Iranian citizen through religious and legal means, especially through the religious obligation of enjoining good and forbidding the evil. 'The imperative of enjoining the good and forbidding the evil is used to control women's hejab, gatherings, associations, parties, weddings, dating, and the consumption of alcoholic beverages' (Kar, 2003:832). Kar (2003:835) concludes that 'women's private lives, their preferences, their personal beliefs, and their convictions are invaded and violated by government agencies more than those of men ...'. Frank Vogel (2003) has made an analysis of the activities of the government of Saudi Arabia reflecting how it abuses the principle of 'ordering good and forbidding evil' to stamp on political dissidents and control women's movement and morality. The activities of the government department called 'General Presidency for Committee of Ordering the Good and Forbidding the Evil' include policing attendance at prayers, enforcing closure of shops at prayer time, assuring that women are properly veiled in public and preventing undue mixing of men and women. Women are banned from driving on the logic that it would give them freedom of movement, which may lead to engaging in immoral behaviour. The practices of the Saudi government, invading the privacy of individuals, is nothing but to continue their political grip over people in general and by keeping women out of public domain simply to perpetuate the patriarchal norms of gender relations.

The discussion above reflects that in Islam the concepts of public and private do exist. The Koran imposes strict restrictions on the invasion of the private sphere from both government and non-government agents unless it is to pre-empt irreparable damage, i.e. domestic violence against women. However, in Muslim states the governments tend to invade and control the private domain through the principle of 'ordering good and forbidding evil' which is a double-edged sword. It can be used for the protection of individuals in cases such as preventing murder or violence against women behind closed doors but repressive regimes can abuse it by intruding into the private lives of political dissidents and use it as tool for subordinating women. The practices of Saudi Arabia and Iran demonstrate that principle of 'ordering good and forbidding evil' is used for twin purposes. First, to invade the private sphere of individuals to control political dissidents and second, to perpetuate the subordination of women in society confining them to their homes. The ultimate goal is the continuation of oppressive regimes and the patriarchal notions of gender relations.

3.5 *IJTIHAD* AS A VEHICLE OF DEVELOPMENT OF ISLAMIC LAW

The discussion of *ijtihad* focuses on its meanings, in which areas *ijithad* is possible, was the gate of *ijtihad* ever closed, and who are qualified to be a *mujtahid* (a jurist who is involved in *ijtihad*) in a Muslim state. The role of *ijtihad* in the evolution of Islamic law is beyond dispute. The need for *ijtihad* emerged when the Prophet Muhammad passed away and the process of revelation, to address new issues, came to an end. It became the responsibility of the Muslim community to make laws within the framework of Islam to meet the exigencies of new circumstances and more importantly when Islam was expanded to other lands and came in touch with new cultures. To derive new laws from *nass* for a new issue, the community relied on the procedure of *ijtihad. Ijtihad* literally means striving, exerting and as a term of jurisprudence it means the application by a lawyer of all his faculties to the consideration of the authorities of law (the Koran and the *Sunnah*) with a view to finding out what in all probability is the law (Rahim, 1911).

> The theory of *ijtihad* presupposes that the process of producing rules is a process of elucidating that which is *present* but yet is not self-evident. In principle, a Muslim jurist never invents rules, he formulates ... rules which God has already decreed and which are concealed in the sources (Weiss, 1998:200).

In other words, *ijtihad* is the maximum effort expended by a jurist to master and apply the principles and rules of legal theory for the purpose of discovering God's law (Hallaq, 1984). This reasoning may take a variety of forms: analogical reasoning (*qiyas*), juristic preference (*istihsan*), consideration of public interests (*istislah*), and even general consensus (*ijma*) of the learned (Kamali, 2000).

3.5.1 Areas Where Ijtihad *is Possible*

The first question that comes to mind after *ijithad* is what are the areas where *ijitihad* is possible? *Ijtihad*, as later instances demonstrate, is possible in all areas of Islamic law except *nass* (the Koran and the *Sunnah*) but some decisions of Caliph Omer, given below, indicate that *ijtihad* is possible even in *nass* if it is according to the spirit of the Koran or the *Sunnah* (Usmani, 1999). Kamali (2000) argues that to say that *Sharia* is contained in the Koran and the *Sunnah,* however, would exclude the scholastic legacy of *fiqh* [*fiqh* is the product of human understanding that has sought to interpret and apply the divine law in space and time] and its vast literature from the *Sharia.* Weiss (1998:199) asserts that Islamic jurisprudence maintains clear distinction between law and its sources:

> This distinction assumes that the Holy Law ... is not self-evident from the sacred text. If it were, the sacred text would not be the sources of the law, but rather the law itself ... in fact, the sacred texts do not, as rule, "state" the law in strict legal sense ... they do, however, *contain* law.

The holy law is the totality of rules for man's behaviour; the rules themselves are 'branches' (*furu*) or 'fruit' (*thamara*), which grow out of 'roots' (*usul*), that is, from the sources. Only the roots are given, not the fruits or branches. They must be made to appear and for this human involvement is required (Weiss, 1998). The Koran (47:24) itself exhorts deep thinking and meditation over its verses: 'do they not then earnestly seek to understand the Qur'an, or are their hearts locked up by them?'

Ahmad Hassan (1970) has catalogued several practical cases from ancient times where resort to *ijtihad* was made. However, a few of them will suffice to illustrate the point here. Two cases of *ijtihad*, done by the great Caliph Omer, are very illustrative of the role human beings played in the evolution of Islamic law. Omer abolished a share of *zakat* (poor due), which used to be given to certain Muslims '... whose hearts have been (recently) reconciled (to Truth) ...' (Koran, 9:60). The Prophet used to give this share to certain chiefs of Arab tribes either to attract them to embrace Islam or prevent them doing harm to Muslims. Omer discontinued this practice arguing that the Prophet used to give this share to strengthen Islam and that now the conditions were changed [Islam was established and expanding to other regions], it was not required. Even if the Prophet were alive, he would have discontinued the practice, said Omer. The decision of Omer apparently seems to be contrary to the Koran and the *Sunnah* but he considered the prevailing conditions and followed the spirit of the Koran (Hassan, 1970). In another instance, Omer refused to distribute the lands of Iraq and Syria (after conquering them) among the Companions (those who had seen and lived during the time of the Prophet are called Companions) contrary to the practice of the Prophet. The Companions showed resentment but Omer argued that if the land were distributed among them how could he maintain the army to defend the borders of newly conquered towns. The Companions acquiesced in his decision. In this case too, Omer went against the Koranic injunctions (59:6-10) regarding distribution of war booty but he 'preferred the general benefit of the Muslims to that of the individuals' (Hassan, 1970:121). Hassan (1970) calls this a significant instance of early *Istihsan*, or departure from the established rule in the interest of equity and public welfare.

3.5.2 Is the 'Gate of Ijtihad*' Closed?*

After understanding the meaning of *ijtihad* and the areas where *ijtihad* is possible, the next question is whether we can do *ijtihad* today. According to the orthodox view, the door of *ijtihad* is closed whereas liberal and progressive scholars strongly believe that it is a continuous process and there is no evidence in Islamic scholarship suggesting that the process of *ijtihad* has ceased. Benjamin Jokisch (1997:119) explains the thinking about the closure of *ijithad* thus:

> In the Western accounts of Islamic law [as well as in some Muslims circles] ... the opinion that the so-called 'door of *ijtihad*' was closed in about the fourth [Islamic] century has predominated, and since that time, it is argued, the Sharia has been unable to take account of changes through times because it has lost its flexibility.

The Muslim apologists maintain that a point has been reached where all questions of law have been thoroughly discussed and settled and further deliberation is deemed unnecessary. After the third century of Islam, the jurists felt an overpowering reverence for the achievements of their predecessors, particularly the founders of the great schools, and were reluctant to claim the same level of competence as their predecessors. At this point the trend of *taqlid* (imitation of the founders of the schools) entered into the Islamic legal system and was 'congealed into a rigid and inflexible system that was regarded as being capable of meeting the needs of all future generations' (Weiss, 1998:208). It is described as an accident of history rather than a requirement of the theory (Weiss, 1998).

The liberal and progressive scholars argue strongly that *ijithad* is a continuous process and an essential part of the Koranic universal message that Islam is for all times and places. Muhammad Iqbal (1934:169) argues that:

> The closing of the door of [i]jtihad is pure fiction suggested partly by the crystallisation of legal thought in Islam, and partly by that intellectual laziness which, especially in the period of spiritual decay, turns great thinkers into idols. If some of the later doctors have upheld this fiction, modern Islam is not bound by this voluntary surrender of intellectual independence.

Iqbal further says that some scholars claim finality for the popular schools of Muhammadan law, though they never found it possible to deny the theoretical possibility of a complete *ijtihad*. 'Did the founders of our schools ever claim finality for their reasonings and interpretations? Never' (Iqbal, 1934:159). Rahim (1911) has put forward the same argument: if the age of *ijtihad* had come to an end with four *imams*, their disciples etc., one should have found mention of such an important doctrine in the books of *usul* (rules) dealing with the sources of law.

> There is no statement to be found anywhere by anyone about the desirability or the necessity of such closure, or of the fact of actually closing the

> gate, although one finds *judgments* by later writers that the "gate of Ijtihad has been closed" (Rahman, 1965:149).

Usmani (1999:118) contends that 'this is sheer propaganda [to say] that the door of *ijtihad* is closed. Nobody has ever closed it'. The Supreme Court of Pakistan (PLD 1967 Supreme Court 118) said that 'the learned Imams never claimed finality for their opinions, but due to various historical causes, their followers in subsequent ages invented the doctrine of *taqlid* [following great *imams*]'. Iqbal (1934) claims that the teaching of the Koran wherein life is a process of progressive creation necessitates that each generation, guided but unhampered by the work of its predecessors, should be allowed to solve their own problems.

Iqbal (1934) gives two examples of *ijtihad*. First, to belong to the tribe of the Prophet, Qureish was considered a precondition for becoming a Caliph. However, Qazi Abu Bakr Balqilani (cited in Iqbal, 1934) dropped this condition keeping in view the political situation, i.e. the political fall of the Qureish and their subsequent inability to rule. Ibn Khaldun (cited in Iqbal, 1934), who personally believed in the precondition of Qureishiyat, also argued that since the power of the Qureish was gone and there was no alternative but to accept the most powerful (politically) man as a Caliph. Second is the recent example of the Grand National Assembly of Turkey vesting power of a Caliph into a body of persons instead of a single person as enunciated by Sunnite doctrine. Turkey's *ijtihad* is according to the spirit of Islam and Iqbal believes that it is perfectly sound. Kamali (2000) has cited a recent example to show the continuation of the process of reinterpretation in Islamic law through *ijtihad*. Yusuf al-Qaradawi (cited in Kamali, 2000) has declared that it is valid for a woman to be unaccompanied by a male relative during air travel. He argued that the rule that a male relative should accompany a woman was formulated in pre-modern times with the aim of securing a woman's physical and moral safety and modern air travel fulfils this requirement. It suggests that '*ijtihad* is the ongoing process which yields the virtually inexhaustibly Law of God' (Weiss, 1998:209). Al-Afghani (cited in Badawi, 1976) argued for reforming Islamic law through *ijtihad* on the authority of the Koran (13:11): 'Allah does not change a people's lot unless they change what is in their hearts'. The observation of the Lahore High Court, Pakistan made in the case of *Rashida Begum* (PLD 1960 Lahore 1142), supports the view that *ijithad* is a continuous process:

> If the interpretation of the Holy Qur'an by the commentators who lived thirteen or twelve hundred years ago is considered as the last word on the subject, then the whole Islamic society will be shut up in an iron cage and not allowed to develop along with the time. It will then cease to be a universal religion and will remain a religion confined to the time and place when and where it was revealed.

3.5.3 Who Can Do Ijtihad *in a Muslim State?*

After investigating the fact that *ijtihad* is essential for the development of Islamic law and society and that its door has not been closed, the next question is who is capable of doing *ijtihad* in a Muslim state. In his discussion of the qualification of the *imam* (ruler), Baghdadi (d. 429/1037) considers the ability to practice *ijtihad* as one of the four conditions that an *imam* must satisfy in order to rule efficiently (cited in Hallaq, 1984).[2] The same condition is required by Mawardi (11th century), who explains that *ijtihad* must be one of an *imam's* skills because knowledge of law and of the means by which new problems can be solved are an essential part of his duties (cited in Hallaq, 1984). Juwayni (d. 478/1085) also deems the quality of *ijtihad* to be a prerequisite for the ideal *imam* and for the well-being of the community (cited in Hallaq, 1984). The *imam* is not the only individual who may practice *ijtihad* within the political institution; officials who are delegated authority by the head of state may also practice it. According to Mawardi, the entire body of state officials are divided into two categories: executive and delegative. The latter are authorised to use their own reasoning – based on the principles of *Sharia* – to tackle any problem that may arise while on government service (cited in Hallaq, 1984). Juwayni argues that where the *imam* does not fulfil the requirement of *ijtihad*, then he must consult the *ulema* (singular, *alim*: Islamic scholars). If the sovereign does not reach the degree of *ijtihad*, then the jurists are to be followed (cited in Hallaq, 1984). Ghazali contends that *ijtihad* is not a requirement for an *imam*. It is a pure legal requirement and is neither required by *Shar* (*Sharia*) nor public interest (*maslaha*). The purpose of the Islamic government is to comply with *Shar* and it makes no difference if the *imam* reaches a legal opinion through his interpretation, or through the interpretation of a *mujtahid* (jurist in-

---

[2] Hallaq has relied on the Arabic sources of Baghdadi and others and I am relying on his account of their Arabic works.

volved in *ijtihad)*. However, he adds that a *mujtahid* must be well qualified and extensively learned (cited in Hallaq, 1984).

In Pakistan, which is discussed in detail in the following chapter, all superior courts and the Federal Shariat Court specifically are empowered by the 1973 constitution (article 203D) to do *ijtihad*: to declare whether or not any law is in accordance with Islam. The constitutional requirement (article 203C (A3)) for a person to be a judge of Federal Shariat Court, *inter alia*, is one 'who is well-versed in Islamic law'. Since its inception in 1980, the Federal Shariat Court has engaged in what Kamali (2000) calls 'judicial *ijtihad*'. The case of *Hazoor Bakhash* (PLD 1980 FSC 145) is a celebrated example wherein stoning to death for adultery was declared extra-Koranic. The Supreme Court of Pakistan overturned the judgment but for different reasons (arguably political pressure), not that the Federal Shariat Court is not competent to do 'judicial *ijtihad*'. The Supreme Court of Pakistan itself was engaged in judicial *ijtihad* before the *Bakhash* case. In the case of *Khursid Bibi* (PLD 1967 SC 97), it validated a form of divorce, known as *khul,* that can take place at the initiative of a wife without the consent of her husband, whereas the legal position was that the right of a wife to separate through *khul* was dependent on the consent of a husband for the return of her dower. The Supreme Court (1967) also said that the subordinate courts are allowed to be engaged in judicial *ijithad*:

> The subordinate courts, the District Judges and the Judges of the High Courts in Pakistan, occupy a position akin to that of a Qazi [judge in Islamic state], since they could effect a divorce on any ground … under the Muslim Law.

In the case of *Abdul Majid* (PLD 2004 FSC 1), the Federal Shariat Court ruled that:

> Islamic Sharia empowers the authorities in power to make legislation for all matters which are not specifically covered by the Injunctions of Islam, as contained in the Holy Qur'an and Sunnah of the Holy Prophet.

The judiciary in Pakistan is a notable example that *ijtihad* is a continuous process but also that the judiciary is allowed and, in the case of Pakistan, is constitutionally empowered to do *ijtihad* in a Muslim nation state.

3.6 CONCLUSION

The foregoing account of the evolution of Islamic law exhibits two trends very clearly: its inherent dynamism and adaptation to new circumstances and its assimilation of external elements. The dynamic aspect of Islamic law is manifested in its revealed as well as non-revealed source. The Koran was revealed over a span of 22 years. The revelation was piecemeal and issue-oriented and some of the verses were revealed because they met the demands of the given time, and when new situations arose new verses were revealed to address them. The recognition of non-revealed sources, *ijma* and *qiyas*, as valid sources of Islamic law not only defies the myth of immutability of Islamic law but also reflects the role of human agency in the process of its evolution through *ijtihad*. There is no evidence to suggest that the door of *ijtihad* was ever closed even in the works of those *imams* who are blindly imitated. To argue that the door of *ijtihad* is closed is against the spirit of the Koran and its message of universality: the Koran is a book for all times to come and for all people. The need-based approach to make or amend rules is at the heart of the Koranic teachings. For instance, during the time of war the Koran (2:239) allowed soldiers to pray on the back of the horse in contrast to normal times. An ablution (washing certain parts of the body) is essential for prayer but again the Koran allowed prayer without it during travel (Koran, 4:43) and lack of availability of water.

The role of Islam in law-making in Pakistan, the Islamisation of its legal system and the application of Islamic laws and its impact on women's rights are discussed in part II.

REFERENCES

Abdul Majid (2004) *All Pakistan Legal Decisions* 2004 Federal Shariat Court 1.

Al-Faruqi, I. R. (1962) 'Towards a New Methodology for Qur'anic Exegesis' *Islamic Studies*. pp.35-52.

An-Na'im, A. A. (1996) *Towards an Islamic Reformation: Civil liberties, Human Rights and International Law*. Syracuse: Syracuse University Press.

Badawi, Z. (1976) *The Reformers of Egypt – A Critique of Al-Afghani, Abduh and Ridha*. Papers 2, The Muslim Institute: The Open University Press.

Badr, G. M. (1978) 'Islamic Law: Its Relation to other Legal Systems' *The American Journal of Comparative Law.* 26 pp.187-198.

Cole, J. R. I. (2003) 'The Taliban, Women, and the Hegelian Private Sphere' *Social Research.* 70 (3) Fall pp.771-808.

Coulson, N. J. (1964) *A History of Islamic Law.* Edinburgh: Edinburgh University Press.

Esposito, J. and DeLong-Bas (2001) *Women in Muslim Family Law.* 2nd ed. Syracuse: Syracuse University Press.

Fitzgerald, S. G. V. (1955) 'Nature and the Sources of Sharia' In: Khadduri and Liebseny (eds.) *Law in the Middle East.* Vol. 1: *Origin and Development of Islamic Law.* Washington, D.C.: The Middle East Institute. pp. 85-112.

Fitzgerald, S. G. V. (1951) 'The Debt of Islamic to Roman Law' *The Law Quarterly Review.* 67.

Fyzee, A. A. (1955) 'Shia Legal Theories' In: Khadduri and Liebseny (eds.) *Law in the Middle East.* Vol. 1: *Origin and Development of Islamic Law.* Washington, D.C.: The Middle East Institute.

Godziher, I. (1981) *Introduction to Islamic Theology and Law.* Andrea and Ruth (trans.). Princeton University Press.

Hallaq, W. B. (1984) 'Was the Gate of Ijtihad Closed?' *International Journal of Middle East Studies.* 16 (1) pp.2-41.

Hamilton (trans.) (1989) *The Hedaya.* Karachi: Darul-Ishaat.

Hassan, A. (1970) *The Early Development of Islamic Jurisprudence.* Islamabad: Islamic Research Institute.

Hazoor Bakhash (1981) *All Pakistan Legal Decisions* 1981 Federal Shariat Court 145.

Iqbal, M. (1934) *Reconstruction of Religious Thought in Islam.* Oxford University Press.

Jokisch, B. (1997) 'Ijtihad in Ibn Taymiyya's Fatawas' In: Gleave (eds.) *Islamic Law Theory and Practice.* I. B. Tauris Publishers.

Kadivar, M. (2003) 'An Introduction to the Public and Private Debate in Islam' *Social Research.* 70 (3) Fall pp.659-836.

Kar, M. (2003) 'The Invasion of the Private Sphere in Iran' *Social Research.* 70 (3) Fall pp.829-836.

Kamali, M. H. (2000) 'Law and Society, the Interplay of Revelation and Reason in the Shariah' In: Esposito (eds.) *Oxford History of Islam.* Oxford University Press.

Khaldun, I. (1398) *Al-Moghaddemah.* Beirut.

Khurshid Bibi (1967) *All Pakistan Legal Decisions* 1967 Supreme Court 97.

Levy, R. (1979) *The Social structure of Islam*. Cambridge: Cambridge University Press.

Libson, G. (1997) 'The Development of Custom as a Source of Law in Islamic Law' *Islamic Law and Society*. 4 (2) pp131-155.

Pakistan (1973) The Constitution of Pakistan.

Rahim, A. (1911) *Muhammadan Jurisprudence*. Lahore: PLD Publishers.

Rahman, F. (1965) *Islamic Methodology in History*. Karachi: Central Institute of Islamic Research.

Rahman, F. (1966) *History of Religion Islam*. London.

Rashida Begum (1960) *All Pakistan Legal Decisions* 1960 Lahore 1142.

Sachedina, A. (1999) 'The Ideal and Real in Islamic Law' In: Khare (eds.) *Perspective on Islamic Law, Justice, and Society*. Rowman and Littlefield Publishers.

Schacht, J. (1950) 'Foreign Elements in Ancient Islamic Law' *Journal of Comparative Legislation and International law*. 32 pp.9-17.

Schacht, J. (1955) 'Pre-Islamic Background and Early Development of Jurisprudence' In: Khadduri and Liebseny (eds.) *Law in the Middle East*. Vol. 1: *Origin and Development of Islamic Law*. Washington, D.C.: The Middle East Institute.

Vogel, F. E. (2003) 'The Public and Private in Saudi Arabia: Restrictions on the Powers of Committees for Ordering the Good and Forbidding the Evil' *Social Research*. 70 (3) Fall pp.749.

Weiss, B. (1998) *The Spirit of Islamic Law*. London: Georgia University Press.

Usmani, M. T. (1999) *Islam and Modernism*. Siddiqui's (trans.) Pakistan: Darul Ishaat.

PART II

WOMEN AND THE LEGAL SYSTEM OF PAKISTAN

CHAPTER 4

The Role of Islam in Drafting the Constitution

The purpose of part II is two-pronged: first, to examine the factors that motivated the process of Islamisation of the legal system in Pakistan and second, to probe the Islamic foundation of the so-called statutory Islamic laws of Pakistan related to women and how the superior courts interpret and implement them. The 1973 constitution (article 227) enjoins that all existing laws should conform to Islamic law and no law shall be made against Islam. Islamic law comprises a vast array of uncodified legal rules contained in juristic treatises. In this context, special attention is given to the role of the judiciary and the Federal Shariat Court of Pakistan as an arbiter of defining the status as to which legal rules are truly Islamic. The impact of the Islamisation process on the rights of women is also analysed. This chapter is focused on the role of Islam in the creation of Pakistan, its status in the successive constitutions and the factors/motives behind the process of Islamisation of the legal system, particularly Zia-ul-Haqq's regime (1976-88).

4.1 ISLAM AND THE BIRTH OF PAKISTAN

Pakistan emerged as an independent Muslim state on the world map on 14 August 1947. Islam played a vital role in its creation. The founder of Pakistan, Muhammad Ali Jinnah, said in 1943 that the aim of Pakistan is to provide a base where:

> We will be able to train and bring up Muslim intellectuals, educationalists, economists, scientists, doctors, engineers, technicians etc. who will work to bring about Islamic renaissance...[and a state] based on the principles which characterised Caliph [O]mar's regime (Iqbal, 1986:33).[1]

---

[1] The speeches of Jinnah and Muhammad Iqbal are taken from Afzal Iqbal and Ghazali's works.

He further elaborated his vision of Pakistan as: 'a modern democratic state, with the sovereignty resting in the people and the members of the new nation having equal rights of citizenship regardless of their religion, caste or creed' (Iqbal, 1986:33). For Jinnah, Pakistan meant a free, independent and sovereign state where the law would protect everyone and everyone would be equal before the law as envisioned in the Koran and the *Sunnah*. Allaying the apprehensions of non-Muslims, Jinnah said that Pakistan would not be a theocracy but a democratic state where every one would be an equal citizen:

> In course of time Hindus would cease to be Hindus and Muslims would cease to be Muslims not in the religious sense, because that is the personal faith of each individual, but in the political sense as citizens of the state (Iqbal, 1986:33).

When Pakistan was achieved, in his first address to the nation, Jinnah said:

> You are free; you are free to go to your temples, you are free to go to your mosques or to any other place of worship in this state of Pakistan. You may belong to any religion or caste or creed – that has nothing to do with the business of the state (Iqbal, 1986:35).

Other leaders of the Muslim League (the main political party of Indian Muslims) shared Jinnah's vision of Pakistan. Muhammad Iqbal said in 1930:

> Nor should the Hindus fear that the creation of an autonomous Muslim state will mean the introduction of a kind of religious rule in such states (Ghazali, 1996:16).

Iqbal wrote to Jinnah that he wanted to see the establishment of social democracy in the proposed Muslim state, which had the approval of the Islamic *Sharia*. However, he pleaded for the reinterpretation of *Sharia* law through *ijtihad* to meet the exigencies of modern times (Ghazali, 1996; see Iqbal, 1934). There is harmony in the views of Jinnah and Iqbal regarding the vision of Pakistan as a Muslim state. They approved of a particular interpretation of Islam on which they founded Pakistan, and according to them it was only through that interpretation that the Muslims could realise their objectives in the newly created Muslim state. Afzal Iqbal (1986:30) argues that 'the sort of Islam he [Jinnah] put forward was simple and straightforward, free of all theological and dialectical subtleties, which the ordinary masses could understand'.

4.2 ISLAM AND DRAFTING THE CONSTITUTION

After the creation of Pakistan, the crucial issue was that of preparing the constitution and the status of Islam in the constitution.

> The most intractable problem that hindered the progress of constitution making ... [was] the character of the proposed constitution with particular reference to the place which Islam should occupy in the constitution (Mahmood, 1990:9-10).

The religious scholars raised the issue of the status of Islam in the constitution of Pakistan although:

> The role of Islam in politics was not at the centre of Muslim politics during the struggle for Pakistan but was brought into the political debate after the nation was created. The issue proved to be the beginning of a decades long quest and debate over just what Pakistan's Islamic character should be (Ghazali, 1996:41).

It is important to note that most of the religious scholars were against the creation of Pakistan, particularly Jamat-i-Islami (hereinafter, Jamat) who later on became the champion of turning Pakistan into an Islamic polity. Maududi [the founding leader of Jamat] had been opposed to the creation of Pakistan (Taylor, 1983). The religious groups did not wait for long to get their share of power in the new state of Pakistan. An Islamic constitution became the prime goal of Jamat, declaring that:

> Pakistan was a Muslim state and not an Islamic state since a Muslim state is any state which is ruled by Muslims while an Islamic state is one which opts to conduct its affairs in accordance with the revealed guidance of Islam and accepts the sovereignty of Allah and the supremacy of His Laws, and which devotes its resources to achieve this end. According to this definition, Pakistan was a Muslim state ruled by secular minded Muslims. Hence, the Jamat-i-Islami and other religious leaders channelled their efforts to make Pakistan an "Islamic state" (Taylor, 1983:41-42).

Thus when it was stated above that Islam was the basis of the creation of Pakistan, it was the notion of a Muslim state as understood and interpreted by the Muslim League leadership, whose notion differed from religious groups such as Jamat and others. The majority of the Muslim League leaders were educated in the West and were more politicians than religious leaders, whereas religious politicians were educated in the well-known Islamic centres of the Indian subcontinent such as Deoband.

4.3 THE OBJECTIVE RESOLUTION OF 1949

Amid these struggles among different political camps on the role of religion, the Constituent Assembly passed a resolution in 1949 embodying the main principles whereon the future constitution of Pakistan should be based. This resolution is commonly known as the 'Objective Resolution'. Because of its great constitutional eminence, it is reproduced below in full:

> Whereas sovereignty over the entire Universe belongs to Almighty Allah alone, and the authority to be exercised by the people of Pakistan within the limits prescribed by Him is a sacred trust;
>
> And whereas it is the will of the people of Pakistan to establish an order: - Wherein the State shall exercise its powers and authority through the chosen representatives of the people;
>
> Wherein the principles of democracy, freedom, equality, tolerance and social justice, as enunciated by Islam, shall be fully observed;
>
> Wherein the Muslims shall be enabled to order their lives in the individual and collective spheres in accordance with the teachings and requirements of Islam as set out in the Holy Quran and Sunnah;
>
> Wherein adequate provision shall be made for the minorities freely to profess and practise their religions and develop their cultures;
>
> Wherein the territories now included in or in accession with Pakistan and such other territories as may hereafter be included in or accede to Pakistan shall form a Federation wherein the units will be autonomous with such boundaries and limitations on their powers and authority as may be prescribed;
>
> Therein shall be guaranteed fundamental rights, including equality of status, of opportunity and before law, social, economic and political justice, and freedom of thought, expression, belief, faith, worship and association, subject to law and public morality;
>
> Wherein adequate provision shall be made to safeguard the legitimate interests of minorities and backward and depressed classes;
>
> Wherein the independence of the judiciary shall be fully secured;
>
> Wherein the integrity of the territories of the Federation, its independence and all its rights, including its sovereign rights on land, sea and air, shall be safeguarded;

> So that the people of Pakistan may prosper and attain their rightful and honoured place amongst the nations of the World and make their full contribution towards international peace and progress and happiness of humanity... (1973 Constitution of Pakistan, article 2A).

Liaqat Ali Khan, the then Prime Minster, described it as the most important occasion in the life of Pakistan, next in importance only to the achievement of Independence (Mahmood, 1990). However, it was not without opposition. The Pakistan National Congress, the main opposition party, opposed the resolution on the ground that it mixed politics with religion and would reduce minority communities to the status of serfs (Mahmood, 1990). Despite opposition from certain political circles, it remained the cornerstone of the constitution and law-making and became a substantive part of the operative 1973 constitution in 1985.

4.4 THE ISLAMIC PROVISIONS OF THE 1956 CONSTITUTION

Study of the Islamic provisions of three different constitutions of Pakistan demonstrates the degree of importance attached to religion in its constitutional system. After nine years of concerted efforts, Pakistan got its first constitution on 23 March 1956. Its Islamic flavour is evident from its numerous Islamic provisions. The Objective Resolution was given the position of the preamble. The Directive Principles of the constitution reaffirmed faith in the preamble and encouraged the state to take steps enabling Muslims to order their lives individually and collectively and understand the meaning of life in accordance with the teachings of the Koran and the *Sunnah* (article 25). The state was to endeavour to promote unity and observance of Islamic moral standards. The state was to secure the proper organisation of *zakat* (poor due) and *awkaf* (religious endowments). Teaching of the Koran was made compulsory. The head of state was to be a Muslim. Islam was not made the state religion but Pakistan was declared an Islamic Republic. Article 197 empowered the President to set up 'an organisation for Islamic research and instruction in advanced studies to assist in the reconstruction of Muslim society on truly Islamic bases'. If any legal practical significance was given to Islam, it was in article 198: no law could be made repugnant to the injunctions of Islam as laid down in the Koran and the *Sunnah* and all existing laws were to be brought into conformity with such injunctions. It also provided that the President should appoint a Commission to give advice on the enactment of laws according to Islam (article 198(3)). The Commission was also required to submit a report to the President within five years, which he would then place before the legislature so that it might enact laws in the light of that report.

The Islamic provisions of the constitution had little practical effect since these provisions were embodied mainly in the preamble and directive principles none of which was enforceable in the court.

> Islam was, in practice, legally enforceable in two major ways only. Firstly, by article 32 requiring the appointment of a Muslim President, and secondly, through articles 107 and 198, providing for the organisation of Islamic research and the appointment of a Commission to bring existing laws into conformity with Islam (Mehdi, 1994:85).

Both the Traditionalists [conservatives] and Modernists [liberals] claimed success after the constitution was adopted. The Jamat said that the preamble of the constitution, its directive principles and article 198 had finally and unequivocally settled the eight-years-old struggle between Islamic and anti-Islamic trends in favour of the former. It explained the fact that the future system of life in the country had to be shaped on the basis of Islam and that the Koran and the *Sunnah* would reign supreme since it was firmly embedded in the constitution (Ghazali, 1996). The Modernists accepted the constitution wholeheartedly because 'Islam was woven into the fabric of the state as matter of policy and not of law' (Mehdi, 1994:86).

> The Constitution of 1956 was basically modern in its character. Islamic provisions were only symbolic in nature. Their practical influence on law was not visible. The Islamic provisions were mostly a compromise and therefore vague (Mehdi, 1994:87).

Rubya Mehdi (1994) argues that the constitution is considered as a compromise between Traditionalists and Modernists but in the end both sides abused it because of its attitude of hypocrisy and vagueness as to its Islamic provisions. Afzal Iqbal (1986:65) contends that: 'the constitution had an Islamic facade but the hard core was missing'.

> The first constitution of Pakistan seems to suggest that its framer decided to borrow the political institutions of the West and made an effort to invest them with the spirit of Islam. A liberal interpretation of Islam was incorporated into the constitution. The institution of representative government was reconciled with the fundamental principles of Islam and

> the idea of restoring medieval political institutions was rejected (Iqbal, 1986:69).

Esposito (1980:143) describes the compromising nature of the constitution in the following words:

> The constitution of 1956 reflected the long years of debate and the difference between [T]raditionalists and [M]odernists. Its final form underscored the lack of any clear idea or consensus regarding an Islamic ideology and how to translate it into programmes and policies. The document represented an eclectic compromise which embodied many of those aspects associated with a secular state while injecting several Islamic provisions.

This war of conflicting tendencies between Traditionalists and Modernists is present throughout Islamic history and is visible in the constitution and law-making processes in Pakistan. The following account of the Islamic provisions of the later constitutions and other laws will further reinforce this argument.

4.5 THE ISLAMIC PROVISIONS OF THE 1962 CONSTITUTION

General Ayub Khan captured power on 7 October 1958. He abrogated the constitution and imposed martial law on the ground that the constitution was 'unworkable'. Ayub Khan announced his own brand of constitution on 1 March 1962. He was a modernist but it was a difficult task to introduce the kind of system he wanted because of possibly strong religious opposition. As a result 'the identification with Islam was formally retained' (Iqbal, 1986:76) in the constitution.

His new constitution differed in many ways from its predecessor but the focus here is only on an analysis of its Islamic aspects. The Objective Resolution was retained as the preamble but with some modifications. The cuts made were merely of a few words and phrases but if these had been allowed to remain as part of the constitution, it would have had a substantial impact on the future polity of Pakistan. In the first paragraph of the preamble of the 1956 constitution, provision is made for: 'authority to be exercised by the people of Pakistan within the limits prescribed by Him is sacred trust'. This sentence is missing in the preamble of the 1962 constitution. The name of the state was changed from the 'Islamic Republic of Pakistan' to the 'Republic of Pakistan'. Another change was that the defunct constitution of 1956 used the phrase 'the Koran and the *Sunnah*' but the new constitution replaced this with one word 'Islam'. A note was appended to article 198 in the 1956 constitution stating that in the application of personal law, the 'Quran and the *Sunnah*' would be as interpreted by a particular sect. This note was meant to appease different sects in the community and thus recognised their existence in society. However, this note was deleted in the 1962 constitution, indicating a desire to cut across differences among various schools of thought as a pre-condition of compiling a code of Islamic law to which all legislation should conform (Iqbal, 1986:77). However, all these words were restored through constitutional amendment in 1963 after the government was pressured by 'the orthodox section of the National Assembly who demanded strengthening of the Islamic provisions of the Constitution' (Iqbal, 1986:77).

The 1962 constitution provided that no law should be made which was repugnant to Islam (article 1) but it did not say, like the 1956 constitution, that all existing laws should be brought in conformity with the injunctions of the Koran and the *Sunnah*. The responsibility to decide whether or not a law is repugnant to Islam was vested in the legislature. Nevertheless, National and Provincial Assemblies and the President and the Governor of a Province could refer a proposed law to the Advisory Council of Islamic Ideology to find out whether or not it was in conformity with Islam. The provision that 'no law could be made which was against Islam' was not enforceable in a court of law in the 1962 constitution whereas article 198 of the 1956 constitution containing the same provision was enforceable in a court of law. However, it was ensured through an amendment that all existing laws should be brought in conformity with the Koran and the *Sunnah*. The head of the state continued to be Muslim. Under article 199, the 1962 constitution provided for the setting up of Advisory Council of Islamic Ideology. The function of the Council was to advise the President, the Provincial Governors and National and Provincial Assemblies on any question referred to it whether or not a proposed law was repugnant to the Koran and the *Sunnah*. The Council was also to make recommendations to central and provincial governments to take steps which would enable and encourage the Muslims of Pakistan to order their lives according to the principles and concepts of Islam. However, the Council was only an advisory body and its advice was not binding on the President or Parliament. The Islamic Research Institute, which was provided for in the 1956 constitution, was retained in the 1962 constitution. The function of the institute was to undertake Islamic research assisting 'in the reconstruction of Muslim society on a truly Islamic basis' (article 207).

It seems that at first efforts were made to avoid including too many Islamic provisions in the 1962 constitution; however, many modifications were made after pressure from the Traditionalists. 'Ayub Khan's period was not a swing towards secularism. It was marked only by an effort for more liberal interpretation of Islam while framing the constitution' (Mehdi, 1996:94). Manzoorudin Ahmad (1963:252) maintains that 'the purpose of rephrasing the Objective Resolution and other Islamic provisions had obviously been to make room for a more liberal interpretation of Islam'. However, these attempts did not succeed due to the presence of strong religious opposition.

4.6 THE ISLAMIC PROVISIONS OF THE 1973 CONSTITUTION

The 1962 constitution was abrogated in March 1969 and the country was run under the 1970 Legal Framework Order as an interim constitution. A new constitution was framed in 1973, which is the operative constitution of Pakistan with 17 amendments. It differs in a number of ways from its predecessors. The first constitution was the product of the Constituent Assembly and the second was the brainchild of an army general. The 1973 constitution was framed by the Parliament, was passed unanimously, and is known as the 'people's constitution'.

The preamble contains the sentiments and aspirations expressed in the Objective Resolution. Pakistan is named as an Islamic Republic and unlike the two previous constitutions, Islam is declared as the state religion (article 2). The President as well as the Prime Minister of the country must be Muslim. Both are required to take a specific form of oath declaring their faith in the unity and oneness of Allah (God), the Books of Allah and the finality of the Prophethood of Muhammad. Article 29, as in the previous constitutions, states that no law shall be made that is repugnant to the Koran and the *Sunnah*. In addition, it states that Quran and the *Sunnah* shall mean the Quran and *Sunnah* are interpreted by the school of law to which the individual belongs. All existing laws shall be brought in conformity with the injunctions of Islam (article 227). Chapter 2 deals with the principles of policy (articles 29-40), which declare, as in the previous constitutions, that the state shall take steps to enable the Muslims of Pakistan to order their lives individually and collectively in accordance with the basic principles and concepts of Islam (article 30). Teaching of the Koran is to be made compulsory and learning Arabic is to be encouraged. Proper organisation of *zakat* (poor due) *awqaf* (religious endowments) and mosques will be secured. Unity and observing of Islamic moral standards is to be promoted (article 31).

4.6.1 The Council of Islamic Ideology

The constitution (article 228) provides for the setting up of a Council of Islamic Ideology as in the previous constitutions but unlike the previous two constitutions it does not mention the Islamic Research Institute. The constitution makes a lofty declaration that no law should be made which goes against Islam and that all existing laws should conform to Islamic teaching. To realise this end, the Council was set up with the following three main functions. First, to advise the Parliament and Provincial Assemblies as to ways and means of enabling Muslims to order their lives according to Islam. Second, to advise any House of the Parliament or Provincial Assemblies, President, Provincial Governors on any proposed law as to whether it is according to Islam. Third, to compile a report in suitable form for the guidance of National and Provincial Assemblies on such injunctions of Islam as can be given legislative effect (article, 230). The Council's duties are only of an advisory and recommendatory nature and it has no independent powers of enforcement. Thus, the constitution only establishes a process by which a constitutional body, the Council, may have an advisory input on the 'Islamic' credentials of existing and proposed law (Ahmad, 1963).

It seems that pressure from the Traditionalists grew with the passage of time as more Islamic provisions were introduced in the new constitution as compared to the previous two constitutions despite the fact that then Prime Minster, Zulfiqar Ali Bhutto, was a liberal and secular-minded politician like his predecessor Ayub Khan. David Taylor (1983:181) observed that: 'Bhutto himself, whose personal vision was entirely secular, was well aware of the ideological significance of Islam … [He] took care to use Islamic symbolism wherever possible'. Bhutto himself said nobody can deny that it is an Islamic constitution. It contains more Islamic provisions than any of the past constitutions of Pakistan as well as any of the other constitutions of Muslim countries (Mehdi, 1996).

4.7 THE RULE OF GENERAL ZIA-UL-HAQ (1976-88): AN ERA OF ISLAMISATION

General Zia captured power on 4 July 1976 in a bloodless military coup and later, seeking public legitimacy, vowed to introduce the Islamic system in the country. During his regime, changes were made in the constitution, in the judicial structure and other laws, mainly criminal laws. The Islamisation programme began in February, 1979 and covered several areas of judicial reforms in implementation of the Islamic Penal Code, economic activity and educational policy (Tolbat, 1998). The first two of these areas are of special relevance to this study.

4.7.1 The Federal Shariat Court

To actualise his agenda of Islamisation, General Zia made changes in the judicial structure as well as the constitution. Through a Presidential Order in 1979, Shariat Benches were established at every High Court in all four provinces with the power to strike down any law which is found repugnant to Islam. Such a law would become invalid from the date set by the Shariat Bench. In 1980, the Federal Shariat Court replaced all Shariat Benches, as they were not working satisfactorily. A person to be appointed as a judge of Federal Shariat Court must be a Muslim and be qualified to be a judge of the High Court. Three out of eight judges must be *Ulema* (Islamic scholars) who are well versed in Islamic law (article 203C (3A)). A Shariat Appellate Bench was set up at the Supreme Court level with the power of hearing appeals from the Federal Shariat Court (article, 203F(3)). It should consist of three Muslim judges of the Supreme Court, two of which must be *Ulema*. The Federal Shariat Court was given the following jurisdiction.

4.7.1.1 Original Jurisdiction

The original jurisdiction of the Federal Shariat Court (in non-criminal cases) is:

> The Court may, either of its own motion or on the petition of a citizen of Pakistan or the Federal Government or a Provincial Government, examine and decide the question whether or not any law or provision of law is repugnant to the Injunctions of Islam, as laid down in the Holy Quran and Sunnah of the Holy Prophet … If any law or provision of law is held by the Court to be repugnant to the Injunctions of Islam...such law or provision shall, to the extent to which it is held to be so repugnant, cease

to have effect on the day on which the decision of the Court takes effect (article 203-D).

4.7.1.2 Criminal Jurisdiction

All cases punishable under *hudood* laws are triable by the District and Sessions Judges and an appeal can be made against their orders/decisions to the Federal Shariat Court. All convictions made under *tazir* by these judges under *hudood* laws are also appealable before the Federal Shariat Court. The Federal Shariat Court is also empowered to examine the record of any case decided by any criminal court under any law relating to the enforcement of *hudood*, to ascertain the correctness of sentence, legality of findings or order recorded or passed by all subordinate courts (article 203DD). The Federal Shariat Court took an extraordinary step in March 2005 and suspended the judgment of the Lahore High Court wherein the court acquitted the accused of gang rape. In a short order, the Federal Shariat Court said:

> The March 3, 2005, judgment pronounced by the [H]igh [C]ourt in these appeals is liable to be treated as coram-non-judice (without jurisdiction), with the consequential result that the appeals would be deemed pending a decision by the Federal Shariat Court (Iqbal, 2005).

Under article 203E(9) of the constitution and section 31-A of the Federal Shariat Court procedural rule 1982, it was empowered to review its own decisions.

4.7.1.3 Suo Moto Power

In February 1982, this Court was given power to take suo moto action by amending article 203-D of the Constitution. The court is now empowered to examine any law on its own motion.

4.7.1.4 Circumscribing Powers of the Federal Shariat Court

It seems that Federal Shariat Court is given vast powers to check the Islamic standing of laws but article 203B(C), defining the word 'law' for the purpose of the remit of the Federal Shariat Court, seriously circumscribes its power.

> 'Law' includes 'any custom or usage having the force of law but does not include the Constitution, Muslim Personal Law … any law relating to the procedure of any Court or tribunal … any fiscal law or any law relating to the levy and collection of taxes and fees or banking or insurance practice and procedure.

After reading article (203B(C), it seems that the powers of Federal Shariat Court were only confined to implement criminal laws and oversee correct implementation of those laws by subordinate judiciary. Whether the Federal Shariat Court remained within or broke this constitutional barrier is discussed in chapter 7.

The subordinate judiciary was also restructured. Ian Talbot (1998:274) has summed up the state of affairs in the following words:

> The piecemeal construction of an Islamic judicial system continued in 1984 with the creation of Qazi [Islamic judge] courts in which cases could be tried according to the Shariat [Islamic law]. The Qazi courts were intended to operate in the locality like the old magistrate courts. Ulema with *sanad* (degree from a religious school) in jurisprudence were eligible for appointment as *qazis* (judges). By this juncture, Pakistan thus possessed federal and lower Shariat courts, civil courts and summary military courts.

General Zia-ul-Haq further Islamised the constitution through the *Revival of the Constitution Order, 1985*. The change was justified on two grounds: 'first to bring it closer to Islam and second to shield it against future national instability' (Tolbat, 1998:104). The Objective Resolution, which was a preamble, was made a substantive part of the constitution (article 2A). The word Parliament was replaced by an Islamic substitute, *Majlis-e-Shoora*. It was a precondition for the members of *Majlis-e-Shoora* (article 62) and Provincial Assemblies (article 113) to possess knowledge of Islam and be honest and righteous. This is perhaps the most Islamised version of the constitution which is now the operative constitution of Pakistan.

General Zia followed a two-pronged approach to realise his goals of Islamisation. First, he empowered the Council of Islamic Ideology to advise the Parliament and Provincial Assemblies on the Islamic standing of laws. Second, he constituted the Federal Shariat Court to strike down any law which is found against Islam. These changes seem symbolic rather than real. The Council of Islamic Ideology has only an advisory role. The Parliament or Provincial Assembly can simply ignore its advice. The role of the Federal Shariat Court as an arbiter of the Islamic standing of laws is restricted to one area: criminal law and its correct application (corrective justice). The most important area of concern for women is the law of personal status and the constitution but they are immune from the scrutiny of the Federal Shariat Court. How far the Federal Shariat Court can intervene in these areas is discussed in the following two chapters.

4.7.2 The Criminal Laws

When we look at the legal history of Pakistan, little or no attention is paid to Islamisation of laws other than the constitution. However, Zia's enthusiasm went beyond the constitution. In 1979, he introduced five ordinances commonly known as the *hudood* laws. They deal with adultery/fornication, *qazf* (false imputation of adultery etc.), theft, armed robbery (*haraba*), prohibiting the taking of alcohol and whipping. The two ordinances dealing with adultery, etc. and *qazf* are discussed at length in chapter 6. The whipping law was abolished in 1996 except in *hadd* cases. Theft and armed robbery are dealt with in the *Property Ordinance* providing severe punishment such as the amputation of a hand if proved guilty beyond reasonable doubt according to the Islamic evidential standard. The *Prohibition Ordinance* prohibits Muslims from drinking all kinds of alcohol but allows non-Muslims to drink in religious ceremonies if permitted by their religion. However drinking in public places is forbidden for non-Muslims. In 1984, the *Evidence Act of 1872* was revised to bring it in line with Islam and renamed as '*Qanun-e-Shahadat Order, 1984*'. Its impact on the rights of women is discussed in chapter 6. Zia also made efforts to Islamise the sections of Pakistan Penal Code pertaining to hurt and murder but could not accomplish the task. These sections were Islamised in 1990 through the *Qisas & Diyat Ordinance,* which is also discussed in chapter 6.

4.8 THE MOTIVES BEHIND ISLAMISATION

Pakistan is a Muslim country and Islam plays a significant role in the lives of the people. The literacy rate is very low particularly among the female population and rural areas. The majority of the people live in rural areas and the economy is mainly agrarian. The majority of people lack sound knowledge of Islam and rely on the way Islam is presented by the *Mullahs* (religious clerics). The existence of effective politico-religious factions is a living reality in Pakistan. Another political reality is that power invariably remained in the hands of non-Islamic parties despite the fact that religious groups remained a formidable force and did exert pressure mainly through street demonstrations. Military *juntas* have always dislodged popularly elected governments, leading to the alienation of mainstream political parties. The option for military rulers was to win over the support of religio-political factions. So the religious outfits were made part of the military administration and their demands were heeded leading to the introduction of their brand of an Islamic system in the country. This provided some political and popular support to the military regimes. Jamat's joining of Zia's military administration is a case in point.

When Zia took power from elected government, he was in desperate search of legitimacy for his rule: legitimacy not in legal sense (as he could easily dictate to the judiciary which he did in many cases with impunity) but rather public and political legitimacy. Mehdi (1994:32) argues that Islamisation was 'the legitimisation of the illegal takeover by the martial law regime'. Esposito (1982) maintains that Zia-ul-Haq from the inception of his regime legitimated his coup and subsequent rule through demands for *Nizam-i-Mustafa* or, as it is more commonly called, *Nizam-i-Islam*. Carroll (1982) argues that initially, General Zia obviously saw Islam, Islamisation, and an emphasis on the Islamic Ideology of Pakistan as the basis for the unification and integration of a state wracked by political regional conflicts, and as a vehicle for securing popular support for his illegal regime. Alavi (1986:45) said that:

> With the assumption of power by the Zia regime another factor has come into play, namely the legitimacy of power. Afraid to face a free electorate and having no mandate to govern, Zia has turned to Allah.

Jehangir and Jillani (1990), supporting this view, argue that Islamisation was used as an instrument of perpetuating his stay in power. 'It is widely accepted that President Zia-ul-Haq had used Islam as an instrument to consolidate his power. It was not a matter of genuine concern with him' (Jehangir and Jillani, 1990:21). Ghulam Jillani (cited in Jehangir and Jillani, 1990) said that the General's excuse to stay in power was his mission of Islamisation which had to be carried out under the umbrella of martial law. Mehdi (1994) writes that Islamisation was not the simple reason to appease the hostile population. There were others as well: the search for identity [after East Pakistan became an independent state of Bangladesh in 1971]; the people's frustration with foreign ideologies, first capitalism under Ayub and then socialism under Bhutto; and lastly, the increased prominence and power of Islamic countries in the 1970s. The National Commission on the Status of Women (2003:1) observed regarding the Islamisation of criminal laws that:

> The motives of the Zia-ul-Haq government ... for the enforcement of these Ordinances [*hudood* Laws] ... essentially lie in the political domain'

and the 'introduction of these Ordinances was meant to give an Islamic appearance to the state.

Taylor (1983:181) puts it this way: 'the programme [Islamisation] itself appears to be concerned only with the husk and not the core of Islam'. Islam was used as a political tool most of the time. The practices of military dictatorships are far removed from the ideals of Islam. Nevertheless, an opportunistic leader may invoke Islam to legitimise his regime: an appeal to faith is compelling, especially among the poorly educated (Taperell, 1985:1180). Taperell (1985:1180) said that 'the selectivity with which some self-styled Islamic governments follow Islamic precepts points to political expediency'.

4.9 CONCLUSION

Religion played a significant role in the creation of Pakistan and has been given a place of prominence in successive constitutions. Islam has always been used as a political tool: any cunning leader can make a smart use of religion to muster popular support. Any government that needed more popular support stressed the role of Islam in the system and life of the country. The need of military regimes was greater as they had snatched power from the popularly elected governments so they relied on religion very heavily. They wooed religious groups indiscriminately. Many fundamentalist groups became a part of various military *juntas* and their interpretation of Islam informed the process of legislation. The marriage of military and fundamentalists give birth to several laws based on their interpretation of Islam. The Federal Shariat Court was set up to check the Islamic standing of laws but its wings were clipped first by article 203B(C) and then by governmental intervention in cases of public importance such as *Hazoor Bakhash* (PLD 1981 FSC 145). It seems that the ultimate aim was the politics of Islam, not the introduction of real Islam. Playing the politics of religion has served the purposes of its proponents but has seriously undermined women's human rights.

REFERENCES

Ahmad, M. (1963) 'Islamic Aspects of the New Constitution of Pakistan' *IslamicStudies*. Vol. II.

Alavi, H. (1986) 'Ethnicity, Muslim Society, and the Pakistan's Ideology' In: Weiss (eds.) *Islamic Reassertion in Pakistan*. Syracuse: Syracuse University Press.

Carroll, L. (1982) 'Nizam-i-Islam: Process and Conflict in Pakistan's Programme of Islamisation, with Special Reference to the Position of Women' *Journal of Commonwealth and Comparative Politics*. p.201.

Esposito, J. L. (1980) 'Pakistan: Quest for Islamic Identity' In: Esposito (eds.) *Islam and Development*. Syracuse: Syracuse University Press.

Esposito, J. L. (1982) 'Islamisation: Religion and Politics in Pakistan' *The Muslim World*. LXXII, July-October.

Ghazali, A. S. (1996) *Islamic Pakistan: Illusions and Reality*. Islamabad: National Book Club.

Iqbal, A. (1986) *Islamisation of Pakistan*. Islamabad: Vanguard Books Ltd.

Iqbal, M. (1934) *Reconstruction of Religious Thought in Islam*. Oxford University Press.

Iqbal, N. (2005) 'FSC Suspends LHC Verdict: Mukhtar Mai Case' *Dawn* 12 March 2005. Islamabad.

Jehangir, A. and Hina, J. (1990) *Hudood Ordinances: A Divine Sanction?* Lahore: Rhotas Books.

Mahmood, S. (1990) *Constitutional Foundations of Pakistan*. Lahore: Jang Publisher.

Mehdi, R. (1994) *The Islamisation of the Law in Pakistan*. Curzon Press Ltd.

National Commission on the Status of Women of Pakistan (2003) *Draft Report on the Meetings of the Special Committee to Review the (Enforcement of Hudood Ordinances*, 1979. http://new.ncsw.gov.pk/index.php [Accessed March 2005).

Pakistan (1956) The Constitution of Pakistan [repealed].

Pakistan (1962) The Constitution of Pakistan [repealed].

Pakistan (1973) The Constitution of Pakistan.

Taperell, K. (1985) 'Islam and Human Rights' *Australian Foreign Affairs*. 56.

Taylor, D. (1983) 'The Politics of Islam and Islamisation in Pakistan' In: Piscatori (eds.) *Islam in the Political Process*. Cambridge University Press.

Tolbat, I. (1998) *Pakistan: A Modern History*. London: C. Hurst.

CHAPTER 5

Gender Equality and the 1973 Constitution

The 1973 Constitution of Pakistan is predicated on a patriarchal view of women's role in Pakistani society but its chapter on fundamental rights provides a number of safeguards to ensure that women are treated equally and to eliminate discrimination on the basis of sex in all spheres of life. Women are entitled to all protections under the constitution but this chapter analyses specific articles on women, how the superior courts interpret and apply them, and whether they meet Koranic and international human rights standards, especially the 1979 Convention on the Elimination of all Forms of Discrimination against Women (hereinafter, the Women's Convention). Pakistan has made a general declaration to the Women's Convention that the accession by Pakistan to the said Convention is subject to the provisions of the country's constitution. This chapter also analyses the justification of this vague and unspecific declaration from the perspective of international law and the constitution of Pakistan.

The constitution contains a long list of fundamental rights applicable equally to men and women but some are designed specifically to protect women's rights. Some women's rights are also recognised as principles of policy. The difference between the fundamental rights and the principles of policy is that the former are justiciable in a court of law whereas the latter are only policy guidelines and no law can be struck down or anyone punished because of their violation (article 30). The constitution recognises almost all human rights guaranteed in the 1948 Universal Declaration of Human Rights, e.g. the right to life and liberty, dignity of person and privacy of home, immunity from torture, freedom of movement and association, freedom of speech and religion and to acquire, hold and dispose of property, access to public places, freedom of assembly, etc. The constitutional provisions of significance to women's rights are the equality clause, the right to employment, human trafficking, political participation, and access to public places, which are discussed below explaining how the superior courts interpret and apply them.

5.1 THE EQUALITY CLAUSE: ARTICLE 25

The constitution has devoted a full chapter to fundamental rights, the most important of which is article 25 prohibiting discrimination of any kind against women:

> 1. All citizens are equal before law and are entitled to equal protection of law.
>
> 2. There shall be no discrimination on the basis of sex alone.
>
> 3. Nothing in this article shall prevent the State from making any special provision for the protection of women and children.

'In its true spirit, it caters to all the principles of equality' the Commission of Inquiry for Women (1997:4) (hereinafter, the Commission) observed. There is, however, one word in article 25, which is different, namely 'alone' in clause (2). It has the potential for biased interpretation. The Commission (1997:4) expressed its concern that the word 'alone' is unnecessary. It suggests that sex, if coupled with some other factor may provide justification for discrimination and has recommended its removal.

The examination of a few judgments of the superior courts illustrates that this clause is usually interpreted and applied to protect women's rights. The Supreme Court clearly explained the intent and scope of article 25 in the case of *Shirin Munir* (PLD 1990 Supreme Court 295). The brief facts of the case are that girls obtained marks in a pre-medical examination, which would have entitled them to admission into one of the seven medical colleges in the province of Punjab. The total number of seats was 1085. After subtracting reserved seats for different categories, 858 were left for open competition. Out of this, 677 were allocated to boys and 181 to girls. As the girls were competing for a small number of seats so as to get admission, the last girl was required to have secured 820 marks. Among the boys who were competing for a relatively large number of seats, the last boy was required to have secured as low as 731 marks. The girls felt discriminated and petitioned the Lahore High Court, which gave a split judgment. On appeal the Supreme Court held that:

> No discrimination on the ground of sex alone can be permitted except on the ground of reasonable and intelligible classification. Such classification in our society for the present permits establishment of educational and professional institutions for the females or exclusively for males. However,

> where co-education is permitted and the institution is not reserved for one sex alone, the fixation of the number on the grounda of sex will directly be opposed to the requirement of article 25(2) unless it is justified as a protective measure for women and children under article 25(3). In other words the number of girl students can be fixed as the minimum but not as the maximum, particularly so where on merit they are likely to get more than the fixed number of seats. The constitution assumes that the women and children in our society need protection and not the males and as long as the constitution mentions that assumption and basis, we cannot reverse it by affording protection to male and adults at the cost of women and children. That would be opposed to the very fundamental mandate of the constitution (PLD 1990 Supreme Court 298).

After elaborate reasoning, the Supreme Court came to the conclusion that the claim of the girl students merited acceptance as they had been discriminated against in the matter of admission to co-educational medical colleges by suppressing their merit as against the boys.

The Supreme Court further spelled out the principles for the application of the equality clause in 1993 in the case of *Azizullah Memon* (PLD 1993 Supreme Court 341) observing that equal protection of law does not envisage that every citizen is to be treated alike in all circumstances but contemplates that persons similarly situated are to be treated alike. Also reasonable classification is permissible but it must be founded on a reasonable distinction or basis. So different laws can be enacted for different sexes, age groups and persons accused of heinous crimes. The court further observed that any law made or action taken in violation of principles contained in article 25 is liable to be struck down. In 2004, the Supreme Court again endorsed the above principles in the case of *Ghulam Mustafa Ansari* (2004 Supreme Court Monthly Review 1903). The cases of *Munir, Memon* and *Ansari* indicate that men and women are treated equally as laid down in the constitution and that special laws are allowed to be enacted in order to protect women's rights when needed (see, Human Rights Committee's view *Shirin Aumeeruddy-Cziffra v. Mauritius* Communication No. R.9/35 (2 May 1978).

However, in 1998 the Lahore High Court interpreted article 25 differently than the Supreme Court in the case of *Sharifan Bibi* (PLD 1998 Lahore 59) where an Indian man married to a Pakistani woman applied for citizenship and his application was denied. It is important to note that the rulings of the Supreme Court are binding on the High Courts and subordinate judiciary under the Constitution (article 189): 'any decision of the Supreme Court shall, to the extent that it decides a question of law or is based upon or enunciates a principle of law, be binding on all other courts in Pakistan'. Before analysing the judgment of the Lahore High Court, it is pertinent to look into the 1951 *Pakistan Citizenship Act* to find out how its discriminatory sections impact upon women's rights. After going through the Citizenship Act, the inescapable conclusion one arrives at is that 'man is the fulcrum' and 'woman an exclusion' in the citizenship law in Pakistan (Kakakhel, 2002). A man is allowed to marry a non-citizen woman (in case of government servants, with the permission of the government, see *Government Servants (Marriage with Foreign Nationals) Rules, 1962*) and the wife acquires the status of citizen after complying with legal provisions and procedures (allegiance to the constitution) without delay. Their children are regarded as 'citizens by descent'. However, section 5 of the Act reads: 'subject to the provisions of section 3 a person born after the commencement of this Act shall be a citizen of Pakistan by descent if his father is a citizen of Pakistan at the time of his birth'. A woman citizen of Pakistan is also allowed to marry a non-citizen man but the Act bars her husband from obtaining the citizenship of his spouse, a right given to men but denied to women.

The contemplation of the Act on the legal status of a non-citizen spouse of a Pakistani woman has a number of implications and reflects 'multi-layered discrimination' (Kakakhel, 2002) against women. The Act restricts the right of a woman to a free choice of marriage, confining its exercise to the borders of Pakistan only. In case she steps out of the limits set by the law, she has to choose between two options: to leave her country of origin and migrate to a country where her spouse resides or to subject her spouse to the subordinate status of non-citizen in her country, no matter how long he remains in Pakistan. The last choice of leaving her country exposes the male chauvinism embedded in the law: that a woman is the domain of a man and has to move as he moves. The Act dissuades foreigners from marrying Pakistani women in and from outside Pakistan, impairing women's right to marriage.[1] Women are not treated equally in the Act because denying

[1] The act does not bar young Muslim men and women living in the UK and USA, etc. from marrying their relations from Pakistan for two possible reasons. First, their parents are originally Pakistanis. Second and most importantly, they are Muslims. A Muslim woman is not allowed to marry a non-Muslim. However, a Muslim man is allowed to marry a Christian or Jewish woman. The interesting point about the citizenship act is that unlike many Islamic legislative pieces, it does not mention that it is based on the principles of Islamic law of citizenship. But in fact, it reflects Islamic principles of citizenship law.

citizenship to an alien husband of a Pakistani woman amounts to 'forcing upon her the nationality of the husband' (Kakakhel, 2002). The discrimination does not end here. It trickles down to the children of a female parent: they are not citizens of Pakistan either by birth or descent since the determining factor in their citizenship is the father's nationality. It is interesting to note that the words used in the Act are 'father' and 'grandfather' instead of 'parent' and 'grandparent'. The children of women married to non-citizens are outside the ambit of the Act.

The Lahore High Court in the case of *Sharifan Bibi* (PLD 1998 Lahore 59) held that the right to citizenship is available only to women who marry Pakistani citizens and not to male aliens who marry Pakistani women. The court found no discrimination in such a case since article 25 of the constitution is available only to citizens, not to an Indian citizen who has married a Pakistani woman. The court clearly failed to recognise that *Sharifan Bibi* as a citizen of Pakistan had made the application, not her Indian husband. It is pertinent to cite the contrasting view of the Sindh High Court in the case of *Nazneen Bibi* (1999 Monthly Law Digest 1250) after one year. Interpreting the concept of 'equality of citizens' contained in article 25, the court observed that: 'a major Muslim woman like a major Muslim man is *sui juris* and entitled to the same rights and liberties'. The interpretation of the Lahore High Court is based on the letter, not the spirit of the law and is very discriminatory, denying women their constitutional right of equality. The constitution is the supreme law of the land but the Lahore High Court went against it. The rulings of the Supreme Court are binding on all courts but the Lahore High Court did not take notice of it.

The view taken in *Sharifan Bibi* also clashes with the 1979 Women's Convention (article 9) which calls on States Parties to grant women equal rights with men to acquire, change or retain their nationality.

> They shall ensure in particular that neither marriage to an alien nor change of nationality by the husband during marriage shall automatically change the nationality of the wife, render her stateless or force upon her the nationality of the husband. States Parties shall grant women equal rights with men with respect to the nationality of their children.

Article 9 has two basic obligations. First, it requires States Parties to guarantee women the same rights as men to acquire, change or retain their nationality. For example, foreign wives of male nationals may be permitted to acquire their husband's nationality, but foreign husbands of female nationals are not granted the same right. The result in such cases is that men who marry foreigners are allowed to remain in their country of origin, whereas women who marry foreigners may be forced to move to their husband's country of origin. Second, States Parties are required to extend to women the same rights as men regarding the nationality of their children. In many countries, children automatically receive the nationality of the father but not their mother (United Nations, Fact Sheet No. 22, 1993). What the Convention and the constitution proscribe actually happened in the case of *Sharifan Bibi.*

These different interpretations of superior courts demonstrate that the provisions of the citizenship act are vulnerable to discriminatory interpretations and application. The equality clause of the constitution could be and should be used as a shield against interpretations undermining women's right to equality. The equality clause of the constitution with its interpretation by the superior courts in majority cases meets international standards and is an effective tool of women's rights protection. However, it may be glossed over or interpreted differently in some cases as in the case of *Sharifan Bibi.*

5.2 EQUAL OPPORTUNITY IN EMPLOYMENT

The constitution also guarantees non-discrimination on the basis of sex in employment. Article 27 reads:

> 1. No citizen otherwise qualified for appointment in the service of Pakistan shall be discriminated against in respect of any such appointment on the ground only of race, religion, caste, sex, residence or place of birth.
>
> Provided that, for a period not exceeding [forty] years from the commencing day, posts may be reserved for persons belonging to any class or area to secure their adequate representation in the service of Pakistan:
>
> Provided further that, in the interest of the said service, specified posts or services may be reserved for members of either sex if such posts or services entail the performance of duties and functions which cannot be adequately performed by members of the other sex.
>
> 2. Nothing in clause (1) shall prevent any Provincial Government, or any local or other authority in a Province, from prescribing, in relation to any post or class of service under that Government or authority, conditions as

to residence in the Province for a period not exceeding three years, prior to appointment under that Government or authority.

The common notion and practice regarding choice of professions in Pakistan is that jobs are divided into women's jobs and men's jobs. Women constitute the majority of teachers, nurses and doctors for these are socially considered women's professions. A few women are visible in the ranks of the army (and that too only in the medical branch), judiciary, administration, etc. The same is the case with employment in the private sectors. The reason is not a legal barrier rather it is social perceptions that determine the choice of professions for women. It should be noted, however, that article 27 is one of the most effective constitutional provisions when it is resorted to. In 1995 the Lahore High Court tested the equality norm of article 25 in conjunction with article 27 in case of *Naseem Firdous* (PLD 1995 Lahore 584). The brief facts of the case are that the petitioner was working in a textile corporation from 1977 and reached the position of Assistant Director, design section. She was prevented from applying for the post of designer in the same department on the ground that the job was for 'male only' applicants. The employers took the view that the job was a male one and covered by the second proviso to article 27 mentioned above. The court declared the action taken pursuant to the advertisement (appointing a male applicant only) to be illegal and ordered the corporation to fill the post according to law.

This is exactly what the Women's Convention seeks to achieve: to ensure women's equality in employment. Article 11 states clearly that women shall enjoy the basic right to work. It then sets out a comprehensive list of obligations for States Parties in order to ensure that this right can be fully and effectively realized. First, among them is that States Parties must guarantee women the same employment rights and opportunities as men. It is not sufficient for a state to outlaw discriminatory hiring practices. It must take positive action to ensure that women exercise this right. Second, women must have the right to free choice in selecting a profession, and must not be automatically channelled into traditional 'women's work'. To discharge this obligation, States Parties must grant women full equality in education and employment opportunities and must work towards the creation of social and cultural patterns, which allow all members of society to accept and work towards the presence of women in many different types of career (United Nations, Fact Sheet No. 22, 1993).

5.3 HUMAN TRAFFICKING AND FORCED LABOUR

The constitution (article 11 (2)) prohibits 'all forms of forced labour and traffic in human beings'. This provision strictly speaking is not women-specific but it can be used to protect women's rights as for all practical purpose in Pakistan human trafficking means women trafficking. Women's trafficking from and to Pakistan is a common practice. Many of these women are forced into the industry of prostitution but this clause does not specifically prohibit prostitution. The Commission (1997:4) said that:

> While article 11(2) of the constitution does not specifically mention 'prostitution', the term 'traffic in human beings' is broad enough to cover the corresponding requirement in article 6 of CEDAW [Women's Convention].

Article 6 of the Women's Convention states that 'States Parties shall take all appropriate measures, including legislation, to suppress all forms of traffic in women and exploitation of prostitution of women.' The Commission (1997:4) recommended that 'the prohibition against "slavery, forced labour, etc." in article 11 should include a specific bar on all forms of sexual exploitation and prostitution of women'. The Commission, however, failed to take notice of article 37(g) of the constitution, which explicitly prohibits prostitution.

It should be noted that article 6 of the Women's Convention does not prohibit the institution of prostitution but the exploitation of prostitution and urges States Parties to take measure to combat trafficking in women although it does not define the term 'traffic'. States Parties are not required to implement measures to prevent prostitution as such. The focus rather is on the exploitation of prostitution. The approach of the constitution is different than the Convention in that the constitution prohibits prostitution and trafficking in women whereas the Convention prohibits the exploitation of prostitution but is silent on the institution of prostitution. The major reason for this is that the constitution (article 2) has declared Islam as a state religion and according to the Koran sex outside wedlock is severely punishable (Koran, 24:2). This is why even the Commission recommended express prohibition of prostitution instead of exploitation alone.

5.4 POLITICAL PARTICIPATION

Article 17 recognises a very crucial right of citizens including women: the political right to form a union or association and be a member of political party. In the male-dominated society of Pakistan, a major change in the situation of women could be effected through their active participation in democratic processes. The constitution was amended through *The Legal Framework Order* in 2002, which allocates women special seats in Parliament (National Assembly and Senate) and Provincial Assemblies. The reserved seats in the National Assembly from each Province, the Federally Administered Tribal Areas (FATA) and the Federal Capital are as follows:

Table 1: Women's reserved seats in the National Assembly

	General	*Women Seats*	*Total*
Balochistan	14	3	17
NWFP	35	8	43
The Punjab	148	35	183
Sind	61	14	75
FATA	12	-	12
Federal Capital	2	-	2
Total	272	60	332

The total membership of the Senate is 100 wherein four women are taken from each Province and one woman from the capital territory of Islamabad. The number of reserved seats for women was also raised in the four Provincial Assemblies. They are as follows:

Table 2: Women's reserved seats in the Provincial Assemblies

	General seats	*Women Seats*	*Total*
Baluchistan	51	11	65
The North-West Frontier Province	99	22	124
The Punjab	297	66	371
Sind	130	29	168

M. Mahmood (2003) argues that the basic right conferred by article 17 does not mean only the right to form a political party but also to contest election and form a government if the party possesses the requisite majority.

5.4.1 Do Women Enjoy Political Rights?

As stated above, the constitution guarantees the right to political participation. However, the contrary happens in practice when it comes to women's direct political participation except in respect of the reserved seats, which are filled indirectly by joint vote of Parliament and the Provincial Assemblies. The local government election of August 2002 is a good case in point. In most of the districts of the North West Frontier Province male electoral candidates/elders of towns decided that women should not cast votes. These decisions were taken either in mosques or district courts in the form of agreements. Anyone violating the agreement had to pay a fine (Aurat Foundation and Information Services Foundation, 2002). The conduct of the candidates in these districts is against the electoral laws but the Election Commission of Pakistan has taken no legal action against these people. The *Code of Conduct for the Candidates: Local Government Elections 2000-2001* states that: 'the candidates and their workers shall not propagate against the participation of any person in the election on the basis of gender'. Article 25 of *The NWFP Local Government Election Ordinance, 2000* prohibits undue influence in order to compel any person to vote, *refrain from voting*, or to induce or compel any person to withdraw his candidature. The dominant practice is that women do not participate actively in all the democratic processes. The situation is worse in rural and tribal areas of the North West Frontier Province. In one district the religious leaders declared women's participation in an election to be against the *Sharia* (Mashriq, 27 May 2001) in contrast to the stark reality that a woman has been twice Prime Minister of

Pakistan. It is interesting to note that religious leaders are not against those laws recognising the political rights of women but resist their actual participation in politics.

Article 7 of the Women's Convention requires States Parties to undertake three levels of action to create equality for women in political and public life. First, States Parties must ensure to women the right to vote in all elections and public referenda. Second, article 7 recognizes that, while it is essential, the right to vote is not in itself sufficient to guarantee the real and effective participation of women in the political process. The article therefore requires States to ensure to women the right to be elected to public office and to hold other government posts and positions in non-governmental organizations. Third, States should ensure the right of women 'to participate in the formulation of government policy and the implementation thereof' (article 7). The constitution of Pakistan has recognised women's right to political participation but they are denied enjoying this right as discussed above. This is not what the Convention stands for and is against Pakistan's international obligations as a State Party to the Convention. States Parties have the obligation to ensure *de jure* and *de facto* equality. The constitution provides for women's political rights but Pakistan has failed to secure this by taking positive steps so that women can enjoy political rights.

5.5 ACCESS TO PUBLIC PLACES

The constitution allows access to public places of entertainment irrespective of sex under article 26:

> 1. In respect of access to places of public entertainment or resort not intended for religious purposes only, there shall be no discrimination against any citizen on the ground only of race, religion, caste, sex, residence or place of birth.
>
> 2. Nothing in clause (1) shall prevent the State from making any special provision for women and children.

This article provides access to public places but places restriction on women to worship freely in places made for religious purposes. The Commission (1997) observed that women must enjoy the right of access to places of worship like mosques, churches and temples and recommended amendment to this article. Article 26 of the constitution is partially in conformity with article 13(C) of the Women's Convention: 'the right to participate in recreational activities, sports and all aspects of cultural life'. It articulates women's rights to recreational activities, sports and cultural life. It obligates States to take measures so that women have real equality of access in these areas (United Nations, 2000:35).

5.6 PRINCIPLES OF POLICY AND GENDER EQUALITY

The 1973 constitution contains a chapter on principles of policy, which aim to eradicate discrimination against women and encourage participation of women wholeheartedly (Shah, 1990). The list of principles of policy embodies special representation of peasants, workers and women in local government institutions (article 32), women's participation in all spheres of national life (article 34), protecting marriage, the family, the mother and the child (article 35), promoting the educational and economic interests of backward classes and areas, better working conditions for women, ensuring maternity benefits (article 37), and ensuring the well-being of people and providing the basic necessities of life irrespective of sex.

In contrast to fundamental rights, the principles of policy are ideals and goals to be achieved 'dependent upon resources being available for the purpose' (article 29(2)). It is the responsibility of each organ and authority of the state to act in accordance with the principles of policy in so far as they relate to each functionary depending upon resources available to them (article 29(2)). The President, as far as the affairs of the Federation are concerned, and the Governor, as far as the affairs of the Province are concerned, shall prepare and lay before the National Assembly or Provincial Assembly as the case may be, a report on the observance and implementation of principles of policy each year. However, if they are not observed, it does not amount to breaching the constitutional provisions. There is no implementing force behind them as no one can be held accountable for not acting in accordance with them and no law can be challenged for breaching them. Their observance is left to the conscience of the various state organs and functionaries. The principles of policy have another inherent weakness: the achievement of goals contained in these principles is dependent on availability of resources. For example, overlooking education and other economic interests of women could be easily justified on lack of resources.

Most of the principles of policy are the repetition of fundamental rights, which are almost compatible with international human rights standards.

Their aim is to help in guiding the policy makers and state organs, and particularly the courts in interpreting laws according to the spirit of the constitution. The Supreme Court has said, in the case of *Shrin Munir* (PLD 1995 Supreme Court 300), that the 'principles of policy are part of the constitution and other provisions should not be interpreted losing sight of them. Harmony should be reached as far as possible without, of course, enforcing [them] in positive terms...' In the case of *Mst. Saima* (PLD 2003 Lahore 474) the Lahore High Court relied on the principle of policy (article 35) together with the corresponding article 16 of the Women's Convention both aiming to protect maternity and family. This may set a new trend of using international human rights law at the domestic level as well as basing a judgment on a principle of policy.

5.7 THE ISLAMIC FOUNDATION OF CONSTITUTIONAL PROVISIONS

The constitution empowers the Federal Sharait Court to look into the Islamic standing of different laws but carefully excludes itself from such Islamic scrutiny (article 203B(C)). The constitution also excludes the law of personal status from such a scrutiny but it is discussed in chapter 7 how it broke this constitutional barrier by declaring some rules of family law against Islam. However, this is not the case regarding the constitution. The record of the Federal Shariat Court indicates no interference with the constitutional provisions for two possible reasons. First, that it is not a trend to challenge the Islamic standing of the constitution before the Federal Sharait Court. Second, that its women-specific provisions are more or less in conformity with Islamic standards. The latter position seems more probable as demonstrated in chapter 2 that the Koran endowed women with equality in all spheres of life and so did the constitution as this chapter indicates. For instance, the constitution prohibits discrimination on the basis of sex and gives women equal right to work and to own property, etc. and so does the Koran. The constitutional standards also meet international human rights standards, which buttress the argument that if statutory Islamic laws of Pakistan are reformed along the lines proposed in this study, it would meet the constitutional and human rights standards.

5.8 PAKISTAN'S DECLARATION TO THE 1979 WOMEN'S CONVENTION

By signing an international treaty, the State Party consents to be bound by its principles and Pakistan has undertaken that responsibility by acceding to the Women's Convention. Pakistan, being a dualist state, does not become liable to implement the provisions of the Convention in the domestic courts like any domestic piece of legislation but it does bind itself to fulfil its international obligation. For instance, reporting to the Committee on the Elimination against Women (CEDAW) and obligations under article 2 (the main thrust of obligations is in the legislative sphere) of the Convention, Rebecca Cook (1990:147) argues that:

> When States assumes membership in international human rights conventions, they agree to give effect to treaty obligation in their municipal legal systems. Treaty responsibilities arise for all states parties, whether their law is contained in comprehensive or exclusive codes or is customary or religious in origin. States parties that do not distinguish secular from religious laws and derive significant portions of their law from interpretation of sacred texts nevertheless obligate themselves in principle to implement human rights norms.

The Women's Convention does allow for reservations to be made by the State Parties to certain parts, which they do not think to be binding on them (article 28(1)). However, it disallows reservations and declarations which are incompatible with the object and purpose of the Convention (article 28(2)). Andrew Byrnes (1989:51-52; see Clark, 1991) contends that: 'the issue of reservations – those limitations to the obligations imposed by a treaty that a State Party specifies when becoming a party – has been one of the most contentious matters that has been arisen in relation to the Convention'. He (1989:51-52) adds that:

> The most contentious reservations and the ones that seem most threatening to the integrity of the treaty regime are the broad reservations which indicate that the obligations of major articles of the Convention are accepted only to the extent that they are consistent with the requirement of Islamic *Sharia* ...

Many States Parties have entered reservations wherein 'significant number are substantive, and some appear inconsistent with the Convention's object and purpose, affecting the enjoyment of women's legally guaranteed rights in all areas' (United Nations, 2000:6). Pakistan acceded to the Women's Convention declaring that her accession to the Convention is subject to the provisions of her constitution. This declaration is of a very unspecific nature raising doubts about Pakistan's commitment to the implementation of the Women's Convention. Other States Parties have raised objection to it. Austria objected that:

> A reservation by which a State limits its responsibilities under the Convention in a general and unspecified manner by invoking internal law creates doubts as to the commitment of the Islamic Republic of Pakistan with its obligations under the Convention, essential for the fulfilment of its object and purpose (CEDAW/SP/2002/2).

The Federal Republic of Germany argued that:

> A declaration which seeks to limit the validity of the Convention by making it contingent upon congruity with the Pakistan Constitution may raise doubts as to Pakistan's commitment to the object and purpose of the Convention. Such a reservation referring generally to the Constitution is not permitted under the Convention (CEDAW/SP/2002/2).

The 1969 Vienna Convention on the Law of Treaties (hereinafter, Vienna Convention) forbids any reservation to an international treaty that: 'is incompatible with the object and purpose of the treaty' (article 19(C)). Austria raised the same point maintaining that:

> A general reservation of the kind made by the Government of the Islamic Republic of Pakistan, which does not clearly specify the provisions of the Convention to which it applies and the extent of the derogation therefrom, contributes to undermining the basis of international treaty law (CEDAW/SP/2002/2).

Pakistan's vague declaration is against another general principle of international law as well. The Vienna Convention (article 27) says that: 'a party may not invoke the provisions of its internal law as justification for its failure to perform a treaty'.

Pakistan's declaration to the Women's Convention is unspecific and vague and is impermissible from the perspective of international law. Many other Islamic countries such as Egypt have entered very clear reservations to specific articles in contrast to Pakistan's blanket declaration. Also, there is no valid constitutional ground for such a declaration as the constitution of Pakistan forbids sex discrimination and most of its provisions meet international standard of equal treatment of men and women.

> Some states enter a reservation to article 2, although their national constitutions or laws prohibit discrimination. There is, therefore an inherent conflict between the provisions of the states constitution and its reservation to the Convention (United Nations, 2000:90).

The case of Pakistan fits into this category. There is greater compatibility, except for minor details, between the constitution of Pakistan and the Women's Convention and Pakistan's declaration cannot be justified from the constitutional point of view either. Pakistan should narrow down its reservation to those specific areas of minor difference as the CEDAW recommends in its General Recommendation No. 19 (1992). For instance, article 6 of the Women's convention is silent on the issue of prostitution but Pakistan being a Muslim state cannot allow prostitution.

5.9 CONCLUSION

The foregoing account of women's rights in the constitution demonstrates that the 'equality clause' of the constitution is the bedrock of the doctrine of equality and anti-discrimination. Some rights such as women's participation in political processes are guaranteed in the constitution but social attitudes hinder its being enjoyed. Pakistan needs to take positive steps to turn these rights into reality in order to fulfil her constitutional as well as her international obligations. The interpretations of constitutional provisions by superior courts, in the majority of cases, are compatible with human rights standards and reflect judicial propensity to extend equal treatment to men and women. The constitution also conforms to the Koranic concept of gender equality except in minor details. In this backdrop where the constitution and its interpretation by the superior judiciary match human rights norms, the vague declaration of Pakistan to the Women's Convention is not warranted. It raises serious doubts about her commitment to the obligations under the Convention. International law also does not allow reservation on the basis of national legislation and Pakistan's position vis-à-vis the Convention is untenable. In cases of absolute incompatibility such as implied approval of prostitution by the Convention and strict proscription by Islamic law, Pakistan should narrow and specify her reservation.

Despite the constitutional principle of gender equality, several legislative decisions in Pakistan discriminate against women such as criminal and evidence laws and some provisions of the law of personal status. These are discussed in the following chapters.

REFERENCES

Aurat Foundation and Information Services Foundation, (2002) *Citizen's Campaign for Women's Representation in Local Government.* Peshawar: Pakistan.

Azizullah Memon (1993) *All Pakistan Legal Decisions* 1993 Supreme Court 341.

Commission of Inquiry for Women (1997) *Annual Report.* Pakistan.

Byrnes, A. C. (1989) 'The "Other" Human Rights Treaty Body: The Work of the Committee on the Elimination of Discrimination against Women' *The Yale Journal of International Law.* 14 (1) pp.1-67.

Clark, B. (1991) 'The Vienna Convention Reservations Regime and the Convention on the Discrimination against Women' *The American journal of International Law.* 85 (2) pp. 281-321.

Cook, R. J. (1990) 'Reservation to the Convention on the Elimination of All Forms of Discrimination against Women' *Virginia Journal of International Law.* 30 pp.643-716.

Ghulam Mustafa Ansari (2004) *Supreme Court Monthly Review* 1903.

Kakakhel, N. A. S. (2002) 'Citizenship Act Violates Women's Rights' *Dawn.* 15 July, Karachi.

Mahmood, M. (2003) *The Constitution of Islamic Republic of Pakistan.* Pakistan: Law Times Publication.

Mashriq (2001) 27 May 2001. Peshawar, Pakistan.

Mst. Saima (2003) *All Pakistan Legal Decisions* 2003 Lahore 474.

Naseem Firdous (1995) *All Pakistan Legal Decisions* 1995 Lahore 548.

Nazneen Bibi (1999) *Monthly Law Digest* 1250.

Pakistan (2002) The Legal Framework Order

Pakistan (2000-2001) The Code of Conduct for the Candidates: Local Government Elections 2000-2001.

Pakistan (2000) The NWFP Local Government Election Ordinance 2000.

Pakistan (1962) Government Servants (Marriage with Foreign Nationals) Rules.

Pakistan (1973) The Constitution of Pakistan.

Pakistan (1951) Pakistan Citizenship Act 1951.

Shah, N. H. (1990) 'Rights of Women before Courts of Law' *All Pakistan Legal Decisions*. p. 80.

Sharifan Bibi (1998) *All Pakistan Legal Decisions* 1998 Lahore 59.

Shrin Munir (1990) *All Pakistan Legal Decisions* 1990 Supreme Court 295.

United Nations (1948) Universal Declaration of Human Rights.

United Nations, Committee on the Elimination of Discrimination against Women, (1992) '*General Recommendation No. 19, Violence against Women*'. http://www.un.org/womenwatch/daw/cedaw/recommendations/recomm.htm#recom19 [accessed Nov. 2005].

United Nations, Human Rights Committee (1978) *Shirin Aumeeruddy-Cziffra v. Mauritius* Communication No. R.9/35 (2 May 1978). http://www1.umn.edu/humanrts/undocs/session36/9-35.htm [accessed Nov. 2005).

United Nations (1993) *Fact Sheet No 22, 'Discrimination against Women: The Convention and the Committee.* http://www.unhchr.ch/html/menu6/2/fs22.htm. [Accessed March 2005].

United Nations (2000) *Assessing the Status of Women: A Guide to Reporting Under the Convention on the Elimination of all Forms of Discrimination against Women*. New York: United Nations.

United Nations (1969) *The Vienna Convention on the Law of Treaties*. http://www.un.org/law/ilc/texts/treaties.htm [accessed Nov. 2005].

United Nations (1979) *Convention on the Elimination of All Forms of Discrimination against Women*. http://www. unhchr.ch/html/menu3/b/e1cedaw.htm [accessed Nov. 2005].

CHAPTER 6

Islamisation of Criminal Laws

The regime of Zia-ul-Haq, in addition to changes in constitutional and judicial structure, amended criminal laws in order to bring them into conformity with Islamic tenets as his regime understood/interpreted them. He introduced five ordinances known as *hudood* laws (singular *hadd,* means cases where punishment is fixed by the Koran and the *Sunnah*). The preambles of the five *hudood* ordinance state: 'whereas it is necessary to modify the existing law … so as to bring it in conformity with the injunctions of Islam as set out in the Holy Quran and Sunnah'. They deal with theft and armed robbery, *zina* (adultery/fornication) and rape, *qazf* (imputation of *zina*/unchastity), drinking alcohol, and whipping. The 1872 *Evidence Act* was also amended in 1984 to Islamise it. The aim of this chapter is to probe the Koranic standing of the two contentious *hudood* ordinances, the 1979 *Offence of Zina (Enforcement of Hudood) Ordinance* (hereinafter, *Zina* Ordinance) and the 1979 *Offence of Qazf (Enforcement of Hudood) Ordinance* (hereinafter, *Qazf* Ordinance) and to explain how the superior courts, particularly the Federal Shariat Court, interpret and apply them. The focus is on the analysis of the case law of these courts. These two ordinances are selected because of their significant impact on the rights of women in Pakistan. The laws of evidence and *qisas* (retribution) and *diyat* (blood money) and their impact on women's rights are also discussed.

6.1 PRE-*HUDOOD* LAW OF ADULTERY AND RAPE

It is important to have an overview of the criminal laws governing sex offences before 1979 before engaging in the analysis of the notoriously famous *Zina* Ordinance. Previously rape was an offence for men alone with the punishment of transportation for life or imprisonment extending up to ten years and a fine. Rape of a wife under the age of twelve years was an offence and had the same punishment. Sex without the consent of a wife above the age of twelve was an offence punishable with two years. Adultery was also a crime but sex between two consenting unmarried individuals was not an offence (Mehdi, 1990). The punishment for adultery was imprisonment for five years or a fine or both. The most fascinating aspect of this law is that adultery was a bailable as well as a compoundable (which can be compromised by the parties) offence. Only the husband of the adulteress could make a complaint of adultery and the prosecution had the power to drop the charge of adultery. The woman partner to adultery could not be punished for adultery but she could not complain either (Pakistan Penal Code, 1860 ss. 375-376 [repealed]).

6.2 THE 1979 OFFENCE OF *ZINA* (ENFORCEMENT OF HUDOOD) ORDINANCE

The *Zina* Ordinance has defined *zina* as wilful sexual intercourse between a man and a woman who are not validly married to each other. Penetration is sufficient to constitute *zina*. The punishment for *zina* liable to *hadd* (section 5) is stoning to death at public place for *muhsan* (married person) and a hundred stripes for non-*muhsan* (non-married). The punishment for rape liable to *hadd* is stoning to death for a married person and a hundred stripes with any other punishment including death for a non-married person (section 6). The punishment for *zina* liable to *tazir* (cases where the court has discretion in sentencing) is ten years rigorous imprisonment, thirty stripes and a fine or both (section 10(2)). Rape liable to *tazir* is punishable by not less than four years and not more than twenty-five years and thirty stripes (section 10(3)). The appellate court (Federal Shariat Court) must confirm *hadd* punishment before execution in any case. The evidential requirement to prove *zina* and rape liable to *hadd* is either a confession by the accused before the competent court or the testimony of four adult male Muslims (section 8). Those cases which do not meet the evidential criterion of *hadd* fall into the category of *tazir* where the court has discretion to make decision on the basis of available evidence.

There is controversy over the fact that the *Zina* Ordinance makes no distinction between *zina* and rape. Rubya Mehdi (1990) argues that in every country in the world rape is categorised as a crime different from adultery and fornication but the *Zina* Ordinance makes no such a distinction. Lucy Carroll (1982:68), however, thinks differently:

> A distinction between rape and consensual sex is clearly recognised and a much more severe maximum penalty is imposed on the person guilty of

the former crime (i.e., twenty five years' imprisonment as opposed to ten years' imprisonment).

Both positions are partially right and partially wrong. According to the *Zina* Ordinance, there is no difference in the standard of proof and punishment for *zina* and rape liable to *hadd*, i.e. confession or testimony of four male adult Muslims and both are punished with stoning to death. However, the Ordinance certainly provides different standards of proof and punishment for *zina* and rape liable to *tazir* as opposed to *hadd*, i.e. ten years rigorous imprisonment, thirty stripes and a fine or both for *zina* and not less than four years and not more than twenty-five years imprisonment and thirty stripes for rape. The trial court may rely on any evidence for sentencing under *tazir*.

The *hudood* ordinances have changed many provisions of the previous law to the great detriment of women although the 'pre-Hudood criminal legal system of Pakistan was by no means an ideal criminal code for women; [y]et it was not repressive and it afforded certain protection to women and children' (Jehangir and Jillani, 1990:85). According to the new law, a woman can be charged for the offence of rape and rape of a wife is not an offence. All the offences under the *Zina* Ordinance are made non-bailable, the offenders cannot compromise the case and the complainant has no option to drop the charge. Any person whether aggrieved or not, including the police, can make the charge of *zina*. Jehangir and Jillani (1990:86) observed that:

> By denying women the right of complaint for adultery and simultaneously exempting them from punishment for adultery, the British legislators relegated women to the status of secondary but protected citizens. The Hudood Ordinances has removed the protection without raising their secondary status.

6.2.1 The Koranic Foundation of the Zina *Ordinance*

The *Zina* Ordinance, as already stated, envisages two types of penalties and evidential tests for the offence of *zina* and rape: one provided under *hadd* and the other under *tazir*. If the required standard of proof for *zina*/rape liable to *hadd* is wanting, then the case falls under the category of *tazir* where the court has discretion in making a decision on the basis of evidence before it. According to Jehangir and Jillani (1990:24), tazir is simply a fallback position from *hadd*. For instance, lack of evidence for *hadd* does not exonerate the accused of the criminal liability. The accused is still liable to *tazir*. The position of the Koran is plain and different from the position of the *Zina* Ordinance. *Hadd* punishment can be imposed when the required standard of evidence is adduced in a court of law otherwise the defendant/s stand exonerated. The Koran (4:15) said: 'if any of your women are guilty of lewdness, take the evidence of four (reliable) witnesses from amongst you against them … ' When this evidential criterion is not fulfilled, the defendant should be acquitted and the accuser punished for *qazf* (false accusation). The Koran (24:4) said:

> And those who launch a charge against chaste women, and produce not four witnesses (to support their allegations) – flog them with eighty stripes and reject their evidence ever after.

This is not the position of the *Zina* Ordinance and the Federal Shariat Court. According to the *Zina* Ordinance, the evidence has to meet a double test: one required by *hadd,* other by *tazir*. In the case of *Rashida Patel* (PLD 1989 Federal Shariat Court 95), the Federal Shariat Court held that if four truthful witnesses are not available to prove *zina*, then the court can award *tazir* punishment for lewdness, etc. other than *zina*. The Ordinance has excluded the evidence of women and non-Muslims for the purpose of imposition of *hadd* punishment whereas from the reading of the Koranic verses it does not transpire that women's testimony can be excluded in *hadd* cases. The Koran does specify the number but not the gender of a witness (see, chapter 2.6). The Federal Shariat Court held that in specific circumstances the testimony of a woman can be accepted but *hadd* punishment cannot be awarded on the basis of such evidence (PLD 1989 Federal Shariat Court 95).

The *Zina* Ordinance applies a similar evidential standard to *zina* and rape liable to *hadd* but the Koran only mentions four witnesses for *zina*. It does not mention rape. This extension of *hadd* evidential criterion to rape cases has seriously jeopardised women's right to a fair trial. The Commission of Inquiry for Women (hereinafter, the Commission) has presented a hypothical situation where a rapist can escape *hadd* punishment because women's testimony is not accepted in *hadd* cases. For instance, the inmates of a women's hostel could be subjected to a daylight orgy of rape but the culprits cannot be punished because women's evidence is not acceptable. In the case of *Rashida Patel* above, the Federal Shariat Court held that rape is an offence different than *zina* and the requirement of four adult male witnesses under section 8(b) to prove rape is against the Koran and the *Sunnah*.

It was further held that it should be two male witnesses instead. This is a slight numerical improvement but far from what is required: admitting evidence that would lead to the conviction of the rapist.

The *Zina* Ordinance provides for stoning to death as punishment for those who are married and guilty of *zina* liable to *hadd* but the Koran (24:2) does not mention it:

> The woman and the man guilty of adultery or fornication, - flog each of them with a hundred stripes ... and let a party of the Believers witness their punishment.

In a landmark case of *Hazoor Bakhsh* (PLD 1981 Federal Sharait Court 145), the Federal Shariat Court ruled that:

> The only punishment that may be called 'Hadd' and which can be imposed on a person, whether married or unmarried, guilty of [zina] is one hundred stripes ... to be inflicted in public.

The court (PLD 1981 Federal Sharait Court 145) also observed that 'according to the principles governing the interpretation of the Holy Qur'an, where the verses of the Holy Qur'an are clear, they are enough and it is not required to turn to anything else for their interpretation'. Subsequently the judgment was reversed in a review filed by the Federal Government after coming under pressure from religious factions. Jehangir and Jillani (1990:29) have given a vivid picture of the circumstances thus:

> As soon as the judgment was reported in the press, the fundamentalists held rallies against it ... under pressure, the President passed a constitutional amendment to grant the FSC powers to review its own judgment. On March 21, 1981 the judgment was announced. On April 13, 1981 the President obliged the fundamentalists. The bench of FSC was reconstituted retaining only one judge from the old bench. Five judges replaced the rest. One out of the five had already given his opinion as amicus curae during the original hearing. He had supported stoning to death as Islamic.

The Islamic standing of *Zina* Ordinance is seriously doubted. The Commission (1997:74) concluded that the Commission: 'is convinced that all the Hudood laws were conceived and drafted in haste. They are not in conformity with the injunctions of Islam'. An 18-member Committee, set up under the auspices of National Commission on the Status of Woman in May 2002 to review *hudood* ordinances, reported that many provisions of the *hu-*

dood laws are un-Islamic and should be repealed. In 2005, the Council of Islamic Ideology hinted to remove features found repugnant to the injunctions of Islam. 'There were many conflicting provisions in the Hudood Ordinance which were not in consonance with the teachings of the Holy Quran' (Dawn, 30 May 2005). In January 2005, a private member's resolution was submitted in the Senate making a declaration that the punishments prescribed under the *Zina* Ordinance for adultery are not Islamic:

> This House is of the view while Islam prescribes Hadd punishments for certain offences, the punishments prescribed under the Enforcement of Hudood (Punishment for Zina) Ordinance 1979, are unIslamic (Dawn, 4 January 2005).

The result of these voices has yet to be seen.

6.2.2 Application of the Zina *Ordinance*

The lower courts have applied the *Zina* Ordinance abusively and the superior courts have set conflicting precedents violating women's right to a fair trial. In the cases of rape, the victims are placed in a no win situation. If a victim reports the matter to the police, she has to prove at the investigation as well as the trial that she was not a consenting party to the act of sexual intercourse. If she does not report the matter immediately and conceives she may be either killed for defiling family honour or convicted for *zina* because the courts consider conception without wedlock as a confession. This places rape victims in a position of defending themselves from prosecution instead of being defended and protected by the law. 'Victims of rape have now been placed in a snare. Silence is as risky as making a complaint' (Jehangir and Jillani, 1990:88). The onus of establishing rape rests with the victim of rape herself. If she is unable to prove her allegation, bringing a case to court amounts to confession of intercourse outside marriage (Mehdi, 1990).

Lower courts have very often converted cases of rape into that of *zina,* turning the victim into a co-accused. In the case of *Mst. Tasleem* (PLJ 1996 Federal Shariat Court 138), the brother of Tasleem made a complaint to the police that Zaman and Muhammad Ali had abducted and raped his sister. After arrest and investigation, the police sent the case for trial. The trial court found Tasleem to be a consenting party to the act of *zina* and convicted her for seven years rigorous imprisonment. At appeal, the Federal Shariat Court set aside her conviction and observed:

> The appellant nowhere stated that she had been consenting party to the sexual intercourse being committed with her. Actually she charged her co-accused for subjecting her to rape and committing sexual intercourse with her forcibly and without her consent ... In such view of the matter she could not be held guilty of the offence of Zina. Actually it appeared that she was a victim of rape and she was not to be blamed for that.

In many cases even the superior courts tend to rely on flimsy grounds giving advantage to the male accused. In 1994, bail was granted to Irshad, an alleged rapist, on the ground that there was no 'mark of violence' on any part of the body of the victim:

> The girl of course is unmarried but there is no mark of violence on any part of body according to the medical report. In any case, prima facie it does not seem to be a case of forcible Zina/rape (1994 Pakistan Criminal Law Journal 2210).

Absence of marks of violence on the body of the victim is not conclusive proof of consent. Most of the time rape victims are in absolute fear, helpless and yield to the perpetrators. In the case of *Muhammad Nawaz* (1990 Supreme Court Monthly Review 886), the Supreme Court asked how a young girl of thirteen years could resist when two armed men overpower her. She remained in a state of helplessness. In the case of *Muhammad Qasim* (1997 Pakistan Criminal Law Journal 1095), the Federal Shariat Court said that the: '... victim was overwhelmed by two armed young persons and was under direct threat of murder or injury to body and, therefore, resistance was not expected from her ... ' In another case in 1997, the Federal Shariat Court said that: 'absence of any marks of violence on the body or private parts of the complainant [victim] could not necessarily prove her consent ... ' (1997 Pakistan Criminal Law Journal 546).

Despite the clear position of the Supreme Court and the Federal Shariat Court on the issue of 'marks of violence' on the victim's body, on 9 March 2005 the Lahore High Court acquitted four accused in the case of *Makhatr Mai* (Dawn, 9 March 2005). The brief facts of the case are that Mai's brother had allegedly been in an illicit relationship with the sister of the accused. To restore their family honour, they demanded public rape of Mai to which the Council of Elders of the area agreed. The Anti-Terrorist Court sentenced the accused to death but the Lahore High Court acquitted them. Beside other reasons for discrediting the victim's story, the High Court said:

> Four adult male persons allegedly committed forcible zina with her turn by turn while she was laid on the ... floor and during the struggle her shirt was also torn, but it is strange that the doctor ... did not observe any marks of violence on her body or private parts (Dawn, 9 March 2005).

The judgment outraged human rights organisations and in a very commendable move, the Federal Shariat Court took *suo moto* notice of the case under article 203DD of the constitution and suspended the order of the Lahore High Court (Dawn 12 March 2005).

The courts are prone to give the benefit of doubt to men as opposed to women. As already indicated, if a woman is unmarried and she becomes pregnant, first she has to establish that she was raped and second, to identify the perpetrator. If the victim fails to do so, the court assumes that she consented to the act and may be convicted under *tazir*. In the notorious case of *Jehan Mina* (Pakistan Law Journal 1983 Federal Shariat Court 134), two persons were accused of raping thirteen-year-old Mina. The matter was reported to the police after her pregnancy reached five to six months. The trial court disbelieved her version and, as there was no other evidence on the file, the accused was given the benefit of doubt and acquitted while she was sentenced to suffer a hundred stripes as *hadd*. The trial took her pregnancy for a confession. On appeal, the Federal Shariat Court agreed with the trial court on the point of acquitting the two accused with the following observation:

> We find that the two accused have been correctly acquitted by the learned trial court because they could not be convicted on the basis of the statement of a co-accused who was throwing the whole blame of the offence of Zina upon the other co-accused and she had not disclosed the offence of Zina-bil-jaber [rape] when it was committed although she had the opportunity of doing the same (Pakistan Law Journal 1983 Federal Shariat Court 134).

The Federal Shariat Court further ruled that as there were not four male witnesses to the act of rape so she could not be awarded *hadd* punishment of a hundred stripes. The court awarded her three years' rigorous imprisonment and ten stripes as *tazir* because of her tender age. The court did not call for semen matching or DNA tests, which would have helped the court immensely in finding the truth.

In later cases the position of the superior courts on the point of pregnancy as a confession of *zina* has changed and seems more balanced. In the case of *Mst. Siam* (PLD 1984 Federal Shariat Court 121), it was held that mere pregnancy/abortion or birth of an illegitimate child by an unmarried girl/widow or a married woman whose husband had no access to her during the relevant period was not sufficient for awarding punishment for *zina*. The Karachi High Court, in the case of *Mst. Rani* (PLD 1996 Karachi 316) made a significant ruling:

> Prosecution in order to get a woman convicted for Zina has to prove on record by positive and independent evidence that she had, actually and in fact, committed Zina with her own free will and consent with another man to whom she was not lawfully married ... proof of pregnancy or some form of medical testimony/report by itself would be of no consequence as the same would at best only serve to be corroborative in nature.

Asifa Quraishi (1997) also argues that the Koranic insistence on four witnesses as proof for intercourse indicates that the act of *zina* must not be public, not its consequences. It is public sex which is deterred, not public pregnancy. A pregnant woman looks the same whether it occurred because of rape, *zina* or marital intercourse.

In many cases the superior courts have discredited the testimony of female witnesses on the basis of their alleged sexual behaviour. There are frequent references to the sexual behaviour of women witnesses in court rulings such as 'woman of easy virtue'. There is, however, no such phrase as 'a man of easy virtue' in the case law of Pakistan. 'In several appeals and trials of rape, the "virtue" of the victim is given great emphasis ... Courts have ruled that testimony of "women of easy virtue" loses its weight' (Jehangir and Jillani, 1990:102-103). In the case of *Muhammad Sadi* (1995 Supreme Court Monthly Review 1403), the Supreme Court held that no implicit reliance could be placed on the statement of a woman of easy virtue unless some other independent evidence of commission of *zina* by the accused with her is available on record. In the case of *Abdul Kalam* (National Law Reporter 1986 Shariat Decisions 61), the accused was granted bail because the woman was of 'easy virtue'. The Commission (1997:70) has drawn attention to this:

> Regrettably, courts, too, reflect their biases in different forms. Words like 'zania', 'woman of easy virtue', and 'habitual' are liberally used in reported cases even where the woman is not an accused in the case. On the one hand, superior courts have discouraged the media from printing the names of women who are victims of rape but on the other hand, some reported judgments are too explicit.

This indicates the patriarchal nature of moral standards informing decisions of the superior courts and tendency among judges who do not sit on the bench with an open mind. They carry their biases with them to the bench.

Hadd law is applicable to adults but the age limit set for adulthood has a discriminatory effect on young girls: eighteen years for male and sixteen for female or attainment of puberty, which is the same for both. Jehangir and Jillani (1990:53) have rightly remarked:

> This definition equates mental development with sexual maturity. Criminal culpability is made to depend on the attainment and non-attainment of puberty. Since female attain puberty earlier, their threshold for criminal liability is lower than that of male children ... Evidence of females is presumably not accepted [in Hadd cases] on the notion that she has no understanding of such worldly matters. However, when it comes to comprehension of a crime as an offender, the logic is reversed.

The criterion of attaining puberty is not applied evenly to boys and girls. Courts recognise female menstruation as a sure sign of puberty but do not put an age limit on male capacity to perform sexual intercourse. In the case of *Muhammad Hussian* (PLD 1982 Federal Shariat Court 11), the Federal Shariat Court fined the accused because of his tender age after establishing that he had raped a minor girl of six years whereas the minimum sentence for an adult guilty of rape is four years and thirty stripes. In contrast to this, Mina, a tender aged girl who became pregnant as the result of alleged rape was awarded three years' rigorous imprisonment and ten stripes as *tazir*. The argument here is not why male non-adults are awarded low punishment but to emphasise that the same treatment is not extended to female non-adults. Interestingly, the Supreme Court does not view the sexual act itself sufficient to establish male puberty but the prosecution must show that the male accused is capable of reproduction (National Law Reporter 1985 Supreme Court 367). This is the most illogical indicator for male puberty. Many men are both pubertal and adults but are not capable of reproduction. By this criterion they could rape as many women as they want but would escape punishment. The age limit for male and female is not mentioned in the Koran; it is a standard set by Muslim jurists.

6.2.3 Abuses of the Zina *Ordinance*

Hudood laws have become a tool of repression for women. According to the National Commission on the Status of Women of Pakistan (2003), 80% of the women languishing in jails are there because of the ambiguous *Zina* Ordinance. The provisions of the Ordinance have been abused in several ways: by parents against their children who marry against their wishes, by former husbands against their ex wives and by the police either as a means of intimidation or as personal vendetta:

> Exploitation takes many forms. Most F.I.R.s [First Information Report, the complaint made to police] are filed by the women's families. Parents complain against their daughters just because the latter have married against their wishes, husbands make allegation against wives only because some estrangement has occurred between them (the Commission, 1997:70).

According to Jehangir and Jillani (1990:110):

> Even married couples are not safe from being implicated in zina charge. In most cases, it is young people who marry out of choice who end up spending their honeymoon in jail.

The study of case law presents a disappointing picture of the way the *Zina* Ordinance is used as a tool of repression against newly-wedded couples. In the case of *Muhammad Imtiaz* (PLD 1981 Federal Shariat Court 308), his father-in-law complained that Imtiaz had abducted his daughter. Both husband and wife were arrested on the charges of *zina*. The police as well as the court declined to accept their marriage certificate and sentenced them for seven years' imprisonment, thirty stripes and a fine of 5,000 rupees. The court held that the permission of the father/guardian was required for a valid marriage, which had not been obtained. The same happened in the case of *Azra Parveen* (PLD 1982 Federal Shariat Court 42). The father of Parveen complained to the police that his daughter was living with Arif Hussian, the co-accused, without being married to him. Both the police and the court turned down their marriage certificate. The trial court sentenced them to ten years' imprisonment and thirty stripes. On appeal, the Federal Shariat Court acquitted them but after spending one year in jail. On several occasions, the Lahore High Court has taken the legally appropriate view of the sad state of affairs in cases of this kind and has quashed a number of complaints against married couples. In the case of *Mst. Nasreen* (1994 Pakistan Criminal Law Journal 1111), the High Court quashed the case observing that the girl was a major and had married voluntarily; therefore, there was no justification for registering a case against her under the *Zina* Ordinance. In the case of *Mst. Faizan Bibi* (1997 Pakistan Criminal Law Journal 416), the court ruled that the accused had proved that they were legally married to each other by documentary evidence. Registration of the case against them was based on *mala fide* and amounted to abuse of the process of law. The Supreme Court has addressed the issue of voluntary marriage by adult girls in the case of *Abdul Hamid* (1994 Supreme Court Monthly Review 475). The father of Shumaila Gul complained that his daughter had been abducted and subjected to *zina* by Hamid, the petitioner; whereas Shumaila Gul made a statement before the Magistrate and Deputy Superintendent of Police denying abduction and claimed that she married Hamid voluntarily and wanted to live with him as his wife. Despite this, the High Court declined a bail petition by Hamid. The Supreme Court allowed the bail petition, ruling that the girl was adult and educated and had contracted marriage out of her own free will. The High Court should have allowed bail in these circumstances. This is a legally correct position but unfortunately trial courts do not follow the course set by the Supreme Court.

Husbands have used the *Zina* Ordinance as an effective device to victimise their divorced wives. The superior courts have given little relief to women in relation to these cases by handing down conflicting judgments on the validity of a woman's second marriage. The Federal Shariat Court upheld the conviction of the accused in the case of *Akbar Hussian* (1997 Pakistan Criminal Law Journal 543), observing that the accused had failed to prove a valid marriage. The facts of the case were that Khadim Ali alleged that his wife Farigha Jan ran away with his nephew Akbar Hussian and they were involved in *zina*. Akbar Hussian and Farigha Jan pleaded that they were validly married after getting a divorce from Khadim Ali but the trial court declined their plea and convicted them. On appeal, the Federal Shariat Court upheld their conviction observing that the accused had failed to prove the dissolution of the first marriage as well as the validity of the second marriage by producing a valid marriage certificate. Therefore, both were involved in unauthorised sexual intercourse and were appropriately convicted. In the case of *Bibi Khudija* (National Law Reporter 1986 Shariat Decision 575), the court adopted a similar approach observing that the accused had to prove not only *nikah* [marriage] but also valid *nikah* in order to obtain a finding of not-guilty. In such cases, the onus to prove a valid marriage is upon the person who sets up a *nikah* plea. A simple *nikah* plea or the frivolous, vexatious or *mala fide* nature of a *nikah* plea would not entitle an accused to acquittal.

However, in two other cases the Federal Shariat Court took a divergent view. In the case of *Aman Ullah* (National Law Reporter 1986 Shariat Decision 30), the court allowed bail when the accused stated that they were husband and wife. The court observed that the male and female co-accused admitted that they were husband and wife and as such the question of commission of *zina* did not arise. In the case of *Mst. Robina Shamim* (National Law Reporter 1986 Shariat Decisions 60), the Karachi High Court followed the same dictum. Robina had contracted a second marriage with Faiyaz after getting a divorce from Shakeel Ahmad. Shakeel complained to the police that Faiyaz has abducted his wife, Robina. Both were arrested and faced trial for commission of *zina*. Robina was in jail for more than fifty days giving birth to a baby in jail. The High Court granted bail on the grounds, *inter alia,* that Robina had entered into lawful wedlock with the male accused after getting a divorce from her previous husband. In 2004, the Lahore High Court quashed a case wherein it was alleged that Raiz Ahmad had enticed away Razia Bibi to commit *zina*. The accused said in the court that they were husband and wife whereon the court ruled that they had married out of their free consent and quashed the complaint (2004 Pakistan Criminal Law Journal 1175).

The aim of introducing the *hudood* laws was to Islamise previous laws dealing with sexual offences and others. However, many provisions of the current *Zina* Ordinance do not meet the Koranic criterion such as stoning to death, requirement of four male witnesses to prove the offence of *zina* and rape, etc. The *Zina* Ordinance is drawn up along the lines of a decontextualised interpretation of relevant verses of the Koran. The Federal Shariat Court and other superior courts have applied and interpreted the *Zina* Ordinance inconsistently. Several rulings and the language used therein reflect gender bias and a patriarchal notion of the family system. Men's sexual behaviour does influence decision making but women are frequently punished for alleged sexual deviancy. Second, the *Zina* Ordinance has not realised the Islamic goal, a society based on justice and equality, since hundreds of women have suffered and are suffering because of the discriminatory legal norms and their biased interpretation and application by courts. Some decisions of the Federal Shariat Court are relatively appropriate but far from sufficient. It depends who sits on the bench (conservative or liberal) and who rules the country (secular or religious parties). The lower courts, family members and the police have abused the *Zina* Ordinance and the abuses go unchecked in the majority of cases. The ordinance has furnished an effective tool for parents and husbands to terrorise and repress their young daughters and wives respectively. The so-called Islamic *Zina* Ordinance contains un-Islamic provisions and is being used to the disadvantage of women breaching their rights.

6.3 THE 1979 OFFENCE OF *QAZF* (ENFORCEMENT OF HUDOOD) ORDINANCE

The *Qazf* Ordinance introduced a new bailable offence into the criminal law of Pakistan. Although its preamble states its objective was to modify the existing law relating to *qazf*, the fact is that there was no specific law relating to *qazf* in Pakistan (except the defamation law). The ordinance has defined *qazf* as the imputation of *zina* to a person either dead or alive with intention or belief to harm the reputation or feeling of that person or family and a close relative in the case of a dead person. The definition allows two exceptions. First, a true imputation of *zina* for the public good and second, an accusation preferred in good faith to an authorised person do not constitute *qazf* except in the following three cases. First, when a complainant makes an accusation of *zina* against another person in the court and fails to produce four witnesses; second, the court finds that a witness has given false evidence of rape; and third, the court finds that a complainant has made a false accusation of *zina* or rape.

There are two kinds of *qazf*: one liable to *hadd* and other liable to *tazir*. *Qazf* liable to *hadd* is punishable with eighty stripes whereas *qazf* liable to *tazir* is punishable with two years imprisonment and up to thirty stripes and a fine. The standard of proof for *qazf* liable to *hadd* is in three forms: (1) confession before the court, (2) commission of *qazf* before the court or (3) testimony of four adult male Muslims. Only those against whom the accusation is made or a person authorised by him/her and in the case of a dead person, his/her ascendants or decedents, can lodge a *qazf* complaint. If spouses allege *qazf* against each other, the ordinance provides the processes of *lian* for them. Under *lian* the husband has to say four times on oath that my accusation against my wife is true and a fifth time that Allah's curse be on me if I am telling a lie. If the wife does not accept the accusation, in the same way the wife has to respond to the husband's accusation saying four times on oath that her husband is a liar and a fifth time Allah's curse be on her if she is telling a lie. The court dissolves the marriage and no criminal proceedings ensue.

6.3.1 The Koranic Foundation of the Qazf *Ordinance*

The Koranic standing of the *Qazf* Ordinance has not been the subject of as fierce a debate as the *Zina* Ordinance. Most of the provisions of the *Qazf* Ordinance seem in congruity with the Koran. A four-member bench of the Federal Shariat Court discussed the Islamic foundation of sections 7 and 14 in the case of *Haji Bakhtiar Muhammad* (National Law Reporter 1986 Shariat Decisions 240 (2)):

> If we read section 7 of Qazf Ordinance in juxtaposition with verse 4 [24:4] ... it would appear that section 7 is almost the restatement of [it]. Hence, there can be no doubt about the legality and validity of section 7 vis-à-vis the Injunctions of Islam.

Regarding section 14, which deals with *lian*, the court observed:

> It must be noted that before attracting the provision of section 14 of Qazf Ordinance, two conditions must be satisfied. First, the accusation is made by the husband during the subsistence of the marriage; and second, the husband has no witness, except himself, to prove the allegation. Both these conditions are deducible from verse 6 [24:6]. The second condition is not specifically mentioned in section 14 but the fact that clause (a) of the section provides for oath to be taken four times suggests that the husband is unable to produce four witnesses and that the four times oath is taken as a substitute for evidence of four witnesses necessary to prove 'zina' liable to Hadd. We shall, therefore, advise that the law makers take steps to amend section 14 by inserting the words "and is unable to produce witnesses except himself to prove the accusation" after the word zina. However, even in the absence of these words, section 14 shall be read as if the second condition referred to above is implied therein (National Law Reporter 1986 Shariat Decisions 240 (2)).

The most serious un-Islamic provision is the absence of the requirement for four witnesses to prove *qazf*. The Koran (24:4) very explicitly states: 'and those who launch a charge against chaste women, and produce not four witnesses (to support their allegations), – flog them with eighty stripes; and reject their evidence ever after'. In the case of *Rashida Patel* (PLD 1989 Federal Shariat Court 95), the Federal Shariat Court took the Koranic view that to avoid *qazf*, four eye-witnesses are required. Those who fail to produce four witnesses should be given eighty stripes and their evidence should not be accepted in future. The un-Islamic nature of these two ordinances is reflected by the fact that the *Zina* Ordinance requires four male witnesses to prove rape which is nowhere mentioned in the Koran but the *Qazf* Ordinance does not require the evidence of four witnesses to prove *qazf* which the Koran expressly demands. The *Qazf* Ordinance, like the *Zina* Ordinance, excludes the evidence of women in cases liable to *hadd*. Section 6(C) requires two male Muslim witnesses apart from the person against whom *qazf* is made. However, when we look at the Koranic verse 24:4, it requires four witnesses to prove *qazf* and does not mention the gender of the witnesses.

6.3.2 The Application of the Qazf *Ordinance*

The aim of *qazf* in the Koran was to provide deterrence against false accusation of *zina*. The *Qazf* Ordinance claimed the same purpose but has failed to turn that claim into reality. However, first, its Koranic standing is challengeable and second, it has not been applied effectively to curb the mounting wave of false *zina* cases. The rules laid down by the superior courts related to *qazf* are not complied with in many cases. The Lahore High Court gave wider interpretation to the *Qazf* Ordinance in the case of *Hussian Bibi* (PLD 1996 Lahore 50). The court ruled:

> Actions under the Enforcement of Huddood Ordinance are two-fold. The petitioner can sue under the ordinary law of tort for libel and also under the dictates of the Holy Quran as envisaged in Surrah Al-Noor [4:24] for Qazf (PLD 1996 Lahore 50).

The court further stated that if a person spreads slander maliciously and vexatiously, the Koran (24:19) says stern action shall be taken against him: 'those who love (to see) scandal published broadcast among the believers, will have a grievous Penalty in this life and in the Hereafter … ' In this case the court awarded 25,000 *rupees* (Pakistan's currency) damages to be paid to the petitioner. The Supreme Court upheld the sentence of an accused when he failed to produce four witnesses to support his allegation of *zina* in the case of *Jamil Hussian Shah* (1997 Supreme Court Monthly Review 897). The Supreme Court said:

> Accused had named the respondent lady in his statement brought on judicial record and the imputation made by him was so specific that she had been dismissed from her service as teacher. Accusation of zina had been made by the accused against the respondent in a court of law which was not substantiated not only by four witnesses but also by any piece of evidence whatsoever (1997 Supreme Court Monthly Review 897).

Many witnesses in *zina* cases are interested witnesses. In most of the cases lower courts faced the issue of whether a discredited witness can be tried under the *Qazf* Ordinance. The Federal Shariat Court ruled on the point in the case of *Bakhat Ali* (1993 Pakistan Criminal Law Journal 1872):

> [T]he injunctions of Islam regarding punishment of Hadd for the offence of Qazf have been given in Sura Noor verse 4 and the trend of that verse indicates that mere failure of the complainant to prove his allegation in the court does not make the witnesses of the said offence liable to Qazf punishment unless it is proved that they had mala fidely concocted a false accusation.

This view of the court indicates that if the witnesses play a part in the making of false accusations and are not *bona fide*, then they are liable to *qazf* punishment if proved so. In the case of *Rashida Patel* (PLD 1989 Federal Shariat Court 95), the Federal Shariat Court took a similar view that if the court comes to the conclusion after scrutinising the statements of witnesses and others attending evidence that the witnesses are malicious and vexatious, then the court can award punishment under *qazf* to them. Witnesses are usually related to the complainants in *zina* cases and they can be caught by this rule if it is proved that they are false and malicious. The *Qazf* Ordinance thus not only prevents false accusations but malicious and vexatious testimony as well.

Another crucial and interesting legal point is whether or not the court can initiate *qazf* proceedings when the complainant fails to prove or the court discredits his/her evidence. Does this failure of adducing the required evidence amount to *qazf* in the presence of the court liable to *hadd* punishment under section 6(b)? It seems from the wording of the section that anyone who deposes in the court that someone is guilty of *zina* but does not establish it, that person commits *qazf* in the presence of the court. Putting the relevant verse (24:4) in its Koranic context, this seems to be the intent of the Koran as *zina* and *qazf* stand side by side in the Koran. The time and reasons of the revelation of verse 24:4 also indicates this view. It was revealed when rumours of adultery against the young wife of the Prophet Muhammad, Aisha, were in the air. And to end and prevent further rumours, this verse was revealed.

However, the Federal Shariat Court has taken a different view in the case of *Masood Shah* (1996 Shariat Decisions 335). In this case a complaint was made against Masood Shah of having sex with a prostitute. The trial court convicted him. On appeal, the Federal Shariat Court set aside the conviction but observed that it is a pity that it cannot take *suo motu* action against the complainant under the ordinance. The court explained that under section 8, three persons have *locus standi* in *qazf* proceedings: (a) the person against whom an imputation of *zina* is made or (b) anyone authorised by him and (c) in case of a dead person, his ascendants or decedents. This does not seem to be the correct interpretation of the ordinance. First, it contradicts section 6(b), which states that one form of proof of *qazf* liable to *hadd* is when it is committed before the court. The ordinance would not make such clearly self-contradictory provisions. Second, section 8 bars public at large and allows only the affected people to make a complaint of *qazf*. The bar does not apply to the court itself. In the case of *Zarina Bibi* (1997 Pakistan Criminal Law Journal 313), the court said that the bar contained in section 8 is against the teachings of Islam. The learned judge (1997 Pakistan Criminal Law Journal 313) said: 'I am of the opinion that such bar is not in accordance to the teachings of Islam'.

When we look at the number of false cases and acquittals regarding *zina* and the lack of application of *Qazf* Ordinance, we reach a conclusion that the ordinance has failed in achieving the purpose for which it was allegedly enacted: furnishing an effective deterrent against false accusation of *zina*. Some of its provisions are also contrary to the Koran. One probable reason for its ineffectiveness is that both *zina* and *qazf* ordinances are not drawn according to the Koranic scheme. In the Koran the verse (24:2) related to *zina* is closely followed by the verse (24:4) related to *qazf* whereas in the legal system of Pakistan both are made the subject of two different ordinances. If the order of *qazf* was inserted into *zina* on the style of the Koran, it will probably prove as a more effective deterrent and remain in the sight of the courts constantly.

6.4 THE LAW OF EVIDENCE (*QANUN-E-SHAHADAT*)

In 1984, the *Evidence Act of* 1872 was revised and renamed as the '*Qanun-e-Shahadat* Order'. Fewer changes were made than in the other laws.

> The Qanoon-e-Shahadat with the exception of nine new sections is drawn up exactly on the old pattern. Most sections have been renumbered … If one were to go by the similarities of the old Anglo-Saxon Evidence Act and the present Qanoon-e-Shahadat, a simplistic conclusion would be that the Anglo-Saxon rules of evidence are quite close to the Islamic rules of evidence. This, of course, is not correct if the view held by the Islamic jurists are studied. The Islamic law of evidence lays much more stress on the number of eyewitnesses and character of the witnesses than the Anglo-Saxon law. The acceptability of evidence varies from crime to crime (Jehangir and Jillani, 19990:30).

The few changes that were introduced are related to the number (article 7) and competence (article 17) of witnesses but 'both of these changes remain vague' (Jehangir and Jillani, 1990:30). The Commission (1997:76) commented on these sections unfavourably:

> These provisions leave much to the discretion of the court. It is the court that will determine the competence of a witness in accordance with the injunctions of Islam. This is bound to lead to varied interpretation … considering that there are usually differences of opinion; strict consistency can hardly be expected. The law thus seems unfair in taxing the courts with laying down the law where varying interpretations of Islamic injunctions are possible. It may lead to much confusion and injustice.

The most important and discriminatory amendment is article 17(2) (a) which says that:

> In matters pertaining to financial or future obligations, if reduced to writing, the instrument shall be attested by two men, or one man and two women, so that one may remind the other … 'and 'in all other matters, the court may accept, or act on, the testimony of one man or one woman …

This section reduces the evidence of women in financial matters to half that of a man but interestingly in all other matters, except *hadd* cases, the court is allowed to accept the evidence of a woman. The section is based on the decontextualised interpretation of the following Koranic verse (2:282) as discussed in chapter 2:

> When ye deal with each other, in transactions involving future obligations ... reduce them to writing ... and get two witnesses, out of your own men, and if there are not two men, then a man and two women ... for witnesses, so that if one of them errs, the other can remind her.

6.5 THE LAW OF *QISAS* (RETRIBUTION) AND *DIYAT* (BLOOD MONEY)

The struggle to Islamise sections of the Pakistan Penal Code (1860) related to hurt and murder etc. started during the Zia's regime (Mehdi, 1994:151) but the goal was not realised until 1990 when the Criminal Law (Second Amendment) Ordinance was promulgated.[1] This law contains several gender-discriminatory provisions. The amended section 330 of the Pakistan Penal Code (1860) states that: 'the diyat shall be disbursed among the heirs of the victim according to their respective shares in inheritance ... ' Obviously a woman's share in inheritance is less than man's who gets double shares. The lesser share of woman in *diyat* was a controversial issue for long but the Ordinance did not settle it but rather legalised it. Anita Weiss (cited in Gottesman, 1991-92) says that despite this disparity, the punishment for a woman culprit was the same as for a man. This change is against the tenets of Islam. The Commission (1997:58) said that:

> There is no warrant for treating *diyat* as inheritance. Inheritance relates to the estate left by the deceased. Diyat on the other hand is a compensation for the loss the heirs have suffered because of the victim's going and cannot be treated as part of the inheritance.

The 1990 Ordinance allows compounding (compromising) of cases related to *qisas* and *diyat* (Criminal Law (Second Amendment), 1990 section: 310). In most cases compensation for compounding turned out to be a woman given in marriage to the member of victim's family. The 1990 Ordinance declared that 'giving a female in marriage shall not be a valid badal-i-sulh [compensation]' but does not make the act punishable. The Commission (1997:57) concluded:

---

[1] Actually the initiative for amending the Pakistan Penal Code came from the Shariat Bench of Peshawar High Court when it declared the relevant sections of Pakistan Penal Code repugnant to Islam in the case of *Gul Hasan* (PLD 1980 Peshawar 1). The Supreme Court upheld the decision (see, PLD 1989 SC 633).

> It leaves the possibility of the intent of the law to be circumvented even though the word is honoured. The practice of handing over a female for *badal-i-sulh* may continue in an informal manner unless the law specifically prohibits this custom.

Another discriminatory aspect of this law is that in a situation where the victim has a *wali* (guardian) who is minor or insane, it allows *qisas* to devolve to the father and if he is not alive, to the grandfather. And if the grandfather too is not alive and the court has not appointed any *wali*, then to the government. The obvious discrimination is the assumption that both mother and grandmother are not qualified to be *wali* in this sort of situation. The whole concept of *walait* (guardianship) is inherently gender-biased. The Commission (1997:56) wrote:

> The law as is conceived and written, it would appear, on the premise that the wali is always male … the use of this biased notion of wali, thus, becomes a mechanism for perpetuating male domination.

The 1990 Ordinance does not consider the testimony of a woman equal to man. Proof for murder liable to *qisas* is either confession or as provided in article 17 of *Qanoon-e-Shahadat order 1984*. (Pakistan Penal Code, 1860 section: 304). Article 17 clearly excludes women's evidence in *hadd* cases as discussed above and murder liable to *qisas* is a *hadd* case.

6.6 CONCLUSION

It is beyond doubt that the much talked about *hudood* ordinances have some serious gender-discriminatory provisions, which are employed systematically to undermine women's human rights. These laws are often employed as a tool of persecution and vendetta against women by parents, husbands and in some instances by police. These laws have also furnished an opportunity to the players in the criminal justice system to vent their gender and patriarchal biases while processing cases under them. The constitutional role of the Federal Shariat Court is to examine whether or not existing laws are in conformity with Islamic standards. However, the court has not discharged its functions very successfully in the case of *hudood* ordinances. In many cases, it followed the official interpretation of Islamic law except in a few bold judgments where judicial *ijtihad* was carried out, such as in the cases of *Rashida Patel* and *Hazoor Bakhash*. There has been strong discontent about the Islamic standing of the *hudood* ordinances, laws of evidence and *qisas* and *diyat*, but the Federal Shariat Court has refrained from engaging in active judicial *ijtihad* regarding criminal laws. Although its recent intervention in the case of *Mai* has received wider commendation, the Federal Shariat Court has used its *suo moto* powers sparingly.

However, on balance, the Federal Shariat Court must be given credit for its strong role as a force of 'corrective justice' on the abusive application of *hudood* laws by trial courts where the tendency is to convict the accused under *hadd*. In contrast to this, the Federal Shariat Court tends to turn convictions into *tazir*. It is because of the role of Federal Shariat Court as an agent of 'corrective justice' that punishments such as stoning to death for adultery and chopping of hands for theft are not executed (Kennedy, 1991:46). Those who sit on the bench and rule the country have invariably played a role in determining the way the Federal Shariat Court interpret *hudood* and other laws and take decisions.

REFERENCES

Ali, Y. (1989) *The Meaning of the Holy Qur'an*. Maryland: Amana Corporation.

Abdual Hamid *(1994) Supreme Court Monthly Review 475.*

Abdual Kalam (1986) *National Law Reporter* 1986 Shariat Decisions 61.

Akbar Hussian (1997) *Pakistan Criminal Law Journal* 543.

Aman Ullah (1986) National *Law Reporter* 1986 Shariat Decisions 30.

Azra Parveen (1982) *All Pakistan Legal Decisions* 1982 Federal Shariat Court 42.

Bakhat Ali (1993) *Pakistan Criminal Law Journal* 1872.

Bibi Khudija (1986) *National Law Reporter* 1986 Shariat Decisions 575.

Carroll, L. (1982a) 'Rejoinder to the Proceedings of the Seminar on 'Adultery and Fornication in Islamic Jurisprudence: Dimensions and Perspectives' *Islamic and Comparative Law Quarterly*. 2 (4) pp.57-95.

Dawn (2005) 'PPP submits resolution against Hudood law in Senate'. 4 January, 2005. Karachi. http://www.dawn.com/2005/01/04/nat5.htm [accessed Nov. 2005].

Dawn (2005) 'CII chief hints at Hudood laws review'. 30 May 2005. Karachi. http://www.dawn.com/2005/05/30/nat1.htm [accessed Nov. 2005].

Gottesman, E. (1991-92) 'The Reemergence of Qisas and Diyat in Pakistan' *Columbia Human Rights Law Review*. 23 pp.433-462.

Haji Bakhtiar (1986) *National Law Reporter* 1986 Shariat Decisions 240.
Hazoor Bakhsh (1981) *All Pakistan Legal Decisions* 1981 Federal Sharait Court 145.
Hussian Bibi (1996) *All Pakistan Legal Decisions* 1996 Lahore 50.
Jamil Hussian Shah (1997) *Supreme Court Monthly Review* 897.
Jehangir, A. and Hina, J. (1990) *Hudood Ordinances: A Divine Sanction?* Lahore: Rhotas Books.
Jehan Mina (1983) *Pakistan Law Journal* 1983 Federal Shariat Court 134.
Kennedy, C. H. (1991) 'Islamic Legal Reform and the Status of Women in Pakistan' *Journal of Islamic Studies*. 2 (1) p.45-55.
Masood Shah (1996) *Shariat Decisions* 335.
Mehdi, R. (1990) 'The Offence of Rape Law in the Islamic Law of Pakistan' *International Journal of the Sociology of Law*. 18 pp.19-28.
Mst. Faizan Bibi (1997) *Pakistan Criminal Law Journal* 1997, 416.
Mst. Nasreen (1994) *Pakistan Criminal Law Journal* 1994, 1111.
Mst. Rani (1996) *All Pakistan legal Decisions* 1996 Karachi 316.
Mst. Siam (1984) *All Pakistan Legal Decisions* 1984 Federal Shariat Court 121.
Mst. Tasleem (1996) *Pakistan Law Journal* 1996 Federal Sharait Court 138.
Mukhtar Mai (2005) *All Pakistan Legal Decisions* 2005 Lahore.
M. Hussian (1982) *All Pakistan Legal Decisions* 1982 Federal Shariat Court 11.
M. Imtiaz (1981) *All Pakistan legal Decisions* 1981 Federal Shariat Court 308.
Muhammad Nawaz (1990) *Supreme Court Monthly Review* 886.
Muhammad Qasim (1997) *Pakistan Criminal Law Journal* 1997, 1095.
Muhammad Sadi (1995) *Supreme Court Monthly Review* 1403.
National Commission on the Status of Women of Pakistan (2003) *Draft Report on the Meetings of the Special Committee To Review The (Enforcement of Hudood Ordinances,* 1979.
http://new.ncsw. gov.pk/index.php [Accessed March 2005).
National Law Reporter 1985 Supreme Court 367.
Pakistan (1997) Commission of Inquiry for Women, *Annual Report*. Pakistan.
Pakistan (1979) The Offence of *Zina* (Enforcement of Hudood) Ordinance.
Pakistan (1979) The Offence of *Qazf* (Enforcement of Hudood) Ordinance.
Pakistan (1984) The *Qanun-e-Shahadat* Order [Evidence Act].
Pakistan (1860) The Pakistan Penal Code.
Pakistan Criminal Law Journal 1994, 2210.

Quraishi, A. (1997) 'Her Honour: An Islamic Critique of the Rape Laws in Pakistan from a Woman-Sensitive Perspective' *Michigan Journal of International Law.* 18 (2) pp.287-320.

Rashida Patel (1989) *All Pakistan Legal Decisions* 1989 Federal Shariat Court 95.

Riaz Ahmad (2004) *Pakistan Criminal Law Journal* 1175.

Robina Shamim (1986) *National Law Reporter* 1986 Shariat Decisions 60.

Zarina Bibi (1997) *Pakistan Criminal Law Journal* 313.

CHAPTER 7

Women's Rights and the Family Laws

The laws that immediately affect women's rights in Pakistani society in every day life are chiefly family laws. The Koran considers the family to be a fundamental social unit and therefore, provides a comprehensive code for its regulation. The Koran also gives a woman an equal role in the family and provides her strong protection within the family. However, in practice, women's rights are greatly violated within this protected circle which is the most vulnerable area for them. The purpose of this chapter is to look at the statutory family laws of Pakistan, their Koranic foundations, how the courts interpret and apply them, and to what extent they protect/undermine women's rights. The focus, therefore, will be on the analysis of the case law of the superior courts. There are quite a few statutes dealing with family matters, e.g. the 1939 *Dissolution of Muslim Marriage Act*, the 1929 *Child Marriage Restraint Act*, the 1964 *West Pakistan Family Courts Act*, the 1976 *Dowry and Bridal Gifts (Restriction) Act*, etc. but this chapter is focused on the 1961 *Muslim Family Laws Ordinance* (hereinafter, MFLO). The main areas of concern here (as understood in the prevalent *Hanafi* School in Pakistan) are the right to marriage, polygamy, right to divorce, registration of marriage and maintenance.

7.1 THE 1961 MUSLIM FAMILY LAWS ORDINANCE

Before proceeding to the analysis of specific provisions of the MLFO, it will be helpful to have an overview of the ordinance from the outset. The ordinance extends to Muslim citizens only and has an overriding effect over all other laws. It provides that the personal law of the parties shall govern all family disputes. Disputes should be referred to the Arbitration Council, comprising representatives of the spouses headed by the Chairperson of the local council (section 2). All Muslim marriages must be registered with *Nikah* (marriage) Registrar and non-registration would be punishable with simple imprisonment up to three months and a fine up to 1,000 rupees or both (section 5). No second marriage can be contracted except with the permission of the wife and the Arbitration Council and marriage contracted without such permission cannot be registered. The applicant must show to the Arbitration Council whether or not the consent of the existing wife/wives has been obtained and breaking this provision is punishable with one-year imprisonment or a fine of 5,000 rupees or both (section 6). An immediate notice of divorce must be sent to the Chairperson of the local council as well as to the wife otherwise he/she is punishable with simple imprisonment extending to one year or with a fine extending up to 5,000 rupees or both. Divorce is ineffective until the expiration of ninety days after such a notice and if the wife is pregnant, until delivery of the child. In the interim period, the Chairperson has to take every step to bring reconciliation between the spouses through an arbitration council (section 7). Besides divorce by the husband, the ordinance recognises other forms of dissolution of marriage: mutual release which may either take the form of *khul* or *mubarah* and the option of puberty (if a girl is married in her minority she may dissolve such a marriage on attaining puberty), and delegating the power of divorce to the wife (section 8). The ordinance provides for adequate, and in case of more than one wife equitable, maintenance during and after the marriage (section 9).

It is interesting to note that the MLFO is mainly related to procedural aspects of the family laws. It does not touch upon what the substantive laws are, thus leaving it to the courts to rely on the uncodified Muslim personal law. For instance, it does not spell out the grounds for divorce, its forms and when a wife can ask for it. However, it does stipulate when it become effective and must be registered. It also does not set out the amount and duration of maintenance but recognises the right of a wife to maintenance. The ordinance is silent on the consent of wife for first marriage but requires the permission of the first wife/wives for contracting a second marriage. The Supreme Court (PLD 1981 Supreme Court 120) has made a nice distinction between the statutory and uncodified Muslim personal law:

> Muslim personal law may have two meaning depending upon context of its use. Such phrase in commonly understood sense may mean religious or Divine law of Muslims by which they believe to be governed as matter of faith. The phrase in second sense may mean all special statutory laws applying only to Muslims as distinct from general law applying to all classes of people in general.

7.2 THE KORANIC FOUNDATION OF THE MFLO

The Islamic nature of the MLFO has remained controversial from the very beginning. The ordinance presents a compromise between Islamic and secular tendencies (Mehdi, 1994:157). The religious groups made many protests when it was promulgated but the military government of Ayub Khan (who introduced the ordinance) did not yield. The secular aspect, aimed at improving the plight of women, did not go well with the people as well as with the superior courts. The superior courts found several provisions of the MLFO contrary to uncodified Islamic family law. Lucy Carroll (1989) argues that section 4 has improved the position of the *Hanafi* daughter (female follower of *Hanafi* School) and should be considered an added benefit of this enlightened legislation. Section 4 reads:

> In the event of the death of any son or daughter of the propositus before the opening of succession, the children of such a son or daughter, if any, living at the time the succession opens, shall per strips receive a share equivalent to the share which such a son or daughter, as the case may be, would have received if alive.

In the case of *Farishta* (PLD 1980 Peshawar 47) the Shariat Bench of the Peshawar High Court declared section 4 to be un-Islamic, observing that:

> [A] person in order to be entitled to inherit his parents or near ones must be alive. Section 4 ... providing for inheritance of predeceased offspring living at time of opening of succession is against injunctions of Islam and liable to be repealed.

However, the Shariat Bench of the Supreme Court (PLD 1981 Supreme Court 120) overturned the ruling on jurisdictional grounds. The Supreme Court did not discuss whether or not section 4 is contrary to Islamic injunctions but said that article 203B(C) of the constitution has excluded the ordinance from judicial scrutiny and that the Shariat Bench of the High Court is not competent to decide cases of this nature. The successor of Shariat Benches, the Federal Shariat Court (PLD 2000 Federal Shariat Court 1) broke this constitutional barrier and declared section 4 repugnant to Islam, instructing the President of Pakistan to amend it and to bring it in line with the injunctions of Islam as interpreted by this court. The section does not seem to have been amended so far (2005) but the 1973 constitution of Pakistan (article 203D(3)(b)) declares that: 'such law or provision shall, to the extent to which it is held to be so repugnant, cease to have effect on the day on which the decision of the Court takes effect'. In 2004, the Supreme Court restrained the Federal Shariat Court from examining the Islamic foundation of family law. The court said:

> Muslim Personal Law cannot be examined by the Federal Shariat Court and Muslim Personal Law in Article 203B(C) means (i) statutory law of Muslim and (ii) it is personal law of a particular sect. If these two conditions are not present, the matter can be examined by the Federal Shariat Court (PLD 2004 Supreme Court 219).

By this interpretation, it is only the statutory family laws which are excluded from Islamic judicial scrutiny, but all other uncodified legal principles may be examined and interpreted by the Federal Shariat Court. Many Islamic legal principles are not codified but are contained in the juristic treatises of Muslim jurists such as *Hedaya* (Hamilton (trans.) 1989). It leaves the Federal Shariat Court with a vast area for examination.

Section 7(3) requires ninety days, after notice to the Chairperson of the local council and wife, for divorce to be effective but the Federal Shariat Court (National Law Reporter 1992 Shariat Decisions 502) ruled that:

> Notice of talaq required by S. 7 … is not mandatory under Injunctions of Islam. Any divorce pronounced or written by husband cannot be ineffective or invalid in Sharia merely because its notice has not been given.

The Lahore High Court (1993 Civil Law Cases 219) adopted similar interpretation ruling that:

> Islam prescribes no particular mode for dissolving a marriage through divorce. Any overt act on the part of husband, which was indicative of a firm intention to sever matrimonial bond, would operate as divorce.

However, the Lahore High Court (2003 YLR 2623) departed from this position and declared section 7 to be in consonance with the injunctions of Islam observing that the Koran never intended a divorce to act as a device of instant magic. Differences of opinion on instant triple divorce (to say three times 'I divorce you') evoked 'legislative compassion' in the form of section 7(3) providing for revocation of divorce within ninety days. The approach of the Supreme Court (1984 Supreme Court Monthly Review 583) towards this section is that divorce would become effective only after notice to the Chairperson and the period of three months provided for reconciliation between parties expires. If the husband does not give notice of divorce to the Chairperson it would be deemed to be revoked. The Supreme Court did not investigate whether or not section 7 is against injunctions of Islam; it applied the law as it stands. These different interpretations tend to result in confusion about the law relating to family matters as in some cases the superior courts go beyond the statutory laws and base their judgement on the uncodified Islamic rules as in the above two cases. In other cases, there is strict compliance with the statutory law such as the above interpretation of the Supreme Court. However, it must be recalled that, according to the constitution (article 189), the judgments of the Supreme Court are binding on all courts in the country.

A similar inconsistent approach is adopted regarding the stipulated registration of marriages. In the case of *Atiya Nasir* (1995 Pakistan Criminal Law Journal 1657) it was held:

> Contract of marriage need not be proved through a written document. If *nikah* is not registered, then either two witnesses can be produced in support of the factum of *nikah* or husband and wife may together certify the factum of their marriage.

Justice Tanzilur Rahman (1997) contends that registration or non-registration of marriage would in no way affect its legality or validity if it is duly performed according to the *Sharia*. Some Islamic scholars argue that it is not proper to treat non-registration of marriage as an offence while others believe that the writing of marriage is desirable (Rahman, 1997; Mehdi, 1994). The current position of the Federal Shariat Court (PLD 2000 Federal Shariat Court 63) is that registration of *nikah* (marriage) is not necessarily the proof of *nikah* as in Islam *nikah* could be performed by an offer and acceptance in the presence of witnesses. Non-registration of *nikah* would only attract a penalty under section 5(4) of the ordinance.

The Koran, according to the conservative interpretation, allows up to four wives but the MFLO (section 6) has put a restriction on it by making permission of the first wife mandatory for contracting a second marriage. The Lahore High Court (1992 Monthly Law Digest 93) held that contracting a second marriage in contravention of section 6 was not only an offence but also gave rise to certain civil consequences in favour of existing wife/wives. However, in another case the court held that failure to obtain permission under section 6 only attracts penal action but does not affect the validity of the second marriage (PLD 1995 Lahore 475). Following the ordinance, it is an offence not to take the permission of first wife for second marriage whereas under Islamic law no such precondition exists. The ordinance does not abolish polygamy but has restricted it. If a husband does not ask permission of a first wife or the Arbitration Council, his second marriage is still valid but he may face imprisonment and a fine. This novel arrangement is neither based on conservative nor contextual interpretation of the Koran. It is also not based on the recommendation of Family Law Commission of 1956 (see *Gazette of Pakistan Extraordinary* 20 June 1956), which recommended abolishing polygamy completely. Shaheen Sardar Ali (2002:323) said:

> As has been the case in Pakistan, elected governments find themselves unable to legislate and implement meaningful reform due to popular pressure. It took an army general ... to promulgate the MLFO and that too only limited/inhibited polygamy rather than abolishing it outrightly.

7.3 INTERPRETATION AND APPLICATION OF THE MFLO

7.3.1 Woman's Consent for Marriage

The ordinance does not mention that consent of a woman is required for a valid marriage but it is a settled principle of *Hanafi* School that 'a marriage of Muhammaden who is of sound mind and has attained puberty, is void, if it is brought without his consent' and 'where consent to a marriage has been obtained by force or fraud, the marriage is invalid' (Hidayatullah, 1968:249-250). Abdual Rahim (1911) maintains that according to the *Hanafi* School every male and female, who is not minor, is competent to contract marriage and cannot be given in marriage without consent either by the father or any other relatives. It is a germane rule of family law in Pakistan that marriage without the woman's consent is invalid. In the case of *Abdul Waheed* (PLD 2004 Supreme Court 219), the Supreme Court settled this issue in very clear terms that the:

> Consent of 'Wali' [guardian] is not required and a sui juris Muslim female can enter into valid Nikah/marriage of her own free will. Marriage is not invalid on account of the alleged absence of consent of Wali.

Islam has also provided protection to girls who are married as minors. When a guardian contracts a marriage for a minor, the minor has the option to repudiate the marriage on attaining puberty, technically known as option of puberty. The option of puberty is lost for a female if she attains puberty and does not exercise it. In the case of a male, it continues until he ratifies the marriage (Hidayatullah, 1968). In the case of *Mst. Irfana Tasneem* (PLD 1999 Lahore 479), the Lahore High Court ruled that 'no exact age, time or specific mode of exercise of option puberty is prescribed in law...Girl, however, should exercise her right of option of puberty before attaining the age of 18'. The court also ruled that it could be 'exercised by a girl even without the intervention of the court' (PLD 1999 Lahore 479; see PLD 1950 Lahore 203; PLD 1953 Lahore 131). In the case of *Mst. Farangeza* (1995 Monthly Law Digest 1439), the Peshawar High Court ruled that 'court order is not essential for conferring validity on the exercise of the option of puberty'. Where a girl, before the consummation of her first marriage as a minor, marries again on attaining puberty, the second marriage would be valid (1995 Monthly Law Digest 1439). In the case of *Said Mahmood* (PLD 1995 Federal Shariat Court 1), the Federal Shariat Court ruled:

> [The] wife whose Nikah had taken place during her minority had the right to repudiate it after attaining puberty provided the marriage had not been consummated, but she must exercise this right immediately after attaining puberty and if there was any delay on her part then she would lose the said right.

Many girls are engaged/married by parents/families when they are minor and this rule is an effective option available to such girls for releasing themselves from unwanted marital bonds. However, to exercise the right is difficult and uncommon because of social pressures. For instance, a divorcee is not considered suitable for remarriage and a woman may want to live with her husband instead of going to her parents/relatives. This is especially true in conservative families and those living in rural areas. Also, in a majority of cases, minor wives are not aware of their right of the option of puberty.

7.3.2 Dower/Maher

Maher or dower is a sum of money or other property which the wife is entitled to receive from the husband for consideration of marriage and is regarded as a mark of respect (Hidayatullah, 1968). Marriage being a settlement, consideration is a precondition of a valid marriage (2003 Civil Law Cases 1213). The Lahore High Court (PLD 1995 Lahore 98), has held that dower or consideration for marriage is an essential ingredient of a valid marriage in Islam. The Karachi High Court (PLD 1992 Karachi 46), held that it 'is essentially the right of the wife and not of her parents'. Parties can enhance the amount of dower at any time subsequent to marriage (1998 Civil Law

Cases 1054). If the husband fails to pay dower to his wife, she has lawful excuse to live away from him and to refuse him sexual intercourse so long as prompt dower is not paid (PLD 1991 Lahore 251).

7.3.3 Right to Divorce

In Islamic law, a man has absolute power to divorce his wife unilaterally, extra judicially and without assigning any cause (Hidayatullah, 1968). According to Rahim (1911:335): 'he can...put an end to the marriage at his uncontrolled option'. But the MFLO has placed a restriction on the right of man to divorce by providing 90 days for reconciliatory efforts during which the divorce remains ineffective. As stated earlier, a marriage tie may be ended by mutual release taking either the form of *khul* or *mubarah*. A husband can also delegate a wife the right to dissolve a marriage. These forms of divorce/separations available to women are discussed one by one below.

7.3.3.1 Mutual Release: Mubarah *and* Khul

Mubarah is kind of mutual release when the desire to separate comes from both spouses and they agree on certain terms and conditions to separate whereas in case of *khul*, the desire to separate comes from a wife and she has to return dower to release herself. *Mubarah* is not a common form of separation in Pakistan as it is considered against the social norms [or man's norms] to release his wife. The dominant form of divorce for women is *khul* but again many men would not take dower from their wives and release them. Women turn to the court to get their marriage dissolved which is why it popularly known in Pakistan as a 'judicial *khul*' (Carroll, 1996).

The Karachi High Court has made a nice distinction between *khul* and *talaq* (divorce) in the case of *Mussarat Jabeen* (2003 Monthly Law Digest 1077; see PLD 2000 Karachi 348). *Khul* is the right of a wife and *talaq* is the right of a husband. The distinction between the two is that *khul* is a form of dissolution of marriage for a consideration to be paid by the wife where a judge decides the same to be a fit case for dissolution. Where a wife has developed such dislike or aversion that she cannot live with her husband under any circumstances and pays him consideration to buy her release, then she has a right to ask the court for the dissolution of the marriage. The Supreme Court clarified the nature and position of *khul* in the case of *Mst. Kaneez Fatima* (2002 Supreme Court Monthly Review 1563) observing that *khul* is a controlled right:

> In case of dislike by wife of her husband, Islam concedes right to wife in circumstances of extreme discord and where life becomes a torture for both, on account of fixed aversion, on part of spouses, to seek dissolution of marriage on ground of Khula. Such right, however, is not an absolute right by which the wife can herself dissolve the marriage but is a controlled right, the success of which depends upon the Qazi's reaching the conclusion that the spouses cannot live within the limits of God.

The Lahore High Court has followed this rule in the case of *Mst. Zanab Mai* (2003 Civil Law Cases 214) holding that a wife is entitled to *khul* as of right, if she satisfies the court that she has developed such a fixed aversion towards the husband that refusing dissolution of marriage would mean forcing her into hateful union. The Peshawar High Court (PLD 2003 Peshawar 146) has further strengthened the rules to protect the rights of women: 'the court has the powers to refuse the return of the dowered property/amount to husband...where due to his cruelty she was compelled to resort to Khula'.

The rulings of the superior courts reflect their liberal and consistent approach towards the application of *khul*. A wife cannot exercise this right as her husband can but she can move and satisfy the court to get dissolution of marriage. If she is forced to seek *khul* by coercion, cruelty, which is found in a good number of cases, and she establishes this in the court, then the court may relieve her from returning dowered property. It seems an effective mode of getting a marriage dissolved but does not empower a woman to divorce herself as a man does. It must be mentioned that for the first time the Supreme Court, resorting to judicial *ijtihad*, granted the right to *khul* in the famous case of *Khurshid Bibi* (PLD 1967 Supreme Court 97). The court ruled that where spouses agree mutually on separation, no resort to court is needed. But when a husband does not agree to release his wife, a third party is needed to decide the case and the court can order separation 'even if the husband is not agreeable to that course'.

7.3.3.2 Delegated Power of Divorce

Hidayatullah (1968:292) notes that the husband 'may delegate the power to the wife or to a third person, either absolutely or conditionally, and either for a particular period or permanently'. 'Once he has conferred such power, he cannot afterwards revoke it and it will depend upon the wife whether to exercise the power or not' (Hidayatullah, 1968:338). In the case of *Mst. Zainab Bashir* (National Law Reporter 1995 Shariat Decisions 558), the Lahore High Court ruled:

> [A] husband under Islamic law enjoys an absolute power to divorce his wife. He may delegate this power to his wife by way of contract. Such delegation may be conditional resting upon happening of some contingencies or delegation may be unconditional. In both cases, a formal pronouncement of talaq by wife would be necessary. Notice sent by wife to Chairman would constitute formal pronouncement of talaq by wife.

Column 18 of the *nikanama* (marriage certificate) in Pakistan asks whether a wife is delegated the power to divorce but unfortunately that column remains blank most of the time or the answer is no. Most of the women do not know this right especially in rural areas. If a wife is given this power from the beginning, it can save women from the ordeals of litigation and may help in reducing the workload of the judiciary as well. The Koran as well as the ordinance recognises this right but is not practised because of social perceptions that a husband and a wife cannot be placed in a position of equality.

7.3.4 Right to Maintenance: During and after Marriage

The ordinance provides for adequate, and in the case of more than one wife, equitable maintenance during and after dissolution of marriage (section 9). In the legal sense, it means providing the necessaries of life to the wife and also to children and parents (Rahman, 1968). *Nafaqh* (maintenance) comprehends 'food, raiment and lodging, though in common parlance, it is limited to the first' (Fyzee, 1999:211). There are other necessary articles as well such as soap, oil, water, medicine etc. Justice Rahman (1968:271-272) observed:

> In Shariat it is duty of husband to provide cooked food and stitched cloths to his wife. A wife cannot be compelled to cook food for herself, much less for the husband, nor is she to be compelled to stitch cloth. The husband is bound to provide her a separate house or a separate portion of house which has an independent entrance and exit, although she can by her free will, live with the parents or other relatives of the husband.

Marriage in Islam is not in the nature of a sacrament or religious right but a pure and simple contract. A duty is cast upon a husband to provide his wife with maintenance (PLD 1957 Dacca 245). This is, however, contingent on two conditions that she is faithful and obeys his reasonable orders. The wife loses her right of maintenance if she refuses herself to her husband except for two reasons: the husband has not paid prompt dower or treats her cruelly (Hidayatullah, 1968). In the case of *Masuda Khanum* (PLD 1978

Quetta 117), it was held that 'non-payment of prompt dower is lawful excuse for wife to refuse herself to her husband until it is paid'. If the wife is living separately on account of her husband's cruelty or non-payment of her prompt dower she is entitled to separate maintenance (PLD 1971 Lahore 151). A wife can also claim past maintenance if neglected. In the case of *Musarat Bibi* (1990 Civil Law Cases 1908), the Peshawar High Court ruled that a husband who had neglected to maintain his wife had violated his duty, which a Muslim husband was under an obligation to perform. She was entitled to past maintenance allowance. In the language of section 9, there is no prohibition for granting past maintenance (PLD 1972 Supreme Court 302) and it can be claimed by a wife and granted according to law (PLD 1978 Quetta 117).

The law in Pakistan is also clear on the period of maintenance for divorcees. In case of the death of a husband, a wife should be provided maintenance for a year. In case of divorce, a wife is entitled to maintenance during *iddat* (waiting period) which is generally recognised as four months (Hiayatullah, 1968; Fyzee, 1999). The prescribed time limitation is not what the Koran says. In 1956, the Family Law Commission recommended that a divorced woman should be allowed maintenance for life or until remarriage but this was not included in the MLFO (Carroll, 1986). This recommendation is in line with the contextual interpretation of the Koran as it obligates Muslims to pay maintenance to ex-wives but does not prescribe a time limit. The classic case in point is that of *Shah Bano* (All India Review 1985 Supreme Court 945) from the Supreme Court of India. In this case a widow, past the age of remarriage, claimed maintenance beyond the four months period of *iddat*. She also asked the court for maintenance under section 125 of the Criminal Procedure Code of India, 1975. The Supreme Court, comprising non-Muslim judges, went into detailed discussion of the relevant verses of the Koran (2:241-2) and concluded that there is 'no doubt that the Qur'an imposes an obligation on the Muslim husband to make provision for or to provide maintenance to the divorced wife' (All India Review 1985 Supreme Court 945). The interpretation of the Supreme Court is in accord with the contextual interpretation of the Koranic verse (2:241): 'for divorced women Maintenance (should be provided) on a reasonable (scale). This is a duty on the righteous'. However, the Muslims may not accept it on technical grounds, i.e. an interpretation done by the non-Muslims which does not meet the requirement of *mujtahid* discussed in chapter 3 (there was strong reaction from the Indian Muslims and a new law was introduced nullifying the effect of the case). The most significant case is from Dhaka High Court (47 (1995) Dhaka Law Reports 54) where all judges were Muslims. The court adopted a similar interpretation:

> Considering all the aspects we finally hold that a person divorcing his wife is bound to maintain her on a reasonable scale beyond the period of iddat for an indefinite period, that is to say, till she loses the status of a divorcee by remarrying another person.

7.4 CONCLUSION

The application and various interpretations of family laws by superior courts reflect a consistent approach towards issues such as consent of a woman for a valid marriage, *khul*/judicial divorce, delegated power of divorce to wife and option of puberty as understood in the classical *Hanafi* law. However, inconsistency and confusion exist regarding interpretation of certain provisions of the MFLO such as the right to maintenance. In some cases, the courts have preferred uncodified Islamic legal rules over the express provision of the ordinance whereas in others they tend to follow both the ordinance and the uncodified rules of *Sharia*: laying down that violation of the ordinance is a punishable act but anything done according to *Sharia* would not be invalid. For instance, non-registration of a marriage and notice of divorce to a wife are punishable under the MLFO but, according to un-codified Islamic law, non-registration will not invalidate the marriage. The Supreme Court seems to follow the letter of the law and does not engage in scrutinising its Islamic foundation in contrast to some of the High Courts where such tendency is frequent. However, the Federal Shariat Court has demonstrated a degree of activism by declaring certain provisions of the ordinance to be un-Islamic but tends to rely more on the uncodified Islamic law instead of the MLFO. This conflicting and inconsistent interpretation and application of family law by the judiciary has generated confusion in some areas to the disadvantage of women as well as men, i.e. several couples are booked under *hudood* laws for not registering their marriages and divorces. However, in contrast to criminal law, most of the issues in relation to family law seem pretty clearly settled and the courts have interpreted and applied the MFLO in a way which protects women's rights to a fair extent.

However, there is greater room for reformation of family law in the areas such as equal divorce rights, maintenance, etc.

REFERENCES

Abdul Waheed (2004) *All Pakistan Legal Decisions* 2004 Supreme Court 219.

Ali, S. S. (2002) 'Testing the Limits of Family Law Reform in Pakistan: A Critical Analysis of the Muslim Family Laws Ordinance 1961' In: Andrew (eds.) *The International Survey of Family Law*. Bainham Andrew International Society of Family Law. pp. 317-335.

Ali, Y. (1989) *The Meaning of the Holy Qur'an*. Maryland: Amana Corporation.

All Pakistan Legal Decisions 1981 Supreme Court 120.

All Pakistan Legal Decisions 1980 Peshawar 47.

All Pakistan Legal Decisions 2000 Federal Shariat Court 63.

All Pakistan Legal Decisions 1995 Lahore 475.

All Pakistan Legal Decisions 1950 Lahore 203.

All Pakistan Legal Decisions 1953 Lahore 131.

All Pakistan Legal Decisions 1995 Lahore 98.

All Pakistan Legal Decisions 1992 Karachi 46.

All Pakistan Legal Decisions 1991 Lahore 251.

All Pakistan Legal Decisions 2000 Karachi 348.

All Pakistan Legal Decisions 2003 Peshawar 146.

All Pakistan Legal Decisions 1957 Dacca 245.

All Pakistan Legal Decisions 1971 Lahore 151.

All Pakistan Legal Decisions 1972 Supreme Court 302.

Atia Nisar (1995) *Pakistan Criminal Law Journal* 1657.

Carroll, L. (1989) 'Section 4 of the Muslim Family Laws Ordinance: Three Alternative Interpretations' *All Pakistan Legal Decisions*.

Carroll, L. (1996) 'Qur'an 2:229: "A Charter Granted to the Wife"? Judicial *Khul* in Pakistan' *Islamic Law and Society*. 3 pp. 91-126.

Carroll, L. (1986) 'Divorced Muslim Women and Maintenance' *All Pakistan Legal Decisions*.

Fyzee, A. A. (1999) *Outlines of Mohammedan Law*. 4th ed. Oxford University Press.

Hidayatullah, M. (1968) *Mullah Principles of Muhammadan Law*. 6th ed. Bombay. 1993 Civil Law Cases 219.

Hamilton (trans.) (1989) *The Hedaya*. Karachi: Darul-Ishaat.
India (1975) *The Criminal Procedure Code of India*.
Khurshid Bib (1967) *All Pakistan Legal Decisions* 1967 Supreme Court 97.
Masuda Khanum (1978) *All Pakistan Legal Decisions* Quetta 245.
Mehdi, R. (1994) *The Islamisation of the Law in Pakistan*. Curzon Press Ltd.
National Law Reporter 1992 Shariat Decisions 502.
Mst. Irfana Tasneem (1999) *All Pakistan Legal Decisions* 1999 Lahore 479.
Mst. Farangenza (1995) *Monthly Law Digest* 1439.
Mst. Kaneez Fatima (2002) *Supreme Court Monthly Review* 1563.
Mst. Bashir (1995) *National Law Reporter* 1995 Shariat Decisions 558.
Mst. Zanab Mai (2003) *Civil Law Cases* 214.
Mussarat Bibi (1990) *Civil Law Cases* 1908.
Mussarat Jabeen (2003) *Monthly Law Digest* 1077.
Pakistan (1973) The Constitution of Pakistan.
Pakistan (1939) The Dissolution of Muslim Marriage Act.
Pakistan (1964) The West Pakistan Family Courts Act.
Pakistan (1976) The Dowry and Bridal Gifts (Restriction) Act.
Pakistan (1929) The Child Marriage Restraint Act.
Pakistan (1961) The Muslim Family Law Ordinance.
Rahim, A. (1911) *Muhammadan Jurisprudence*. Lahore: PLD Publishers.
Rahman, T. (1997) *Essays on Islam*. Lahore: Islamic Publication.
Rahman, T. (1968) 'Maintenance of Wife in Islamic Law' *All Pakistan Legal Decisions*: Lahore.
Report of the Family Law Commission of Pakistan (1956) Gazette of Pakistan Extraordinary. 20 June 1956.
Shah Bano (1985) *All India Review* 1985 Supreme Court 945).
Said Muhammad (1995) *All Pakistan Legal Decisions* Federal Shariat Court 1.
2003 *Yearly Law Reporter* 2623.
2003 *Civil Law Cases* 1213
1998 *Civil Law Cases* 1054.
1984 *Supreme Court Monthly Review* 583.
1992 *Monthly Law Digest* 93.
47 (1995) *Dhaka Law Reports* 54.

PART III

WOMEN'S HUMAN RIGHTS SYSTEMS: A COMPARISON

CHAPTER 8

Towards an International Women's Human Rights Regime

Part III looks critically at the women's human rights regime in the international human rights system together with its strengths and weaknesses. Women's human rights norms and values are analysed and then compared with the Koranic women's rights standards and the statutory Islamic law of Pakistan. The purpose of this chapter is to look into the international women's human rights protection regime, especially the 1979 Convention on the Elimination of All Forms of Discrimination against Women (hereinafter, the Women's Convention). An analysis of the pre-Women's Convention rights system is made to explain how it evolved over the decades. Post-Women's Convention developments are also discussed to show whether and how some weaknesses of the women's rights system have been changed. The chapter also discusses how certain women's human rights principles may conflict with other equally recognised norms such as the right to freedom of religion and cultural rights.

Gender equality and non-discrimination on the basis of sex is one of the most frequently recognised norms of international human rights law (Bayfesky, 1990; see Hevener, 1986) and is considered the 'cornerstone of every democratic society, which aspires to social justice and human rights' (United Nations, Fact Sheet No. 22, 1993). Hosken (1981) contends that a human relationship based on equality between women and men is the foundation of human rights and justice in each family and community within each nation, and finally among all nations. In virtually all societies and spheres of activity women are subject to inequalities in law and in fact. John Stuart Mill (1998) said that the principle which regulates the existing social relations between the two sexes – the legal subordination of one sex to another – is wrong in itself and one of the chief hindrances to human improvement. This situation is both caused and exacerbated by the existence of discrimination in the family, in the community and in the workplace. While the causes and consequences may vary from country to country, discrimination against women is widespread. It is perpetuated by the survival of stereotypes and of traditional cultural and religious practices and beliefs detrimental to women (United Nations, Fact Sheet No. 22, 1993). The concept of equality means much more than treating all persons in the same way. Equal treatment of persons in unequal situations perpetuates rather than eradicates injustice (Machkinnon, 1987). True equality can only emerge from efforts directed towards addressing and correcting these situational imbalances. It is this broader view of equality which has become the underlying principle and the final goal in the struggle for recognition and acceptance of the human rights of women (Machkinnon, 1987).

8.1 WOMEN'S HUMAN RIGHTS BEFORE THE WOMEN'S CONVENTION

'Equality of rights for women is a basic principle of the United Nations' (United Nations, Fact Sheet No. 22, 1993) and 'discrimination on the basis of sex is singled out among the list of items specifically prohibited' (Morsink, 1991:230). One of the purposes of establishing the United Nations was 'respect for human rights and for fundamental freedoms for all without distinction as to race, sex, language, or religion' (United Nations Charter 1945, article 1). The Charter (article 13) encourages 'promoting international co-operation in the economic, social, cultural, educational, and health fields, and assisting in the realization of human rights and fundamental freedoms for all without distinction as to race, sex, language, or religion' and 'universal respect for, and observance of, human rights and fundamental freedoms for all without distinction as to race, sex, language, or religion' (article 55). Courtney Howland (1997:325) argues that 'the Charter is the foundational treaty of contemporary international law and prevails over all other international obligations'. Fraser (1999:886) says that 'the equal rights of men and women clause in the UN Charter established a legal basis for the international struggle to affirm women's human rights'.

The 1948 Universal Declaration of Human Rights (hereinafter, UDHR), which is considered an authoritative interpretation of the human rights guaranteed in the Charter, contains aspirational goals and United Nations member states are expected to work towards the achievement of these goals (Howland, 1997). Article 2 states that everyone is entitled to the enjoyment of human rights and fundamental freedoms set forth in this Declaration 'without distinction of any kind, such as race, colour, sex, language, religion, political or other opinion, national or social origin, property, birth or other status'. Morsink (1991:229) maintains that article 2 is 'an expansion of the Charter's mandate that the new world organisation promote human rights for all without discrimination'. Article 16 has given equal rights to men and women of full age to enter into marriage based on their free consent.

However, despite its non-discriminatory tenure, the language of the UDHR is tainted with sexism. Schwab and Polis (1982:7) argues that the Declaration is informed by the 'notion of man as an autonomous, rational and calculating being ... a notion of man but not of women ...'. Robert Nelson (cited in Morsink, 1991:233) has pointed out the sexist word 'brotherhood' for all human beings in article 1. Another sexist phrase is 'his family' and the strong statement about family in article 16 (Morsink, 1999). This argument can, however, be countered by an argument that when it comes to interpretation, the word 'man' is interpreted as including both men and women. This type of language is used in other human rights instruments as well (see Convention against Torture 1984, article 1) and the jurisprudence of United Nations treaty bodies such as the Human Rights Committee (hereinafter, HRC) and country reports to different human rights bodies strongly suggest that these instruments are interpreted in a way which certainly include women. Nonetheless, it is more appropriate and desirable to avoid using sexist language.

The two covenants, the Covenant on Civil and Political Rights (hereinafter, CCPR) and the Covenant on Economic, Social and Cultural Rights (hereinafter, the Economic Covenant) strengthen and extend the emphasis on the equal rights of men and women laid down in the Charter and the UDHR. Most of the provisions of the Charter and the UDHR are reflected in the two covenants. The two covenants are legally binding on State Parties in contrast to the UDHR except those principles of the UDHR which have acquired the status of *jus cogens* or customary international law with a binding effect on all states. The covenants clearly state that the rights set forth therein are applicable to all persons without distinction of any kind including sex. The articles of the two covenants dealing with women's rights are identical, explicitly recognising the equality of men and women (United Nations, Fact Sheet No. 2, 1996). Two separate committees, the Committee on Economic, Social and Cultural Rights (hereinafter, CESCR) and the Human Rights Committee (HRC), are set up to monitor the implementation of each of the two covenants. Both committees are competent to deal with issues of gender-based discrimination raised under the provisions of their respective covenants despite a separate reporting and communication procedure under the Women's Convention and the Optional Protocol thereto. The HRC is the most active forum for women's rights in contrast to the CESCR, which has done very little in the form of making some guidelines for States Parties to achieve rights recognised under the covenant. Because of its significant role in the protection of human rights, the CCPR and the HRC are discussed below in some detail.

Before discussing the role of the HRC in protecting women's human rights, it is relevant to look at the women's specific article of the CCPR. The rights contained in the CCPR are mainly negative rights whereas, as we will see later, the Women's Convention imposes the positive obligation to end gender discrimination. Article 2 of the CCPR obligates State Parties to respect and ensure to all persons within the territory subject to its jurisdiction, the rights recognized in the covenant without distinction of any kind, such as race, colour, sex, language, religion, political or other opinion, national or social origin, property, birth or other status. Article 26 entitles all persons to equality before the law as well as equal protection of the law. It prohibits any discrimination under the law and guarantees to all persons equal and effective protection against discrimination on any ground such as race, colour, sex, language, religion, political or other opinion, national or social origin, property, birth or other status (General Comment No. 18, 1989). While article 4 allows States Parties to take measures derogating from certain obligations under the covenant in time of public emergency, the same article requires, *inter alia*, that those measures should not involve discrimination solely on the ground of race, colour, sex, language, religion or social origin.

The Human Rights Committee has been particularly active in preventing women's rights breaches and providing remedies for discrimination against women. The two notable examples are the cases of *Shirin Aumeeruddy-Cziffra v. Mauritius (Communication No. R.9/35 1978) and Brooks v Netherlands* (Communication No. 172/1984). In the first case the authors claimed that the enactment of the Immigration (Amendment) Act 1977, and the Deportation (Amendment) Act 1977, by Mauritius constitutes discrimination based on sex against Mauritian women as their husbands, who are of foreign origin, do not have the same status of residence, work permit etc. as the foreign wives of male nationals of Mauritius. Before the enactment of the new laws, the spouses of both men and women enjoyed equal rights. Hence, the new laws were violative of the CCPR. Accepting the arguments of the applicant, the HRC held:

> It is of the view that the facts ... disclose violations of the Covenant, in particular of articles 2 (1), 3 and 26 in relation to articles 17 (1) and 23 (1) with respect to the three co-authors who are married to foreign husbands, because the coming into force of the Immigration (Amendment) Act, 1977, and the Deportation (Amendment) Act, 1977, resulted in discrimination against them on the ground of sex.

The brief facts of the *Brooks* case are that the woman was married at the time when the dispute in question arose (she has since divorced and not remarried). She was employed as a nurse from 7 August 1972 to 1 February 1979 when she was dismissed for reasons of disability. She had become ill in 1975, and from that time she benefited from the social security system of the Netherlands until 1 June 1980 (as regards disability and as regards unemployment), when unemployment payments were terminated in accordance with a new law of the Netherlands. Mrs. Brooks claimed that under the new law an unacceptable distinction has been made on the grounds of sex and status, hence against the CCPR. The HRC held:

> The circumstances in which Mrs. Brooks found herself at the material time and the application of the then valid Netherlands law made her a victim of a violation, based on sex, of article 26 of the International Covenant on Civil and Political Rights, because she was denied a social security benefit on an equal footing with men.

8.2 WHY A SEPARATE WOMEN'S HUMAN RIGHTS REGIME?

As the foregoing account of human rights demonstrates that most of the existing human rights instruments provided for gender equality and all the remedial mechanisms and implementation procedures were equally available to men and women, why then was it felt that there was need to have a separate regime dealing with women's human rights? United Nations (Fact Sheet No. 22, 1993) gives two reasons. First,

> Additional means for protecting the human rights of women were seen as necessary because the mere fact of their "humanity" has not been sufficient to guarantee women the protection of their rights. The preamble to the Convention on the Elimination of All Forms of Discrimination against

> Women explains that, despite the existence of other instruments, women still do not have equal rights with men. Discrimination against women continues to exist in every society.

The second reason was 'to reinforce the provisions of existing international instruments designed to combat the continuing discrimination against women'. It further claims:

> It [the Women's Convention] identifies many specific areas where there has been notorious discrimination against women, for example in regard to political rights, marriage and the family, and employment. In these and other areas the Convention spells out specific goals and measures that are to be taken to facilitate the creation of a global society in which women enjoy full equality with men and thus full realization of their guaranteed human rights (United Nations, Fact Sheet No. 22, 1993).

8.3 THE 1979 CONVENTION ON THE ELIMINATION OF ALL FORMS OF DISCRIMINATION AGAINST WOMEN

On 18 December 1979, the Convention on the Elimination of All Forms of Discrimination against Women was adopted by the United Nations General Assembly and came into force on 3 September 1981. As of March 2005, 180 countries were party to the Convention (Division for the Advancement of Women, 2005). The Women's Convention is described as:

> Essentially an international bill of rights for women and a framework for women's participation in the development process … [and] spell[ing] out internationally accepted principles and standards for achieving equality between men and women (International Women's Rights Watch, 1988).

Rebecca Cook (1990) maintains that the Convention is the definitive international legal instrument requiring respect for and observance of the human rights of women; it is universal in reach, comprehensive in scope and legally binding in character. Theodor Meron (1986:53) argues that 'while other conventions address particular aspects of women's rights, the Convention is the first universal instrument which focuses on the general prohibition of discrimination against women'. According to Noreen Burrows (1986:85) 'the main thrust of the Convention is the elimination of discrimination and it is not intended to provide a list of rights for women'. In contrast to other human rights instruments, e.g. the CCPR, the Women's Convention imposes positive obligations on States Parties to end gender discrimination.

Prohibition of discrimination per se is not enough; States Parties must take positive steps to achieve gender equality.

The Committee on the Elimination of Discrimination against Women (hereinafter, CEDAW), set up under the Women's Convention, monitors the implementation of the Convention. At least every four years, the States Parties are required to submit a country report to the CEDAW, indicating the measures they have adopted to give effect to the provisions of the Convention. The Committee also makes General Recommendations to the States Parties on matters concerning the elimination of discrimination against women. An Optional Protocol to the Women's Convention was adopted in 1999 and entered into force in 2000. The Protocol provides for two procedures: communication and inquiry. Article 2 provides a mechanism how to make a complaint against women's rights violations to CEDAW and article 8(2) enables the CEDAW to conduct inquiries into 'grave or systematic abuse' of women's rights by the States Parties. As we will see later in this chapter that implementation of the Women's Convention was/is one of the major weaknesses of the women's rights system but the Protocol has added some strength to the rather frail implementation mechanism. As of January 2005, the Protocol had 71 States Parties (Division for the Advancement of Women, 2005a).

8.4 SUBSTANTIVE PROVISIONS OF THE WOMEN'S CONVENTION

Before analysing the strengths and weaknesses of the women's rights system, it will be helpful to have an overview of what the Women's Convention stands for. Following is the discussion of each provision of the Convention.

8.4.1 Definition of Discrimination

Article 1 has defined discrimination as:

> Discrimination against women' shall mean any distinction, exclusion or restriction made on the basis of sex which has the effect or purpose of impairing or nullifying the recognition, enjoyment or exercise by women, irrespective of their marital status, on a basis of equality of men and women, of human rights and fundamental freedoms in the political, economic, social, cultural, civil or any other field.

Article 1 provides a comprehensive definition of discrimination, which is applicable to all provisions of the Convention. It encompasses any difference in treatment on the grounds of gender which intentionally or unintentionally disadvantages women; prevents society as a whole from recognizing women's rights in both the domestic and public spheres; or which prevents women from exercising the human rights and fundamental freedoms to which they are entitled (United Nations, Fact Sheet No. 22, 1993). The definition makes it clear that, in addition to establishing the criterion of differentiation (sex), it is also necessary to consider the outcome of the differentiation. If the result is a nullification or impairment of equal rights in any of the forms set out above then the differentiation is discriminatory and therefore prohibited under the Convention. 'The Convention does not seek to eliminate discrimination based on sex but only to eliminate discriminatory behaviour which is adverse to women' (Burrows, 1986:424).

The provisions of the Convention apply to a broad range of activities: unintentional as well as intentional discrimination is prohibited (as indicated by the 'effect' clause); private as well as public actions are regulated (as indicated by the phrase 'any other field'). Moreover, the definition of discrimination against women encompasses discrimination with regard to all rights and fundamental freedoms, whatever their source in contrast to the more limited prohibition contained in article 3 of the CCPR requiring States Parties to ensure the equal rights of men and women to the enjoyment of the rights set forth in the covenant only (Meron, 1986). The definition of discrimination against women does not prohibit certain distinctions *per se*, but only when they have the purpose of or the effect of denying women the enjoyment of human rights and fundamental freedoms on a basis of equality with men (Meron, 1986). Donna Sullivan (1992:800) argues that:

> The object of the basic guarantee of gender equality articulated in the Women's Convention is not to ensure that women receive treatment identical to that of men, nor that laws and practices will impact men and women in the same way. Rather, the aim is to ensure that gender does not impede women's ability to exercise rights protected by international human rights law, and to dismantle the political, economic and social structures that perpetuate their subordination.

8.4.2 Obligations of States Parties

Article 2 establishes, in a general way, the obligations of States Parties under the Convention and the policy to be followed in eliminating discrimination against women. The main thrust of obligations is in the legislative sphere. By becoming Parties to the Convention, States accept the responsibility to take positive steps to integrate the principle of equality between men and women into their national constitutions and other relevant legislation. States should also eliminate the legal bases for discrimination by revising existing laws and civil, penal and labour codes. States Parties to the Convention must take steps to eliminate discrimination in both public and private spheres. Article 2 recognizes that legislative changes are most effective when made within a supportive framework, i.e. when changes in the law are accompanied by a simultaneous change in the economic, social, political and cultural spheres. To this end, subparagraph (f) requires States Parties not only to modify laws, but also to work towards the elimination of discriminatory customs and practices.

Certain sections of article 2 reach interpersonal private acts of discrimination and the language of these sections requires State Parties to restrict privacy and associational rights if restrictions are necessary to prevent discrimination. Meron (1986:62) has expressed concern regarding the reach of the Women's Convention to private interpersonal relations:

> There is a danger, however, that state regulation of interpersonal conduct may violate the privacy and associational rights of the individual and conflict with the principles of freedom of opinion, expression, and belief. Such regulation may require invasive state actions to determine compliance, including inquiry into political and religious beliefs.

Paragraph (f) may not only conflict with associational rights but also with the rights of ethnic or religious groups. There is a certain overlap between paragraphs (f) and (g). The former requires measure 'including legislation, to modify or abolish existing laws' whereas the latter specifically addresses discriminatory 'national penal provisions' (Meron, 1986:64-65). Most of the obligations of article 2 are reiterated in article 24 stating that States Parties shall adopt measures to achieve the rights recognised in the Convention, which in a sense makes article 24 redundant (Burrows, 1985).

8.4.3 Special and Temporary Measures

Article 3 defines appropriate measures in all fields: in particular in the political, social, economic and cultural fields which should be taken to implement the policies set out in article 2. It also serves to demonstrate the indivisibility and interdependence of the rights guaranteed by the Women's Convention and the basic human rights contained in other human rights instruments to which all persons are entitled. Article 3 recognizes that, unless States take active steps to promote the advancement and development of women, they will not be able to enjoy fully the basic human rights guaranteed in the other instruments (United Nations, Fact Sheet No. 22, 1993). The phrase 'all fields' in this article extends the obligation of the States Parties to interpersonal and familial activities and may pose the problem as discussed in relation to article 2.

Article 4 recognizes that, even if women are given legal (*de jure*) equality, this does not automatically guarantee that they will be treated equally in reality. To accelerate women's actual equality in society and in the workplace, States are permitted to use special remedial measures for as long as inequalities continue to exist. The Convention thus reaches beyond the narrow concept of formal equality and sets its goals as equality of opportunity and equality of outcome. Positive measures are both lawful and necessary to achieve these goals. These special measures should be used simply to speed up the achievement of *de facto* equality for women, and should not create separate standards for women and men. In other words, the appropriateness of any special measures should be evaluated with regard to the actual existence of discriminatory practices. Consequently, once the objectives of equality of opportunity and treatment are reached, these special measures are no longer needed and should be discontinued (United Nations, Fact Sheet No. 22, 1993). Paragraph (2) states that adoption of special measures aimed at protecting maternity shall not be considered discriminatory but the Convention does not define the term 'maternity' and it might be used as a pretext for justifying discrimination against women, when a 'protective' purpose can be articulated (Meron, 1986:73). For instance, in certain countries women's role is to rear and look after children and a woman with children may be prevented from entering into certain types of employment which might be detrimental to her interests. This is more likely as: 'each state is the arbiter of its own special measures as the Convention does not provide for any procedures for evaluating such measures' (Burrows, 1985:428).

8.4.4 Modification of Social and Cultural Patterns

Article 5 recognizes that, even if women's legal equality is guaranteed and special measures are taken to promote their *de facto* equality, another level of change is necessary for women's true equality, i.e. States should strive to remove the social, cultural and traditional patterns which perpetuate gender-role stereotypes and to create an overall framework in society that promotes the realization of women's full rights. Sub-paragraph 5(*b*) calls on States Parties to ensure that education includes a proper understanding of the important role of 'maternity as a social function'. It also requires that States recognize the raising of children as a responsibility that should be shared by women and men, not as a task that is borne by women alone.

This provision might permit States to curtail to an undefined extent privacy and associational interests and the freedom of expression and opinion. Social and cultural behaviour may be patterned according to ethnicity or religion, State action under paragraph (a), which is directed towards modifying the way in which a particular ethnic or religious group treat women, may conflict with the principles forbidding discrimination on the basis of race or religion (Meron, 1986). Paragraph (b) gives States the power to define 'proper understanding' of maternity as a social function, which in fact empowers States to inform the way its citizens should think. It allows States to intervene in areas which are more crucial to women's lives. If maternity has a social function and is recognised as such, then parent's rights to choose the number and spacing of children may be called into question in cases of under or over population, e.g. China's sterilization policy. This also seems to be in conflict with the equal right of men and women to decide on the size of their family contained in article 16 (Burrows, 1985).

8.4.5 Women Trafficking and Prostitution

'States Parties shall take all appropriate measures, including legislation, to suppress all forms of traffic in women and exploitation of prostitution of women' (article 6). This reflects that article 6 does not prohibit the practice of prostitution but rather seeks that States prohibit the exploitation of prostitution and urges them to take measures to combat trafficking in women although it does not define the term 'traffic'. States Parties do not undertake to implement measures to deter prostitution as such. This uncertainty on the issue of prostitution or its tacit approval should have generated strong reaction from the Muslims states as it conflicts with the Koranic moral code but interestingly Muslim States Parties have not entered reservations/declarations to that aspect of the article (see chapter 10).

8.4.6 EQUALITY IN POLITICAL AND PUBLIC LIFE

Article 7 requires States Parties to undertake three levels of action to create equality for women in political and public life. First, States must ensure women's right to vote in all elections and public referenda. Second, article 7 recognizes that, while it is essential, the right to vote is not in itself sufficient to guarantee the real and effective participation of women in the political process. The article, therefore, requires States to ensure for women the right to be elected to public office and to hold other government posts and positions in non-governmental organizations. Third, States should ensure that women can 'participate in the formulation of government policy and the implementation thereof' (United Nations, Fact Sheet No. 22, 1993). Article 8 requires States Parties to take all appropriate measures to ensure to women, on equal terms with men and without any discrimination, the opportunity to represent their Governments at the international level and to participate in the work of international organizations. The CEDAW (General Recommendation No. 8, 1988) recommended that States Parties make use of temporary special measures such as affirmative action and positive discrimination as envisaged by article 4. States should also use their influence in international organizations to ensure adequate and equal representation to women. It is interesting to note that in various United Nations bodies women are not represented equally.

8.4.7 EQUALITY IN NATIONAL LEGISLATION

Article 9 urges States Parties to grant women equal rights with men to acquire, change or retain their nationality. They shall ensure in particular that neither marriage to an alien nor change of nationality by the husband during marriage shall automatically change the nationality of the wife, render her stateless or force upon her the nationality of the husband. States Parties shall also grant women equal rights with men with respect to the nationality of their children. This article contains two basic obligations. First, it requires States Parties to guarantee women the same rights as men to acquire, change or retain their nationality. For example, in Pakistan, foreign spouses of male nationals may be permitted to acquire their husband's nationality, but foreign husbands of female nationals are not granted the same right (see chapter 5.1). The result in such cases is that men who marry foreigners are allowed to remain in their country of origin, whereas women who marry foreigners may be forced to move to their husband's country of origin. Second, States Parties are required to extend to women the same rights as men regarding the nationality of their children. In many countries, children automatically receive the nationality of the father but not mother. Pakistan's citizenship law is a good example in this case too (see chapter 5.1).

8.4.8 Equality in Education

Article 10 recognizes that equality in education forms the foundation for women's empowerment in all spheres: in the workplace, in the family and in wider society. The obligations of States Parties under this article can be conveniently divided into three categories. The first obligation is equality of access to education. Second, States Parties have an obligation to eliminate gender-role stereotyping in and through the education system. Third, the obligation of States Parties is to close the existing gap in education levels between men and women. Article 10 has negative and positive aspects. It is negative in the denial of discrimination and positive in the encouragement of forward educational planning to improve the status of women (Burrows, 1985). Paragraph (c) does not mandate the introduction but only the encouragement of co-education but even this may give rise to conflict with religious freedom, especially when religious organisations provide education (Meron, 1986). Paragraph (g) provides for the same opportunities to participate actively in sports and educational facilities but apparently not the right to play on a team with men.

8.4.9 Equality in Employment and Labour Laws

Article 11 states clearly that women shall enjoy the basic right to work. It then sets out a comprehensive list of obligations for States Parties in order to ensure that this right can be fully and effectively realized. First, States Parties must guarantee women the same employment rights and opportunities as men. It is not sufficient for a State to outlaw discriminatory hiring practices. Second, women must have the right to free choice in selecting a profession, and must not be automatically channelled into traditional 'women's work'. To discharge this obligation, States Parties must grant women full equality in education and employment opportunities and must work towards the creation of social and cultural patterns, which allow all members of society to accept and work towards the presence of women in many different types of career. Third, women in the workplace must have the right to equal remuneration and all work-related benefits. States Parties must guarantee women equal pay for equal work, as well as equal treatment for work of equal value and equal treatment in evaluating the quality of work. Women are also to enjoy the protection of social security. Provision should be made for paid leave as well as retirement, unemployment, sickness and old-age benefits. Fourth, women in the workplace must be protected from discrimination based on marital status or maternity. States Parties must prohibit employers from using pregnancy or marital status as a criterion in the hiring or dismissal of women employees. States must also take measures that allow parents to combine family obligations with work responsibilities, by giving them benefits such as paid maternity leave, child-care subsidies and special health protection during pregnancy. It is interesting that paragraph 2(a):

> Does not outlaw dismissal on marriage but merely outlaws discriminatory practices. If both men and women are dismissed when they marry that is permissible under the terms of the Convention, what is outlawed is dismissal of one sex only (Burrows, 1985).

Finally, true equality in employment requires the implementation of measures to protect women from all forms of violence in the workplace and that is why the CEDAW (General Recommendation No. 12, 1989) called on States Parties to include in their reports to the Committee information on legislation against sexual harassment in the workplace. In 1992, the CEDAW (General Recommendation No. 19, 1992) recommended that States Parties adopt effective legal measures, including penal sanctions, civil remedies and compensatory provisions, to protect women against all kinds of violence, including sexual assault and sexual harassment in the workplace.

8.4.10 Equal Access to Health Facilities

Access to health care is a problem affecting women, men and children in many regions of the world. Therefore, paragraph 1 of article 12 specifically requires States Parties to ensure the equality of women and men in access to health care services. This requires the removal of any legal and social barriers, which may operate to prevent or discourage women from making full use of available health care services. Steps should be taken to ensure access to health care services for all women, including those whose access may be impeded through poverty, illiteracy or physical isolation. Article 12 makes specific reference to the area of family planning. Both women and men must have a voluntary choice in planning their families, and States must accordingly make available information and education about medically approved and appropriate methods of family planning. Any laws that operate to restrict a woman's access to family planning or any other medical services would be contrary to article 12 and consequently should be amended. Where laws requiring the spouse's authorization for medical treatment or for the provision of family planning services have previously existed and subsequently been amended, States Parties should ensure that medical workers as well as the community are informed that such authorization is not required and that the practice is contrary to the rights of women. Paragraph 2 of article 12 recognizes that women need extra care and attention during pregnancy and the post-natal period. States Parties must recognize women's needs both as providers and receivers of health care during these times, and must ensure that they have access to adequate health care facilities and resources, including adequate nutrition during and after pregnancy. The issue of abortion is relevant to this article but the Convention does not mention it. In many countries family planning services and information includes abortion but requiring free health services only in connection with childbirth indicates that the Convention does not favour the alternative of abortion (Meron, 1986). In addition to that, there is no explicit protection to women in two principal areas: discrimination in hiring on grounds of maternity or pregnancy and discrimination in job assignment and promotion (Meron, 1986).

8.4.11 Equality in Finance and Social Security

Article 13 recognizes that unless States Parties guarantee women financial independence they will not have true equality with men because they will not be able to head their own households, own their own homes, or start their own businesses. States must take positive steps to ensure that women have equal access with men to credit and loans and family benefits. Equal rights of participation in sporting, recreational and other cultural activities presume the existence of real equality of access. To achieve this, States should ensure that all legal or social obstacles to the full participation of women in these areas are removed and that funding, grants or other forms of support are implemented under a principle of equality of opportunity.

8.4.12 The Rights of Rural Women

The Convention requires States Parties to eliminate discrimination against women in rural areas; to implement their right to adequate living conditions; and to take special measures to ensure for them, on a basis of equality with men, the same participation in and benefits of rural development (article 14). Special measures to achieve these goals could include: ensuring the participation of women, especially rural women, in the elaboration and implementation of development planning in order that they may work to create a better environment for themselves; encouraging and providing assistance for the establishment of self-help groups and cooperatives; and providing rural women with access to adequate health care, family planning facilities and social security programmes to give them greater financial and social control over their lives. States should also give women in rural areas the opportunity to break out of traditional roles and choose different lifestyles by ensuring they have equal access to training and education programmes, as well as to agricultural credit, loans and marketing facilities. Article 14 recognizes that rural women are a group with special problems needing careful attention and consideration by States Parties. In addition, by extending the convention to women in rural areas, States Parties are explicitly recognizing the importance of the work of rural women and their contribution to the well-being of their families and the economy of their countries. This emphasis on development is unique in a human rights treaty and represents clear acknowledgement of the fundamental link between achieving equality and involving women in the development process.

8.4.13 Equality before Law and in Civil Matters

Article 15 focuses on four important areas for women who have been subjected to discriminatory treatment. First of all, women are accorded equality with men before the law. Second, States Parties are required to guarantee women equality with men in areas of civil law, particularly to conclude contracts and to administer property. Women are to be treated in the same way as men in all legal proceedings in courts and tribunals. Burrows (1985:448-449) argues that:

> The 1979 Convention does not provide for the recognition of a right in this respect but only that where legal systems do recognise the capacity of individuals to contract or to administer property then that right should be afforded equally to men and women.

Third, 'states Parties agree that all contracts and all other private instruments of any kind with a legal effect which is directed at restricting the legal capacity of women shall be deemed null and void' (article 15(3)). Finally, 'states Parties shall accord to men and women the same rights with regard to the law relating to the movement of persons and the freedom to choose their residence and domicile' (article 15(4)). A law which makes a woman's domicile dependent upon her husband's would be considered discriminatory under this provision, as would a law which operated to restrict the right of a woman to choose where she lives. In Pakistan, the fact that the domicile of women depends on their parents when unmarried and after marriage on husbands clearly conflicts with this provision (see chapter 5.1).

8.4.14 Equality in Family Law

The Convention breaks new ground for international human rights law in that it provides that States Parties will take measures 'to eliminate discrimination against women in all matters relating to marriage and family relations' (article 16(1)). In particular States Parties must guarantee men and women the same rights as to (a) entry into marriage; (b) choice of spouse and entry into marriage with full and free consent; (c) rights and responsibilities in marriage and its dissolution; (d) rights as parents whether married or not; (e) rights on the number and spacing of children and the right to have access to family planning; (f) rights in regard to guardianship, wardship and adoption; (g) personal rights such as the right to choose a family name or occupation and (h) rights in respect of property. Paragraph 2 goes further and prohibits child betrothal and marriage but does not give a definition of the child. Many States Parties have entered reservations to this article, particularly Muslim states. Pakistan's blanket declaration is a case in point (see chapter 5.8). It is, as argued above, against the purpose of the Women's Convention. Egypt and Bangladesh are other Muslim States Parties which have entered substantive reservations to article 16. (See, Fact Sheet 22, 1993 of United Nations for full summary).

8.5 THE WEAKNESSES OF THE WOMEN'S CONVENTION

Broad as its substantive provisions are, the Convention fails to address a number of areas of concern to women, and in addition includes provisions that are distinctly detrimental to its purpose of eliminating discrimination against women (Zearfoss, 1990). Perhaps most noticeable is the Convention's complete lack of attention to domestic violence and marital rape as women's human rights. In fact, the Convention does not explicitly address a woman's right to decide whether to have sexual intercourse. Nonetheless, there are provisions that arguably could have an implicit impact on the question of sexual abuse within marriage. Article 16 requires that men and women have the same rights during the marriage, the right to decide freely on the number and spacing of children and the same personal rights as husband and wife. Concluding that the rights referred to include the right to choose whether to have sexual intercourse seems reasonable, since the right of deciding on the number and spacing of children should include rights regarding intercourse ((Zearfoss, 1990). The Convention likewise fails to address pornography and the relationship between pornography and sex discrimination.

The Women's Convention also fails to clearly address the issue of right to abortion. While article 12(1) requires States Parties to ensure access to health care services, including those related to family planning, the article explicitly specifies only 'services in connexion with pregnancy, confinement and the post-natal period ... as well as adequate nutrition during pregnancy and lactation'. Meron (1986:71) argues that 'in requiring free health services only in connection with childbirth (Art. 12(2)), it is obvious that the convention disfavours the alternative of abortion'. Jack Greenberg (1984) argues that men have equal rights with women in matters of family planning, abortion under the Convention, if recognized at all, would not be a woman's individual right which she might exercise independently of consent of the father. Men claiming paternity could challenge, as a denial of their rights, a woman's decision to have an abortion. Greenberg (1984:330) adds that the Convention has not expressly settled the issue of abortion:

> Like all fundamental instruments written in general terms, [the Conven tion] leaves unanswered many questions which will be resolved only when concrete applications are attempted. For example ... if men and women are to have "equality" in deciding spacing of children, may a man require

> his pregnant spouse to undergo, or may a father-to-be prohibit the woman who is pregnant by him from undergoing, an abortion?

Similarly disturbing is the Convention's acceptance, which at times what appears to be a requirement of the use of 'protective legislation' that is, legislation prohibiting all fertile women from engaging in certain activities in the interest of protecting foetuses, whether the foetus is real or only potential. Article 11(3) does provide some small safeguard by requiring that: 'protective legislation should be reviewed periodically in the light of scientific and technological knowledge and shall be revised, repealed or extended as necessary'. In addition, in other articles of the Convention the drafters correctly recognized that pregnancy and motherhood might not be utilized as a basis for discrimination against women if the goal of equality is ever to be achieved. Nonetheless, it is clear that the potential for abuse is great because the provisions permit great discretion to States Parties in designing legislation. There is much evidence that:

> The effect of protective legislation has been to lower the economic status of women as a group, to deny them employment or force them into unskilled, low-paying positions, often in sex-segregated industries, and to deter their professional advancement' (Meron, 1986:73-74).

The Convention, then, provides flawed coverage in two ways. First, it fails to provide explicit substantive coverage of areas that are of great concern to women, areas that would be ideally addressed in a document that aims to eliminate discrimination against women; and second, it permits States Parties to legislate in the name of protecting women, but with such wide discretion that the legislation could harm women and might even be only a cover for discriminatory action.

Sarah Zearfoss (1990:916) argues that the Women's Convention embodies an understanding of sex equality that revolves largely around women's functions as wives and mothers. The Convention's failure to include abortion among the rights it guarantees and its allowance of protective legislation at the possible sacrifice of women's employment rights reflect this understanding, as does its repeated caveat following the articulation of a right, 'the interest of the children is the primordial consideration in all cases'. This understanding is important and beneficial for women insofar as it prescribes action in private arenas historically ignored by legislation. It also contemplates the special difficulties of women in the employment arena. Yet, this understanding is negative for women insofar as it neglects issues such as domestic violence, abortion, pornography, and rape – acts and conditions that impair or nullify the fundamental freedoms and human rights of women, and that occur because they are women. Furthermore, the Convention fails to address special concerns of lesbians and unmarried heterosexual women. The net effect of the Convention's understanding may be to strengthen a traditional image of women as mothers, albeit mothers with rights.

8.6 WEAK IMPLEMENTATION PROCEDURE

A major problem with the Women's Convention was/is the lack of an effective implementation procedure. The Convention provides for a Committee (CEDAW) to which the States Parties are required to submit periodic reports. However, if the CEDAW finds from the reports that no steps have been taken or there has been violation of women's rights, it cannot compel a State Party to observe what the Convention requires. It can only communicate its concern over these breaches and make recommendations. This situation has changed for those States Parties who have ratified the 1999 Optional Protocol which came into force in 2000. Under the Optional Protocol women or someone on their behalf can complain against a State Party having allegedly violated their rights. This is a step forward within the women's human rights system and has brought the CEDAW on a par with other human rights bodies such as the Human Rights Committee. However, the decisions of these quasi-judicial bodies of the United Nations have no binding force and their implementation is left to the conscience of the States Parties. They seem to be advisory in nature and if the States Parties fail to implement no sanctions follow except the displeasure of other States Parties. This is one of the major weaknesses of the international human rights system as a whole.

8.7 WOMEN'S EQUALITY AND THE RIGHT TO FREEDOM OF RELIGION

Several provisions of the Women's Convention, particularly articles 5, 15 and 16, may conflict with the right to freedom of religion recognised by other international instruments, i.e. article 18 of the CCPR and the 1981 Declaration on the Elimination of All Forms of Intolerance and of Discrimination Based on Religion or Belief (hereinafter, the Declaration). The

Women's Convention calls on States Parties to eradicate religious and cultural norms, which are detrimental to women. What constitutes 'detriment' would be determined by international human rights standards? On the other hand, several human rights instruments recognise the right to freedom of religion and cultural rights. For instance, article 18 of CCPR declares:

> 1. Everyone shall have the right to freedom of thought, conscience and religion. This right shall include freedom to have or to adopt a religion or belief of his choice, and freedom, either individually or in community with others and in public or private, to manifest his religion or belief in worship, observance, practice and teaching.
>
> 2. No one shall be subject to coercion, which would impair his freedom to have or to adopt a religion or belief of his choice.
>
> 3. Freedom to manifest one's religion or beliefs may be subject only to such limitations as are prescribed by law and are necessary to protect public safety, order, health, or morals or the fundamental rights and freedoms of others.
>
> 4. The States Parties to the present Covenant undertake to have respect for the liberty of parents and, when applicable, legal guardians to ensure the religious and moral education of their children in conformity with their own convictions.

The Human Rights Committee (General Comment No. 22, 1993) interpreted the right to freedom to mean:

> The freedom to manifest religion or belief in worship, observance, practice and teaching encompasses a broad range of acts … The observance and practice of religion or belief may include not only ceremonial acts but also such customs as the observance of dietary regulations, the wearing of distinctive clothing or head coverings, participation in rituals associated with certain stages of life, and the use of a particular language customarily spoken by a group.

The Committee (General Comment No. 22, 1993) said further that 'the fundamental character of these freedoms is also reflected in the fact that this provision cannot be derogated from, even in time of public emergency, as stated in article 4.2 of the Covenant'. This clearly conflicts with article 5 of the Women's Convention, which requires that States should strive to remove the social, cultural and traditional patterns which perpetuate gender-role stereotypes. Most of these norms may be based on religion or attributed to religion and anyone may rely on the protection provided in article 18 of the CCPR. As argued in chapter 9.2, it is enough to say here that genuine religious norms must be sifted from the vague patriarchal traditions and cultural norms ascribed to religion.

The 1981 Declaration also recognises that 'everyone shall have the right to freedom of thought, conscience and religion' (article 1(1)) and prohibits 'discrimination by any State, institution, group of persons, or person on the grounds of religion or other belief' (article 2 (1)). Meron (1986:153) contends that 'although not a treaty, the Declaration has normative character reflected in articles 4 and 7'. Article 4 requires States:

> To make all efforts to enact or rescind legislation where necessary to prohibit any such discrimination, and to take all appropriate measures to combat intolerance on the grounds of religion or other beliefs in this matter.

Article 7 goes beyond the duty imposed by article 4 requiring that:

> The rights and freedoms set forth in the present Declaration shall be accorded in national legislation in such a manner that everyone shall be able to avail himself of such rights and freedoms in practice.

Greenberg (1984:330) rightly asks the question 'if a religion relegates women to a certain societal or familial status which would otherwise be deemed discrimination on the basis of sex, which convention governs?' Some Muslim States Parties may justify religious laws discriminatory towards women on the basis of article 18 whereas women's rights advocates will stress the principles of the Women's Convention. International law does provides that domestic law shall not be made a basis for reservations to international treaties (The Vienna Convention on the Law of Treaties, 1969, article 19) but it does not provide a mechanism to cover a situation where the provisions of two treaties or human rights instruments clash with each other.

Article 15 of the Women's Convention addresses only women's capacity in civil matters whereas in some countries and legal systems matters pertaining to family are within the domain of a religion. For example, where Jewish religious laws give less evidentiary weight to women's testimony in civil matters and certain countries allow those laws to be administered in this discriminatory way, a violation of article 15 occurs. Adjudication purporting to affect only women's rights within a religious community or group, but not their rights in civil matters, would not breach article 15. Thus, for instance, refusing a woman a religious divorce for reasons of sex-based discrimination would not go against article 15, unless that refusal affected her ability to obtain a civil divorce (Meron, 1986:157). In the same fashion, in an Islamic legal system a husband can divorce his wife orally (known as *Sharee* divorce, according to the classical Islamic law) and that is considered a valid divorce by the courts for all legal and religious purposes. 'It is therefore regrettable that the Convention does not address the question of the status of women in tribunals which adjudicate matters of family status on the basis of religious law and in religious courts' (Meron, 1986:79). This phenomenon indicates a potential area of clear conflict among articles of different human rights instruments on the one hand and national legal norms based on religious values and human rights law on the other. How can this be resolved in these two situations? The Women's Convention (article 23) provides a mechanism for conflicting situation between domestic legislation and the Convention's principles:

> Nothing in the present Convention shall affect any provisions that are more conducive to the achievement of equality between men and women which may be contained (a) in the legislation of a State Party or (b) in any other international convention, treaty or agreement in force for that State.

This article gives primacy to those principles, both in domestic and human rights instruments, which are more *conducive* to the achievement of equality, but it does not indicate how to affect those provisions which are *less or not conducive* or when there is an apparent conflict. Meron (1986:154) argues that:

> The saving clause of the Convention, Art. 23 does not 'protect' the provisions of the [1981] Declaration from the reach of the Convention, not only because the Declaration is not an 'international convention, treaty or agreement in force' for a particular state but because it does not state norms 'more conducive to the achievement of equality between men and women'. Similarly, the saving clause of the Declaration, art. 8 does not protect the Convention from the reach of the provisions of the Convention ... [Therefore], the potential is great for unregulated conflicts between religious freedom and other norms, such as women's equality.

Catherine Tinker (1981:40) argues that the Women's Convention: 'is legally binding upon [S]tates [P]arties who ratify or accede to it ... The Convention supersedes all other documents, conventions, and declaration' except those national and international norms which are more conducive to the realisation of equality between men and women. The argument of Tinker is a sweeping statement and cannot be justified from the perspective of international law. All human rights treaties have the same legal worth and one cannot supersede another equally valid treaty. As indicated above, international human rights system does not provide any criterion where the principles of the Women's Convention may trump the principles of other human rights instrument such as the CCPR.

8.8 THE POST 1979 WOMEN'S CONVENTION DEVELOPMENTS

The process of development of a women's human rights system is neither perfect nor did it came to an end with the coming into force of the Women's Conventions in 1981. As discussed above, there are weaknesses at the normative as well as the implementation levels of the Women's Convention. However, later developments indicate an effort to remove those weaknesses but they do not seem to be very successful. Numerous developments have taken place, but three of them are important and have great bearing on the women's rights movement. The net result of these developments, as we will see later, is the building of an international consensus on important women's rights issues rather than concrete legally binding rules and the problems still remain.

8.8.1 The 1993 UN World Conference on Human Rights

A global women's human rights movement had taken definite shape by the 1993 UN World Conference on Human Rights (Friedman, 1995) and as result of the efforts made by the women's rights groups, several of their recommendations were included in *The Vienna Declaration and Program of Action* (hereinafter, the Declaration). The significant achievement of the World Conference, in relation to women's rights, was the central commitment of the Declaration to integrate women into the human rights mechanisms of the United Nations (Roach cited in Friedman, 1995). The final document identifies particular examples of gender-specific abuses as human rights violation (Sullivan, 1994). The Declaration reaffirms the principle of universality and that women's human rights are: 'an inalienable, integral, and indivisible part of *universal* human rights' [and] the human rights of women should form an integral part of the United Nations human rights activities (paragraph 18). The Declaration identifies the issue of violence against women and declares that:

> All forms of sexual harassment and exploitation, including those resulting from cultural prejudice and international trafficking, are incompatible with the dignity and worth of the human person, and must be eliminated (paragraph 18).

The Conference also endorsed the draft Declaration on the Elimination of Violence against Women (adopted by General Assembly in 1993), which highlights the rapidity of progress made towards clarifying the norms applicable to violence against women (Sullivan, 1994). There are, however, significant omissions. For example, it did not consider means for more effective implementation of women's economic, social and cultural rights. According to Friedman (1995:30-31):

> Appropriately gendered language was not found through the document, nor was there any mention of transcending the public/private dichotomy so as to make states accountable for all violations of women's human rights. Finally, it [Declaration] did not sufficiently address the problem of ensuring compliance with recommendations.

8.8.2 The 1995 UN Fourth Women's Conference

Another development of great importance for women's human rights movement is the 1995 United Nations' Fourth Women's Conference in Beijing (hereinafter, Beijing Conference), which will go down in history as one of the largest global conferences of women (Yost, 1995). The message of the Beijing Conference was seeing the world through women's eyes (Yost, 1995). The Beijing Declaration (1995:5) recognised that:

> The status of women has advanced in some important respects in the past decade but that progress has been uneven, inequalities between men and women have persisted and major obstacles remain.

The Declaration (paragraph 8, 14) reaffirms 'the equal rights and inherent dignity of men and women' and recognises that 'women's rights are human rights'. The Declaration calls for empowerment of women including participating in decision-making, equal opportunities and access to resources, eradication of poverty, the right of women to control all aspects of their health particularly their fertility, and to prevent all forms of violence and discrimination against women. The Beijing Conference identified twelve areas of concern such as poverty, education, health, violence, armed conflict, decision-making power, women and media and environment, etc. and provides an elaborate platform of action. In international terms, the Platform for Action (hereinafter, the Platform) has taken gender issues further than they have ever been taken (Hunt, 1996).

Both the Declaration and Platform for Action is not free from weaknesses and reflect political compromises and limitations like other international documents. Hunt (1996) argues that there are areas where the Platform is weak or silent on important issues. The most important areas are macro-economic issues, and resources for development and peace/disarmament. The Platform concedes that men and women live in poverty and most of them live in the developing countries but it avoids criticising the effects of global capitalism and the production on income inequalities. It seeks equality of men and women in each country, not across national borders. International agencies are asked to contribute a tiny fraction of their resources to a process, which can best be described as equalising the exploitation of men and women in developing countries (Bullbeck, 1996). The language of rights disappears altogether in those sections of the Platform which address women's poverty and inequality in economic structures (Otto, 1999). The Platform calls for women's participation in decision-making in most of the twelve priority areas but Dianne Otto (1999:127) argues that:

> In the absence of a recognition that the decision-making structures must themselves change, it is not clear what difference women's equal participation could make. Ultimately, it may merely equally implicate women in the perpetuation of the masculinist liberal forms of minimalist representative democracy and capitalist economics.

Women's diversities were also discussed in the 'universality' versus 'cultural relativity' debates in the Beijing Conference. The result was an ambiguous compromise (Otto, 1999) repeating the language adopted at the 1993 Vienna Conference stating that while States must protect all human rights 'cultural and religious backgrounds must be born in mind' (Platform of Action, paragraph 9). The text of the Platform (paragraph 9) has not recognised 'violence against women' as an independent human right of women. It is considered as 'impairing' and 'nullifying' women's enjoyment of human rights, not as a violation of women's human rights in itself. While the goals and objectives of the Beijing Conference are admirable, the five-year deadline set for meeting its objectives is unrealistic. It is even worse for the Third World countries. Even the developed countries, where the objectives may not be as 'lofty', they still are not likely to be accomplished within five years (Streeter, 1996). Even the language of the Platform gives little guidance on the development of time-bound quantified targets (Bullbeck, 1996). According to Otto (1999), a woman of international legal discourse who emerges after the Beijing Conference has acquired a new entrepreneurial role in the marketplace and expanded access to decision-making in masculine structures, but at the same time, retains her pivotal role in the family.

8.8.3 The 1999 Optional Protocol to the Women's Convention

The last and most important development in the evolution of a women's human rights regime is the adoption of the 1999 Optional Protocol and its coming into force in 2000. The Protocol (article 2) provides for a communication procedure:

> Communications may be submitted by or on behalf of individuals or groups of individuals, under the jurisdiction of a State Party, claiming to be victims of a violation of any of the rights set forth in the Convention by that State Party.

The Protocol (article 8) also provides for an inquiry in the territories of States Parties 'if the Committee receives reliable information indicating grave or systematic violations by a State Party of rights set forth in the Convention' and 'the Committee may designate one or more of its members to conduct an inquiry and to report urgently to the Committee'. This provision of inquiry has taken women's rights system a step further than other human rights mechanisms such as the Human Rights Committee. However, this will not change much as the decisions of the CEDAW and its inquiry findings are only reflective of the Committee's views and States Parties may not implement them. What the Protocol has achieved is that it has brought women's human rights system into line with the mainstream human rights system by sharing its general characteristic: a weak implementation mechanism.

8.9 CONCLUSION

The equality of men and women and the principle of non-discrimination on the basis of sex runs throughout human rights debates and instruments beginning from the 1945 UN Charter until the 1979 women's own convention and subsequent conferences and declarations. The chronology of different instruments plus documents dealing with women's human rights indicate the steady evolution of women's human rights norms and implementation mechanisms. Women can presently rely on two different human rights systems, the one available to everyone such as the Human Rights Committee and their own such as the CEDAW. The current women's human rights system is a great advance but certainly needs improvement on two levels. First, at the normative level to bring into its legal fold issues such as violence against women, abortion and to provide a mechanism for resolving conflicts with other human rights norms. Second, at the implementation level: more compelling procedures may be installed obligating States Parties to comply with the Convention principles and implement the decisions of the CEDAW.

REFERENCES

Bayefsky, A. F. (1990) 'The Principles of Equality or Non-discrimination in International Law' *Human rights Law Journal*. 11 (1-2).

Bulbeck, Chilla. (1996) 'Less Than Overwhelmed by Beijing: Problems Concerning Women's Commonality and Diversity'. 6 pp.31-37.

Burrows, N. (1985) 'The 1979 Convention on the Elimination of All Forms of Discrimination against Women' *Netherlands International Law Review*. 32.

Burrows, N. (1986) 'International Law and Human Rights: the Case of Women's Rights' In: Campbell et al (eds.) *Human Rights: From Rhetoric to Reality*. Oxford: Basil Blackwell. pp.80-98.

Cook, R. J. (1990) 'Reservation to the Convention on the Elimination of All Forms of Discrimination against Women' *Virginia Journal of International Law*. 30 pp.643-716.

Fraser, A. S. (1999) 'Becoming Human: The Origins and Development of Women's Human Rights' *Human Rights Quarterly*. 21 (4) pp.853-906.

Friedman, E. (1995) 'Women's Human Rights: The Emergence of a Movement' In: Peters (eds.) *Women's Human Rights: International Feminist Perspective*. Routlege. p.18.

Greenberg, J. (1984) 'Race, Sex and Religious Discrimination in International Law' In: Meron (eds.) *Human Rights in International Law: Legal and Policy Issues*. Oxford: Clarendon Press.

Hervener, K. N. (1986) "An Analysis of Gender Based Treaty Law: Contemporary Development in Historical Perspective' *Human Rights Quarterly*. 8 (1) p.70-88

Holland, C. W. (1999) 'Introduction' In: Holland (eds.) *Religious Fundamentalism and the Human Rights of Women*. Macmillan.

Hosken, F. P. (1981) 'Towards a Definition of Women's Human Rights' *Human Rights Quarterly*. 3 (2) pp.1-10.

Hunt, J. (1996) 'Reflections on Beijing' *Australian Feminist Law Journal*. 6 p.39.

MacKinnon, C. A. (1987) *Feminism Unmodified: Discourses on Life and Law*. Harvard University Press.

Meron, T. (1986) *Human Rights Law-Making in the United Nations: A Critique of Instruments and Process*. Clarendon Press.

Mill, J. S. (1998) *The Subjection of Women*. Oxford World Classic.

Morsink, J. (1991) 'Women's Rights in the Universal Declaration' *Human Rights Quarterly*. 13 (2) pp.229-256.

Otto, D. (1999) 'A Post-Beijing Reflection on the Limitations and Potential of Human Rights Discourse for Women' In: Askin and Keoing (eds.) Vol. 1 *Women and International Human Rights Law*. New York: Transnational Publishers, Inc. Ardsley, p 128.

Schwab and Polis (eds.) (1982) *Towards a Human Rights Framework*. New York: Praeger.

Streeter, N. (1996) 'Beijing and Beyond' *Berkeley Women's Law Journal*. 11 p.200.

Sullivan, D. (1994) 'Women's Human Rights and the 1993 World Conference on Human Rights' *American Journal of International Law*. 88 (1) p.164.

Sullivan, D. (1992) 'Gender Equality and Religious Freedom: Towards a Framework for Conflict Resolution' *New York Journal of International Law and Politics*. 24, p 800.

Tinker, C. (1981) 'Human Rights for Women: The UN Convention on the Elimination of All Forms of Discrimination against Women' *Human Rights Quarterly*. 3 (1), pp.32-43.

United Nations (1945) The Charter of the United Nations.

United Nations, Division for the Advancement of Women '*General Recom-*

mendation No. 8, 1988. http://www.un.org/womenwatch/cedaw/cedaw/recommendations/recomm.htm [accessed Nov. 2005).

United Nations (1993) World Conference on Human Rights 'Vienna Declaration and Programme of Action'.
http://www.unhchr.ch/huridocda/huridoca.nsf/(Symbol)/A.CONF.157.23.En?OpenDocument [accessed Nov. 2005].

United Nations, Department of Public Information (1996) *Platform for Action and the Beijing Declaration*. New York.

United Nations (1981) Declaration on the Elimination of All Forms of Intolerance and of Discrimination Based on Religion or Belief.

United Nations (1948) Universal Declaration of Human Rights.

United Nations (1966) International Covenant on Economic, Social and Cultural Rights.

United Nations, (1966) International Covenant on Civil and Political Rights.

United Nations (1979) Convention on the Elimination of All Forms of Discrimination against Women.

United Nations (1999) Optional Protocol to the Convention on the Elimination of Discrimination against Women.

United Nations (1969) The Vienna Convention on the Law of Treaties. http://www.un.org/law/ilc/texts/treaties.htm [accessed Nov. 2005].

United Nations (1984) Convention against Torture and Other Cruel, Inhuman or Degrading Treatment or Punishment.

United Nations (1993*) Fact Sheet No 22, 'Discrimination against Women: The Convention and the Committee.* http://www.unhchr.ch/html/menu6/2/fs22.htm. [Accessed March 2005].

United Nations (1996) *Fact Sheet No. 2 (Rev. 1), The International Bill of Rights.* http://www.ohchr.org/english/about/publications/docs/fs2.htm. [Accessed Jan. 2005].

United Nations, Human Rights Committee (1978) *Shirin Aumeeruddy-Cziffra v. Mauritius* Communication No. R.9/35 (2 May 1978).
http://www1.umn.edu/humanrts/undocs/session36/9-35.htm [accessed Nov. 2005).

United Nations High Commissioner for Human Rights (1993) *CCPR General Comment No. 22: The right to freedom of thought, conscience and religion (Art. 18).*
http://www.unhchr.ch/tbs/doc.nsf/0/9a30112c27d1167cc12563ed004d8f15?Opendocument [Accessed Nov. 2004].

United Nations, High Commissioner for Human Rights (1989) *CCPR General Comment No. 18: Non-discrimination.* http://www.unhchr.ch/tbs/doc.nsf/(Symbol)/3888b0541f8501c9c12563ed004b8d0e?Opendocument. [Accessed Nov. 2004].

United Nations, Human Rights Committee (1984) 'Communication No. 172/1984: *Brooks v. Netherlands*. 09/04/87'. http://www.unhchr.ch/tbs/doc.nsf. [Accessed March 2005].

United Nations, Committee on the Elimination of Discrimination against Women (1989) *General Recommendation No. 12.* http://www.un.org/womenwatch/daw/cedaw/recomm.htm#recom12.

United Nations, Committee on the Elimination of Discrimination against Women, (1992) '*General Recommendation No. 19, Violence against Women*'. http://www.un.org/womenwatch/daw/cedaw/recommendations/recomm.htm#recom19 [accessed Nov. 2005].

United Nations, Division for the Advancement of Women (2005) '*Text of the Convention/States Parties/Reservations*'. http://www.un.org/womenwatch/daw/cedaw/states.htm [accessed Nov. 2005].

United Nations, Division for the Advancement of Women (2005a) 'Text of the Optional Protocol/Signatures and Ratifications'. http://www.un.org/womenwatch/daw/cedaw/protocol/sigop.htm [accessed Nov. 2005).

United Nations (1995) 'Beijing Declaration and Platform of Action'. http://www.un.org/womenwatch/daw/beijing/platform [accessed Nov. 2005].

Yost, B. (1995) 'Women's World Conference Was Eye-Opener for Attendees From Valley' *Phoenix Gazette.* September 23.

Zearfoss, S. C. (1991-92) 'The Convention on the Elimination of All Forms of Discrimination against Women: Radical, Reasonable, or Reactionary? *Michigan Journal of International Law.* 12 pp.903-942.

CHAPTER 9

Universality of Human Rights: Its Challenges

As outlined in the preceding chapter, human rights in general and women's human rights in particular have weaknesses both at the normative and implemental levels. If we accept the simple natural law theorists' definition of human rights,

> ... [t]here are some basic or fundamental rights that we have simply because we are human beings. Because all persons everywhere share that which makes us human, the rights that belong to us naturally are also universal (Hayden, 2001:5; see Paine, 1994),

then we face two robust challenges to the definition and the universality of the human rights system: feminism and cultural relativism. Feminists have three main arguments. First, they argue that the human rights system overlooks the issues and experience common as well as specific to women and therefore, the claim of its universality is unfounded. Second, they say that human rights law is mainly concerned with the public sphere – the male domain. Third, some feminists argue that the priority given to civil and political rights over economic and social rights is misplaced. The thrust of the cultural relativists' argument is that current human rights principles are the product of the Western liberal tradition and do not encompass notions of wrong and right specific to other cultures. Hence, its claim to universality is untenable. In fact, both ask one question: where does the system of human rights come from? For the feminists, it comes from the male perspective and excludes female experience. For the relativists, it comes from the Western liberal tradition and excludes other cultures' concepts of rights and duties. Some feminists would go further and argue that human rights are for the 'white propertied male' of the West (Bunch, 1995).

The purpose of this chapter is to highlight the arguments of the feminists and cultural relativists with the aim of explaining that human rights norms are neither sacrosanct nor a monolithic whole. There can be different notions of human rights. Genuine voices and concerns from different regions of the world must be accommodated, otherwise the universalism and universal application of human rights system would remain a farce. Of course, the target should be our common humanity. The best example to support this point is the existence of different regional human rights systems such as the European human rights system and the African and Inter-American human rights systems. The main arguments of feminists and relativists are analysed below.

9.1 FEMINISM AND UNIVERSALITY OF HUMAN RIGHTS

Feminists basically have three main arguments: current human rights are 'male standards'; they exclude the private sphere where women live out their lives and some would argue that the present human rights system stresses civil and political rights whereas women need economic and social independence. Therefore, the prevalent international human rights system has got its priorities wrong.

9.1.1 The Male Standard

Despite the inclusion of the principle of equality between men and women and the prohibition of discrimination on the basis of sex in several human rights instruments, women's human rights proponents do not accept the view that human rights are universal in their scope and application.

> Human rights are not what they claim to be, feminists say. They are product of the dominant male half of the world, framed in their language, reflecting their needs and aspirations. Whereas the "rights of man" as originally conceived by the great liberal thinkers were not intended to include women, today's "universal human rights" still overlook them as a matter of fact (Brems, 1997).

Among the feminists, the radical feminists maintain that: 'all theories based on equality or difference makes the same mistake of using a "male yardstick". They warn against valuing differences, which are a product of a patriarchal society, which needs to be dismantled (Mackinnon, 1987). Shelly Wright (1989-90) states that the term 'human rights' is a modern euphemism for the 'rights of man' which has meant, for most of history, 'men's rights' in the literal, gender-specific, masculinist sense of the words. The problem of 'men's rights' masquerading as human rights is not merely one of language, but is culturally and historically specific to the development of these rights in modern Western Europe. The substance of the rights, and the political/economic foundation on which they rest, are also 'male' and not 'human' (Wright, 1989-90). Marilyn Waring (1989-90:179) argues that '*[m]en* make the rules and the law, and decide their scope and application'. To substantiate her point, Waring quotes the masculine language of the UDHR (article 1) requiring that human beings 'should act towards one another in a spirit of brotherhood. More than half of the people on the planet are physically incapable of that particular spiritual relationship'. As argued in chapter 8, this argument is without substance but it would be more appropriate to avoid sexist language.

9.1.2 The Public/Private Dichotomy

The second argument of the feminists is about the dichotomy of public and private spheres. They maintain that while human rights were designed to regulate the relations between men and the state, women's oppression is largely situated in a private context: in practices and traditions in society or in the home, an arena outside the remit of many human rights instruments. Katherine O'Donovan (1985:3) defines the private realm as the 'area of life into which the law will not intrude, which is "not the law's business". Feminists of all strands argue for the inclusion of women's rights into the human rights protection regime (Brems, 1997). Charlesworth and Chinkin (1991:621) argue that:

> The structure of the international legal order reflects a male perspective and ensures its continued dominance. The primary subjects of international law are states and, increasingly, international organizations. In both states and international organizations the invisibility of women is striking.

The normative structure of international law [including human rights law] has allowed issues of particular concern to women to be either ignored or undermined. For example, modern international law rests on and reproduces various dichotomies between the public and the private spheres, and the 'public' sphere is regarded as the province of international law. Noreen Burrows (1986:82) argues that it is precisely this area that legal reforms have traditionally ignored:

> The areas ... which have been defined by states as being areas of private life ... are often thought not to be areas where the discourse of human rights is relevant, yet they are areas in which the majority of the world's women live out their days.

Issues such as domestic violence, childcare, family planning, the marital relationship, and deeply ingrained societal perceptions and prejudices are recognized as some of the most pressing concerns for women today, but because states have defined them as 'private', they are often outside the scope of governmental control. Bunch (1985:488) says that the responses to women's rights violations tend to be that 'abuse of women, while regrettable, is a cultural, private, or individual issue and not a political matter requiring state action'. Charlesworth and Chinkin (1991:626) maintain that:

> At a deeper level one finds a public/private dichotomy based on gender. One explanation feminist scholars offer for the dominance of men and the male voice in all areas of power and authority in the [W]estern liberal tradition is that a dichotomy is drawn between the public sphere and the private or domestic one. The public realm of the work place, the law, economics, politics and intellectual and cultural life, where power and authority are exercised, is regarded as the natural province of men; while the private world of the home, the hearth and children is seen as the appropriate domain of women.

To illustrate the grip that the public/private distinction has on international law, and the consequent banishment of women's voices and concerns from the discipline, Charlesworth and Chinkin (1991) give the example of torture contained in human rights law. The basis for the right not to be tortured is traced to 'the inherent dignity of the human person'. The 1984 Convention against Torture and Other Cruel, Inhuman and Degrading Treatment or Punishment (article 1) has defined torture as:

> Any act by which severe pain or suffering, whether physical or mental, is intentionally inflicted on a person for such purposes as obtaining from him or a third person information or a confession, punishing him for an act he or a third person has committed or is suspected of having committed, or intimidating or coercing him or a third person, or for any reason based on discrimination of any kind, when such pain or suffering is inflicted by or at the instigation of or with the consent or acquiescence of a public official or other person acting in an official capacity.

This definition has been considered broad because it covers mental suffering and behaviour 'at the instigation of 'a public official'. However, despite the use of the term 'human person' in the preamble, the use of the masculine pronoun alone in the definition of the proscribed behaviour immediately gives the definition a male, rather than a truly human, context. More importantly, the description of prohibited conduct relies on a distinction between public and private action that obscures the injuries typically sustained by women's dignity (Charlesworth and Chinkin, 1991). The crucial aspect of the definition is that it is confined to the public realm: a public official and or a person acting officially must be implicated in the pain or suffering.

> [S]evere pain and suffering that is inflicted outside the most public context of the state—for example, within the home or by private persons, which is the most pervasive and significant violence sustained by women—does not qualify as torture despite its impact on the inherent dignity of human person (Charlesworth and Chinkin, 1991).

Shelly Wright (1989-90:250) asserts that:

> The basic foundation of liberal democracy, and classic civil and political rights, is the division between public and private. Usually this is characterised as the separation of the State from interference in the "private" sphere of commerce and individual initiative...The modern liberal emphasis on the freedom of the individual in matters relating to sexuality, morality and family life are a continuation of the this theme. The State is obliged to refrain from interfering in the "private" matters...includ[ing] the home, or the domestic sphere, the domain of women and children.

This is why Celina Romany (1993:87) says that:

> Women are the paradigmatic alien subjects of international law. To be an alien is to be an *other*, an *outsider*. Women are *aliens* within their states and *aliens* within an exclusive international club of states which constitutes international society.

As demonstrated above, feminist legal scholars have made a valid criticism of international human rights law in that it excludes women's rights and issues specific to them. The most important among them is the private sphere where women 'live out their life'. However, the 1979 Women's Convention is a clear departure from previous human rights instruments, i.e. the CCPR and the CESCR in that it extends its reach to the private sphere. Zearfoss (1990-91) says that extending the Convention's reach to private spheres by use of the 'any other field' language is uniquely important to a convention meant to eradicate discrimination against women. That the Convention did not distinguish between public and private in structuring and shaping the substantive rights was a key element of its potential strength in the field of women's rights. Julie Minor (1994:137) contends that 'a unique and important feature of the Convention is its recognition of discrimination outside of the public sphere, as is evidenced by the "any other field" language.' According to Zearfoss (1990-91:920):

> While its reach into private behaviour is perhaps the most controversial element of the Convention, it is also one of its greatest strengths and separates it from most legal action taken to achieve equality for women.

Meron (1986) has, however, expressed his apprehension regarding the extension of state power into the realm of the private arena arguing that it can be abused, resulting into the violation of the right to privacy (see chapter 8).

The reach of law into the private sphere is a delicate issue and needs to be approached with care. Any wrongs or rights violations taking place in private must not go beyond the pale of law but clear guidelines regarding when and how to intervene are required. A balance should be struck between the right to privacy and family life and pre-empting the private sphere from becoming an arena of women's rights violations. This is what the Women's Convention fails to do: to draw a thin line between the two positions.

9.1.3 A Hierarchy of Human Rights

The third argument of the feminists is questioning the priority given to civil and political rights over social, economic and cultural rights in the current human rights system.

> Identifying the political sphere as male and the socio-economic sphere as more central to women's advancement, feminists object to the general priority accorded to civil and political rights and the second rate status of social and economic rights. The rights they advance as priorities (for instance, the rights to food, clothing, shelter, work, health, and education) belong to this second category (Friedman, 1995:139-1400).

Bunch (1995) argues that much of the abuse of women is part of a larger socio-economic and cultural web that entraps women. The inclusion in so-called socio-economic human rights of food, shelter, and work is vital to addressing women's concerns fully.

The feminists' arguments are valid in that human rights norms in their present form are 'male standards' and that they exclude the private sphere where women live their lives. They have also got a strong point that women need economic independence and more so in the Islamic and non-Western world. Some of the concerns of women's human rights advocates have been answered as we see more women's engagement in the formulation of human rights standards, which answers the 'masculine norm' argument. The implied reach of the Women's Convention into the private sphere is a step in the right direction but certainly more precise principles of intervention are required. Women's rights advocates were successful in inserting in the [action plan] final document of the 1993 Vienna World Human Rights Conference that 'all human rights are universal, indivisible and interdependent and interrelated'.

This was considered the most significant success of the World Conference. The document also proclaimed that the 'human rights of women and of the girl-child are an inalienable, integral and indivisible part of universal human rights'. In addition, the integration of the human rights of women into the mainstream of the United Nations system was mentioned as a concern, as was the elimination of violence against women in the public and in the private life. The 1995 Beijing Platform for Action reaffirms, as stated before, the universality of human rights, including the human rights of women.

9.2 CULTURAL RELATIVISM AND UNIVERSALITY

The cultural relativists have also challenged the argument of the Universalists. They argue that every culture has its own rights and duties system and even if, as a matter of customary or conventional international law, a body of substantive human rights norms exists, its meaning varies substantially from culture to culture. Vincent (1986) states that the doctrine of cultural relativism entails three things. First, that rules about morality vary from place to place. Second, that the way to understand this variety is to place it in its cultural context. Third, that moral claims derive from and are enmeshed in a cultural context, which is itself the source of their identity. Jack Donnelly (1984:400) asserts that:

> Cultural relativity is an undeniable fact; moral rules and social institutions evidence an astonishing cultural and historical variability…[It] holds that (at least some) such variations are exempt from legitimate criticism by outsiders.

Vincent (1986:28-37) argues that:

> There is no universal morality, because the history of the world is the story of the plurality of cultures, and the attempt to assert universality…as a cri-

> terion of all morality, is a more or less well-disguised version of the imperial routine of trying to make the values of a particular culture general.

Fernando Teson (1985:870-871) believes that:

> A central tenet of relativism is that no transboundary legal or moral standards exist against which human rights practices may be judged acceptable or unacceptable... [and that] human rights standards vary among different cultures and necessarily reflect national idiosyncrasies. What may be considered as human rights violation in one society may be...lawful in another and Western ideas of human rights should not be imposed upon Third World.

Raimundo Panikkar (1982:28) says that 'we should approach this topic with great fear and respect'. He maintains that human rights are trampled upon in the East and West as well as in the North and the South and that:

> Could it not also be that human rights are not observed because in their present form they do not represent a universal symbol powerful enough to elicit understanding and agreement?

He adds that 'it is a fact that the present-day formulation of human rights is the fruit of a very partial dialogue among the cultures of the world'. 'Is the concept of human rights a universal concept?' asks Panikkar and 'the answer is plain no' (Panikkar, 1982:32). Polis and Schwab (1979:viii) argue that:

> The prevailing conception of human rights as embodied in the Universal Declaration of Human Rights might be an essentially Western doctrine of little relevance to cultures other than those of the West and to ideologies other than those of capitalist pluralist societies.

They (1979: viii) further argue that 'although all societies have human rights notions, some are rooted in the individual as the core unit of society, some in the "group". Likewise in some societies economic rights have priority, in others, political rights'.

> The core of the cultural relativist critique ... is made up of a "difference" argument, in the style of cultural feminism. Typically, in a first step it is shown how human rights historically and conceptually reflect Western values. In the next step, some particularities of a non-Western culture are highlighted and contrasted with those Western concepts' (Polis and Schwab, 1979:143).

The conclusion from these premises could either be a complete rejection of human rights as 'foreign to and incompatible with a particular non-Western culture' or to reject 'specific rights, or reject the specific content or interpretation of those rights' (Polis and Schwab, 1979:143). Donnelly (1984:401) has divided these positions into strong and weak cultural relativism. The former holds that 'culture is the principal source of the validity of a moral right or rule' and the latter holds 'that culture may be an important source of the validity of a moral right or rule. 'In other words, there is a weak presumption of universality, but the relativity of human nature, communities, and rights serves as a check on the potential excesses of universalism' (Donnelly, 1984:401). Donnelly (1984:401) has made a nice distinction among three levels/types of relativity: 'involving cultural relativity in the *substance* of lists of human rights, in the *interpretation* of individual human rights, and in the *form* in which particular human rights are implemented'.

The cultural relativists have a valid point in arguing that all current human rights standards are not universal. We can see that in the fact that only a few of them have acquired the status of *jus cogens* and customary international law. They are also right that each culture has its own rights and duties system which may not seem similar to international standards but may aim to achieve the same goal: human dignity and a just society. This is what some Islamic scholars would argue. Their argument must be listened to very carefully so that human rights breaches are not justified on the basis of some vague and harmful cultural traditions ascribed to Islam. Donnelly (1984:410) argues that the cultural basis of cultural relativism must also be considered: 'especially in the light of the fact that numerous contemporary arguments against universal human rights standards strive for the cachet of cultural relativism but in fact are entirely without cultural basis'. The cultural relativists normally turn to religion: asserting that this or that cultural norm is based on religion. Two notable instances from Islamic tradition are *purdah* (dress code for women covering them from head to toe) and Female Genital Mutilation (FGM). The so-called Islamic repressive regime of the *Taliban* in Afghanistan forced women to observe full *purdah* outside their house and required male members of the family to accompany a woman in public. This directive was part of their drive for establishing a pristine Islamic society. The fallacy of *Taliban* style *purdah* can be seen in a neighbouring Muslim county, Pakistan. The North West Frontier Province (NWFP) of Pakistan has the same ethnic origin (*Pushtoon*), speaks the same language

(*Pushtoo*), and religiously follows the same Sunni sub-school: the *Hanafi* School. There, however, women do not follow the *Taliban* style dress code despite the fact that the people have exactly the same culture. In similar fashion, the practice of FGM is believed to be based on the teachings of Islam:

> Most women believe that, as good Muslims, for example, they have to undergo the operation. Among women in ... Somalia and the Sudan, circumcision is performed to reduce sexual desire and also to maintain virginity until marriage. A circumcised woman is considered to be 'clean' (United Nations, Fact Sheet No. 23, 1994).

The practice of FGM is not consistent among Muslim countries. Those who practice it attribute it to Islam but it is not practised in many Muslim countries such as Pakistan or Afghanistan where Islam is a state religion. There is no Koranic standing for it. Both *Taliban* style women's dress code and FGM have no foundation in the Koran but seem to be mere patriarchal concepts perpetuating women's subordination. Both violate women's basic rights to dignity and freedom and cannot be justified on the ground of cultural relativism or freedom of religion. What Donnelly (1984:412) said is very true that 'appeals to traditional practices and values all too often are a mere cloak for self-interest or arbitrary rule'. The 1992 UN Declaration on Minorities (article 4(2)) said:

> States shall take measures to create favourable conditions to enable persons belonging to minorities to express their characteristics and to develop their culture, language, religion, traditions and customs, except where specific practices are in violation of national law and contrary to international standards.

9.3 BRINGING TOGETHER THE UNIVERSAL AND THE CULTURAL

To hold that the entire corpus of human rights is universal and should be enforced across the continuum of world cultures while overlooking different authentic cultural values and norms is an extreme position. It does not help the cause of human rights movement for two reasons. First, it ignores the fact that many cultures have notions of rights and duties aiming at achieving the goals of human rights system, i.e. human dignity and a just society. Second, several articles of the human rights instruments recognise the right to culture and to freedom of religion. Polis and Schwab (1979:14) contend that:

> Efforts to impose the Declaration [UDHR] as it currently stands not only reflect a moral chauvinism and ethnocentric bias but are also bound to fail. In fact, the evidence of the last few decades shows increasing violations of the Declaration rather than increasing compliance.

To think of the human rights regime as 'foreign and alien' and a symbol of 'Western neo-imperialism', as the relativists would have us believe, is another extreme that refuses to acknowledge the consensus of international community on core human rights issues and their moral underpinning. Teson (1985:897-98) states that even if 'some Western plot created human rights philosophy, that fact alone would not necessarily undermine its moral value' since 'international human rights law embodies the imperfect yet inspired response of the international community to a growing awareness of the uniqueness of the human being and the unity of human race'. Teson's point is a good response to the conservative Muslim scholars' position (see introduction, B) that current human rights values are Western in origin and Islam has its own human rights system. Susan Waltz (2004) argues that it is often supposed that international human rights standards were negotiated without active participation by Middle Eastern and Muslim states but that was not the case. Waltz has given an extensive list of United Nations documents indicating the contribution of Arab and Muslim diplomats in the making of various human rights instruments from 1946-1966 [and, of course, later].

A mechanism to bring together the universal and the particular must be found to achieve the goals of human rights movement across a variety of cultures. Such a mechanism must allow accommodation of different concepts and notions of human rights. Different voices must be listened to and adjusted. Abdullahi An-Na'im (1994:121) argues that:

> The paradox can only be resolved by first acknowledging the historical facts and then by arguing that although the universal validity of these standards cannot be assumed or taken for granted, they are not necessarily or inherently invalid from the perspective of other cultures. The question of whether and to what extent there is fundamental and irreconcilable difference between a particular international human rights standard and the norms, values and institution of any other culture, can be debated internally and across the cultures.

An-Na'im (1994:122) further explains that how to broaden this dialogue:

> If dialogue is to broaden and deepen global consensus it must be undertaken in good faith, with mutual respect for, and sensitivity to, the integrity and fundamental concern of respective cultures, with an open mind and with the recognition that existing formulation may be changed---or even abolished---in the process. Ideally, participants should feel on equal footing but, given existing power relations, those in a position to do so might seek ways of redressing the imbalance.

Like An-Na'im, Polis and Schwab (1979:17) believe in the:

> Rethinking of the conception of human rights that both take into account the diversity in substance that exists and recognizes the need for extensive analysis of the relationship of human rights to broader societal context. Through this process it may become feasible to reformulate human rights doctrines that are more validly universal than those currently propagated.

No matter what mechanism is employed for reconciling the two positions, it is certainly essential for achieving universality and infusing vitality in the human rights system to bring the universal and particular together. As An-Na'im has suggested, all nations representing various cultures should be taken on board and everyone must have an equal footing in reaching a consensus on standards acceptable to all. Otherwise, many nations would either not ratify the agreed instruments, e.g. the CCPR and the CESCR, as many nations were not the part of the formulating process or like the Women's Convention where many States Parties did participate but their concerns were not adjusted (although it impossible to adjust the concern of every state). The result was that many States entered reservations to the Women's Convention virtually undermining its efficacy. Another point to be borne in mind is that authentic cultural practices must be sifted from fallacious ones such as the *Taliban's* style of women's dress code. The relativists must be careful to differentiate Western concepts such as an 'overemphasis on work at the expense of family' (Howard, 1993:337) from universal ones such as human dignity, in their process of finding 'common ground and standards acceptable to all' (UDHR, preamble).

9.4 CONCLUSION

All principles of human rights law, in its current formulation, are not universal. The arguments of the natural law theorists and universalists are valid to the extent that some human rights, such as the rights to life and not to be tortured, etc. are universal and have acquired the status of *jus cogens* and customary international law. United Nations records of the process of formulation reflect disagreements on several issues. Several states did not accept these principles totally which is why some of them entered reservations while others did not ratify various human rights instruments. For example, the CCPR was mainly not signed by Third World countries. Some states stressed economic and social rights instead of civil and political rights, e.g. the former Communist states. The arguments of the feminists are valid and, as said above, they have achieved great success in several areas such as women's visibility in the formative process of human rights conventions and declarations. They have got their 'own' separate convention, which impliedly reaches into the private sphere, and, under the 1999 Optional Protocol thereto, have separate inquiry and communication procedures.

The cultural relativist argument is a sensitive issue and must be approached with care from all sides. The universalists should refrain from imposing their 'sole' standards on the rest of the world while relativists should refrain from justifying human rights breaches on the basis of vague and harmful cultural traditions. Particular care should be taken when dealing with the issues of women's human rights. If the rich Western nations, as they do now, keep on stressing what they think are right 'rights standards', there will be more violations and oppression than compliance and protection. I agree with Shand Watson (1998: x) that:

> We in the academic community [as well as human rights organisations] would be well advised to stop making extravagant claims about what the international [human rights] law can do for the oppressed, and instead analyse the reasons for the lack of success of the human rights idea. It is only when one understands a problem that one can begin to change reality. Indignation and wishful thinking is not enough.

REFERENCES

An-Na'im, A. A. (1994) 'What Do We Mean by Universal?' *Index on Censorship*. 4/5

Brems, E. (1997) 'Enemies or Allies? Feminism and Cultural Relativism as Dissident Voices in Human Rights Discourse' *Human Rights Quarterly*. 19 (1) pp.136-164.

Bunch, C. (1995) 'Transforming Human Rights from Feminist Perspective' In: Peters and Wolper (eds.) *Women's Rights Human Rights: International Feminist Perspectives*. Routledge.

Burrows, N. (1986) 'International Law and Human Rights: the Case of Women's Rights' In: Campbell et al (eds.) *Human Rights: From Rhetoric to Reality*. Oxford: Basil Blackwell. pp.80-98.

Burrows, N. (1985) 'The 1979 Convention on the Elimination of All Forms of Discrimination against Women' *Netherlands International Law Review*. 32.

Charlesworth, H., and C. Chinkin (1991) 'Feminist Approaches to International Law', *American Journal of International Law*. 85 (4) pp.613-645.

Donovan, K. O. (1985) *Sexual Division in Law*. London, Weidenfeld.

Donnelly, J. (1984) 'Cultural Relativism and Universal Human Rights' *Human Rights Quarterly*. 6 (4) pp.400-420.

Friedman, E. (1995) 'Women's Human Rights: The Emergence of a Movement' In: Peters (eds.) *Women's Human Rights: International Feminist Perspective*. Routlege. p.18.

Hayden, P. (2001) *The Philosophy of Human Rights*. Paragon House.

Howard, R. E. (1993) 'Cultural Absolutism and the Nostalgia for Community' *Human Rights Quarterly*. 15 (2) pp.315-338.

MacKinnon, C. A. (1987) *Feminism Unmodified: Discourses on Life and Law*. Harvard University Press.

Meron, T. (1986) Human Rights Law-Making in the United Nations: A Critique of Instruments and Process. Clarendon Press.

Minor, J. A. (1994) 'An Analysis of Structural Weaknesses in the Convention on the Elimination of All Forms of Discrimination against Women' *Georgia Journal of International and Comparative Law*. 24 (1) pp.137-153.

Panikkar, R. (1982) 'Is the Notion of Human Rights a Western Concept?' *DIOGENES*. 120 pp. 28-42.

Romany, C. (1993) 'Women as Aliens: A Feminist Critique of the Public/Private Distinction in International Human Rights Law' *Harvard Human Rights Law Journal*. 6 p.87-125.

Schwab and Polis (eds.) (1982) *Towards a Human Rights Framework*. New York: Praeger.

Teson, F. (1985) 'International Human Rights and Cultural Relativism' *Virginia Journal of International Law*. 25 (4) pp.869-898.

United Nations (1984) Convention against Torture and Other Cruel, Inhuman or Degrading Treatment or Punishment.

United Nations (1948) Universal Declaration of Human Rights.

United Nations (1966) International Covenant on Economic, Social and Cultural Rights.

United Nations, (1966) International Covenant on Civil and Political Rights.

United Nations (1979) Convention on the Elimination of All Forms of Discrimination against Women.

United Nations (1999) Optional Protocol to the Convention on the Elimination of Discrimination against Women.

United Nations (1993) World Conference on Human Rights 'Vienna Declaration and Programme of Action'. http://www.unhchr.ch/huridocda/huridoca.nsf/(Symbol)/A.CONF.157.23.En?OpenDocument [accessed Nov. 2005].

United Nations (1994) *Fact Sheet No 23 'Harmful Traditional Practices Affecting the Health of Women and Children.* http://www.unhchr.ch/html/menu6/2/fs23.htm. [Accessed March 2005].

United Nations, Department of Public Information (1996) *Platform for Action and the Beijing Declaration*. New York.

United Nations (1992) Declaration on the Rights of Persons Belonging to National Or Ethnic, Religious and Linguistic Minorities.

Vincent, R. J. (1986) *Human Rights and International Relations*. Cambridge University Press.

Waltz, S. (2004) 'Universal Human Rights: The Contribution of Muslim States' *Human Rights Quarterly*. 26 (4) pp.799-844.

Watson, J. S. (1998) Theory & Reality in the International protection of Human Rights. New York: Transnational Publisher.

Wright, S. (1989-90) 'Economic Rights and Social Justice: A Feminist Analysis of Some International Human Rights Conventions' *Australian Year Book of international Law*. 12 pp.241-264.

Zearfoss, S. C. (1991-92) 'The Convention on the Elimination of All Forms of Discrimination against Women: Radical, Reasonable, or Reactionary? *Michigan Journal of International Law*. 12 pp.903-942.

CHAPTER 10

Koranic, Pakistani and Human Rights Standards: A Comparison

In the preceding chapters three different standards of women's rights were discussed: the Koranic; the statutory Islamic law of Pakistan; and the international human rights. Now we are in a position to put them in comparative perspective to find out how much compatibility exists between them. In the Koranic standard, a clear line is drawn between the two different interpretations of the Koranic verses regarding women's rights: the conservative interpretation (decontextualised), on which the statutory Islamic law of Pakistan is based, and a contextual interpretation proposed in this study. Each substantive provision of the 1979 Women's Convention is compared with each interpretation, to demonstrate that it is the conservative interpretation and the statutory Islamic law of Pakistan that conflict with the international human rights standards, not the Koranic standards. It is important to note one major point from the very outset: that is that the spirit and overall approach of the Koran and the Women's Convention are the same – equal and human treatment of women. The Koran started the reformation of 7th century Arab society by liberating women and enjoining men to treat them as human beings. The Women's Convention has the same liberating and human thrust. The 1973 constitution of Pakistan follows a similar approach of gender equality but its inconsistent application of the equality clause (article 25) and also sex-discriminatory criminal, evidence and personal status laws defeat that spirit.

10.1 GENDER DISCRIMINATION

The Women's Convention prohibits discrimination on the basis of sex (article 1; see chapter 8.4.1). However, it does not simply seek the elimination of discrimination on the basis of sex but rather that which adversely affects women (Khaliq, 1995-96). The Koran is against discrimination on the basis of gender. It says that men and women are equal by birth as they are created from a single soul (Koran, 4:1) and both are equal morally and spiritually (Koran, 33:35). Everyone is responsible for his/her actions (Koran, 2:286) and no one shall carry the burden of other people's actions (Koran, 74:38). Both men and women have the right to enjoy what they earn (Koran, 4:32). The Koran (49:19) describes one criterion for different treatment, i.e. righteousness. However, the Koran does prescribe different social roles for different sexes, such as the role of woman as a mother in the family. These different roles are complementary rather than discriminatory and no one should be discriminated against because of her/his specific role as a member of society. For instance, a pregnant woman or a mother cannot be discriminated against because of her temporary situation. The constitution of Pakistan (article 25) prohibits gender discrimination (see chapter 5.1). In contrast to the Koranic, constitutional and human rights standards, the statutory Islamic law of Pakistan such as criminal law, law of evidence and personal status discriminates on the basis of gender (see chapter 6.2.2; chapter 7.1). These provisions are discussed one by one in the following pages.

The Convention extends its reach to the private sphere unlike most other human rights instruments. Both the Koran and law in Pakistan cover private spheres as understood in the human rights scholarship. The Koran does protect the right to privacy but does not exclude the regulation of harmful actions taking place in the private sphere (see chapter 3.4). The same is the case with the legal system in Pakistan.

10.2 STATES PARTIES OBLIGATIONS

The Convention (article 2) obligates States Parties to undertake positive actions to prevent and eliminate discrimination by changing laws and abolishing harmful social and cultural traditions adversely affecting women. So does the Koran. The Koran not only obligates the ruler of the time to prevent all kinds of discrimination but also imposes a duty on every member of society to refrain from such behaviour or activities. The constitution of Pakistan forbids all sorts of discrimination specifically on the basis of gender (article 25) and any custom or tradition inhibiting the enjoyment of fundamental rights contained in the constitution. Everyone is entitled to all fundamental rights and some provisions are designed to protect women's rights. For instance, the constitution (article 8) declares that any law, custom or usage having the force of law, in so far as it is inconsistent with fundamental rights, shall be void to the extent of that inconsistency. Pakistan has also several statutory laws, which protect women's rights. They are all discussed below in comparison with each article of the Convention and Koranic standards.

10.3 GENDER EQUALITY

The Convention (articles 3-5) outlines how to implement States' obligations and to achieve actual (*de facto*) gender equality by adopting certain measures. Article 3 obligates States to take all appropriate measures in all fields so as to implement the policies mentioned in article 2. Recognising that even if women enjoy legal equality (*de jure*), they do not necessarily enjoy equality in fact. Article 4 permits States to employ special measures (affirmative actions) as long as inequalities continue to exist. Article 5 recognises that despite efforts to achieve legal and *de facto* equality for women, true advancement towards equality requires fundamental changes in social and cultural patterns. This is why it requires States to address the social and cultural patterns that lead to discrimination and stereotyped roles for men and women in society.

The Koran makes no distinction between *de jure* and *de facto* equality but provides an elaborate system of rules for the equal and human treatment of women which are to be followed in letter and spirit by each individual as well as the ruler (see chapter 2). The specific Koranic rules are permanent, e.g. the ban on sex without marriage, but its general rules can be interpreted differently as the society requires. They cannot be replaced, in contrast to the provisions of the Convention. The Koran is against all harmful social and cultural traditions and seeks to abolish anti-women traditions such as infanticide in Arab society. The laws in Pakistan provide legal (*de jure*) equality as we shall see later from the discussion of some women-specific constitutional provisions and other laws such as maternity benefits. Several of these legal rules exist on paper but are not enjoyed in practice. This signifies that legal equality exists but actual equality is missing. Also, certain customs and traditions are adhered to so strictly that they seriously inhibit women's enjoyment of their basic rights, for instance, full and effective participation in the democratic process (see chapter 5.4). The constitution does afford a remedy against such customs and traditions but in practice the constitution is ignored and customs prevail.

10.4 EXPLOITATION OF WOMEN FOR PROSTITUTION

The Convention (article 6) addresses the trafficking and exploitation of women for prostitution but it does not require States to abolish the institution of prostitution. This silence may mean tacit approval or leaving it to the conscience of each State Party in contrast to the 1949 Convention on the Suppression of Traffic in Persons and of the Exploitation of the Prostitution of Others, which outlaws the procurement and enticement of others for prostitution, exploitation of the prostitution of other persons as well as forbidding the keeping of brothels. The position of the Koran and the Islamic law in Pakistan is very clear and completely different than that of the Convention. The Koran (17:32) clearly forbids sex outside wedlock: 'nor come nigh to adultery: for it is a shameful (deed) and an evil, opening the road (to other evils)' and provides the punishment of whipping: 'the woman and the man guilty of adultery or fornication – flog each of them with a hundred stripes' (24:2). The *hudood* laws in Pakistan forbid sex without wedlock and the enticing away and procurement of someone for the purposes of prostitution (*Zina* Ordinance 1979; see the West Pakistan Suppression of Prostitution Ordinance, 1961; the West Pakistan Vagrancy Ordinance, 1958). Keeping brothel houses is against the law.[1] The approach of the constitution is slightly different to the Koran in that it does not mention the issue of prostitution in article 11 but forbids human trafficking and forced labour. However, the phrase 'trafficking in human beings' is broad enough to cover prostitution (Commission of Inquiry for Women, 1997). This interpretation signifies that the constitution prohibits prostitution which is more in congruity with the general tenor of the constitution for it recognises Islam as a state religion and Islam certainly does not allow the profession of prostitution. Also, article 37, which is a principle of policy, says that steps should be taken to prevent prostitution.

The problem of the exploitation of prostitution is ancillary to the institution of prostitution. If prostitution is legalised, then the issue of exploitation would arise but in a situation where it is not permitted in the first place then there would be no dispute on the question of exploitation. Interestingly,

[1] In practice, however, there are many brothels in big cities and, of course, the law enforcing agencies and Islamic political groups are aware of the fact. For example, *Heera Mundi* (gem market), a popular brothel and the headquarters of Jamat-e-Islami, one of the religious political parties, are both in the city of Lahore.

it is not a trend for Muslim States Parties to enter reservations to article 6 of the Convention, presumably accepting the Convention position on the question of prostitution. The practice of Muslim States Parties is in contravention of the Koranic standard, which they always use as a basis to enter reservations to the substantive provisions of the Convention destabilising its object and purpose. There is a clear conflict between the Koranic and the Convention standards on the question of prostitution but the question is that is it desirable to reconcile the two standards. It is neither desirable nor feasible to reconcile Islamic standards to international norms on the issue whether or not prostitution should be allowed. It is not desirable since prostitution is not a dignified use of human bodies. Some would argue that it should be allowed if it is an individual choice of profession. This can be rebutted by two arguments. First, some scholars argue that it is not an independent individual choice; rather it is forced upon women in disadvantaged positions (Leidholt, 1993-4). Second, many individual choices fail to respect the principle of human dignity enshrined in the human rights instruments, e.g. contracting oneself into slavery or selling children for financial gains. The prevalent exploitation of prostitution and trafficking in women for prostitution compound the issue further. Reconciliation of Islamic law regarding prostitution is a legal impossibility because an express verse of the Koran forbids any sexual relationship outside marriage and Muslim societies are not ready to accept such a change, at least at this stage of human history. Nonetheless, it must be mentioned that keeping war captives as concubines was a common practice in the early days of Islam but it gradually went out of practice despite its existing Koranic approval (4.3).

10.5 PARTICIPATION IN POLITICAL AND PUBLIC LIFE

Article 7 reaffirms women's right to vote and to be eligible for election to elected bodies. It also obligates States to create certain conditions that facilitate women's participation in political processes. This article also refers to women's participation in non-governmental organisations and associations concerned with the public and political life of the country. Article 8 requires States to ensure that women have equal opportunities to represent their government internationally and to participate in international organisations. Shaheen Sardar Ali (1995:60) argues that:

> A detailed study of the Koran indicates that there is no bar on the participation of women in political and public life including the right to vote, hold any office such as head of the state or judicial office.

Chaudhry (1991) argues that the Koran is silent on this point and silence on the issue means that the decision to allow women as political leaders is one for the Muslim community to decide, according to how their interests would best be served. The constitution of Pakistan recognises women's rights to political participation and public life. A woman, Benazir Bhutto, twice became Prime Minister of Pakistan and currently several women are ministers in the Central and Provincial cabinets. The Parliament and Provincial Assemblies have reserved seats for women (see chapter 5.4). There are many women working in the judiciary, the army, in medicine, in academia, etc. However, in some regions of Pakistan women do not enjoy political rights or the right to work outside home (see chapter 5). Women are allowed to represent their country at the international level. 'Since there is no prohibition on women's employment or holding public office or political office, therefore it may be inferred that there is no bar on women representing their country at the international level' (Ali, 1995:66). Several women represent Pakistan at international level today. The current Pakistani High Commissioner to the United Kingdom is a woman, Dr Maleeha Lodhi, and Pakistan has sent a female judge, Khalida Raschid, to the special international tribunal for Rwanda. Two United Nations special rapporteurs, Asma Jehangir and Hinna Jillani, are Pakistani women. Bangladesh had two women Prime Ministers: Khalida Zia and Hasina Wajed. The practise of Muslim states negates the religious theoretical norm that women cannot be either heads of states or represent their country internationally. It must, however, be acknowledged that the scale of women representation internationally is far less than required. Muslim states such as Saudi Arabia and Iran deny all these rights to women.

10.6 RIGHT TO NATIONALITY

Article 9 of the Convention grants women equal rights with men to acquire, change or retain their nationality and grants them equal rights with respect to their children. Any law under which children automatically acquire the nationality or citizenship of their fathers but not their mothers would contravene this article. 'Within the Islamic tradition, right to a name and identity is a basic right accorded to every human being irrespective of sex, class, race or colour' (Ali, 1995:67). All Muslims belong to the one *Ummah* (Muslim community) transcending geographical boundaries. The Koran (49:13) says that all human beings are born equal and the division into groups and communities is only for recognition. Conversely, the 1951 *Pakistan Citizenship Act* flagrantly contravenes both the Koranic and the Convention standards. The act does not treat men and women equally and seriously discriminates against the children of Pakistani females married to foreigners. The foreign husband of a Pakistani woman cannot get his wife's citizenship or nationality as is evidenced in the case of *Sharifan Bibi* (PLD 1998 Lahore 59). The children get the citizenship of their father automatically but not that of their mother, according to the act. So a Pakistani woman married to a person not from Pakistan would not get citizenship for her husband or her children (see chapter 5.1). The act not only clashes with the Koranic and the Convention standards but also with the constitution, which forbids discrimination on the basis of sex. The act needs overhauling to bring it in line with the Koran, the constitution and the Convention.

10.7 RIGHT TO EDUCATION

The Convention recognises women's equal right to education and requires that States Parties take all appropriate measures to ensure women the same conditions, opportunities and quality of education at all levels. Article 10 also seeks to eliminate stereotyped conceptions of the roles of men and women at all levels and in all forms. The Koran stresses education for all and the very first revealed verse begins with:

> Read in the name of thy Lord and Cherisher (96.1).
> He who taught (The use of) the Pen (96.4).
> Taught man that which he knew not (96:5).

In another place, the Koran says:

> It is He [God] who has taught the Quran (55:2).
> He has created man (55:3).
> He has taught him speech (and intelligence) (55:4)

The constitution of Pakistan (article 37) says in its principles of policy that the state shall remove illiteracy and provide free and compulsory secondary education within the minimum possible period. The state will also make technical and professional education equally accessible to all on the basis of merit. There are other several special laws such as the *Literacy Ordinance*, 1985, the *Provincial Primary Education Ordinance*, 1962 and the *Workers Children (Workers) Ordinance*, 1972 dealing with issues related to education.

There are several laws relating to education in Pakistan but a huge gap exists between theory and practice. Generally, very little money is earmarked for education in the national budget and only a paltry sum is spent on female education (Human Rights Commission of Pakistan, 2004). Women have fewer educational institutes and there too the facilities are negligible. The female literacy rate is 36 per cent in contrast to 60 per cent for men (Human Rights Commission of Pakistan, 2003). Men and women attend different schools until they reach university level, which is co-educational, but the majority of girls do not reach the university for various reasons, e.g. early marriage, family opposition to education away from home, poverty, the preference for male education, etc. Some elitist schools are co-educational but this is not what a common girl can dream of. According to Khaliq (1995-96:23-24):

> The text of the Convention can be interpreted to allow for the segregation of sexes, something which Islamic teaching would require, but segregation would only be permissible under the terms of the Convention, if both male and female education establishments provided exactly the same standard and type of education.

This is, however, not the case in Pakistan. According to Ali (1995:72): 'the segregation at high school and college level has resulted in not providing any facilities for girls as the demand for the education of boys is more pressing according to cultural norms'. The laws exist but are not enforced. In contrast, the Convention's aim is to achieve *de jure* and *de facto* equality. Pakistan needs to take positive action enabling men and women to get equal access to all levels and types of education according to the spirit of the Koran and the Convention.

10.8 RIGHT TO EMPLOYMENT

Article 11 obligates States to take measures to eliminate discrimination against women in employment providing them the same opportunities, choices, benefits, promotion etc. as men. Women must not be confined to traditional work in home and all direct and indirect discrimination should be ended. The Koran (4:32) allows women to earn their livelihood in the same way as men and insists that whatever they earn belongs to them, not their fathers, husbands or family: '…to men is allotted what they earn, and to women what they earn…' The constitution of Pakistan guarantees women the right to employment and the interpretations of the superior courts, as we saw in the case of *Naseem Firdos* (PLD 1995 Lahore 584), meet the standards of the Koran and the Convention. Despite the Koranic foundation and constitutional backing of the right to work, women in some regions of Pakistan do not get access to employment at all and in some cases cannot go for the job of the their choice for it is considered against cultural taboos which restrict women to homely chores. Again, women's choice of profession is limited to very few jobs – those branded as women's jobs, for instance, teaching and nursing.

10.9 EQUAL ACCESS TO HEALTH CARE

Article 12 recognises that the unequal status of women hampers their equal access to health care. Accordingly, States are obliged to ensure that women have access to care on an equal basis with men. All legal and social barriers that obstruct women's access to health care should be removed including disability, illiteracy or where they live (United Nations, 2000). There are several verses in the Koran dealing with different aspects of women's health care which impose a duty on men towards women. For example, the Koran (2:233) says:

> The mothers shall give suck to their offspring for two whole years, if the father desires to complete the term. But he shall bear the cost of their food and clothing on equitable terms … No mother shall be treated unfairly on account of her child … If ye decide on a foster-mother for your offspring, there is no blame on you, provided ye pay (the mother) what ye offered, on equitable terms.

In another place the Koran (4:1) declares an obligation to revere God and mothers: 'reverence Allah, through whom ye demand your mutual (rights), and (reverence) the wombs (that bore you): for Allah ever watches over you'. Several women's specific legal norms may be derived from these general Koranic statements. The issues of family planning and abortion are central to women's health care generally and in the context of the Convention specifically. There is no clear statement in the Koran on the issue of birth control. Hassan (1990) argues that in a sense the subject is open and Islamic state can legislate according to the needs and protection of women.

There are three articles in the constitution of Pakistan which do not reflect exactly what the Convention stands for but they do come close to the spirit of the Convention. Article 35 declares that the state shall protect marriage, mother and children. Article 37 urges the state to make sure that women are not employed in vocations unsuited to their sex and that they get maternity benefits in employment. Article 38 requires the state to provide the basic necessities of life including medical relief irrespective of sex. It must be noted that these three articles belong to the principles of policy, which are not to be relied in a court of law like fundamental rights. There are other laws such as the *Mines Maternity Benefit Act*, 1941, the *West Pakistan Maternity Benefit Ordinance*, 1958, etc. designed for the protection of women's rights. Collectively, this legal protection does not seem enough and would not match the strong commitment required under the Convention and certainly there is a need to build a stronger legal framework. Practically, inadequate health care is a problem for both men and women but access to the meagre available resources is more difficult for women (Ali, 1995:84). There are few governmental awareness programmes concerning family planning, birth control and contraceptives available to women. A few non-governmental organisations, funded by international donors mainly, are active in awareness projects but they face hardship and resistance particularly in rural areas as they are considered to be Western agents and what they do is considered to be against Islam and local culture. Incidents of attacks on some teams of these organisations have been reported in the North West Frontier Province.

Abortion is allowed under the amended Islamised sections of the Pakistan Penal Code (1860) subject to certain conditions. Section 338 says that whoever causes a woman with a child whose organs have not been formed, to miscarry, if such miscarriage is not caused in good faith for the purpose of saving the life of the woman or providing necessary treatment to her, is said to cause *isqat-i-haml* [abortion]. A woman who causes herself to miscarry is within the meaning of this section. Such abortion is punishable for three years imprisonment if caused with the consent of woman and ten years if without her consent (section 338A). The punishment is seven years and *diyat* (blood money) if the limbs and organs of the miscarried baby are formed (section 338B&C). The law thus allows abortion only to save the life of a woman. The Koran and the Convention are both silent on the issue of abortion but the statutory Islamic law in Pakistan allows conditional abortion: it must be done in good faith to save the life of the mother and it must have resulted from necessary treatment to her. The abortion law in Pakistan seems more conducive in the absence of international human rights law and the Convention (article 23) allows such laws to be relied.

10.10 SOCIAL AND ECONOMIC BENEFITS

The Convention aims at eliminating economic discrimination against women and seeks to ensure that women have equal rights to participate in recreational and cultural life (article 13). This requires the State not only to eliminate discrimination by government but also to take appropriate steps to ensure that no private actor such as an employer or financial institution discriminates against women (United Nations, 2000). The Koran has given women the right to work and they are entitled to own property. They can also open and run a business of their choice. In the same fashion, the Koran does not place any bar on the enjoyment of recreational and cultural activities. The constitution of Pakistan states that steps should be taken to ensure women full participation in all spheres of national life (article 34). In general, there are few recreational facilities for both men and women but of whatever is available women get the lesser share and women's sporting events are open to women only. Also most families, particularly in rural areas, think women's participation in sports is against their culture. In extreme cases, people may think women's sports and recreation are against Islam as they require women to go out of the home. However, the traditional thinking seems to be eroding gradually. Several women, particularly students, now participate in national and international sports. The recent 4th Annual Muslims Women Games in Iran is good example (Muslim Women's League, 2005). Regarding the economic benefits as envisaged in the Convention, no special system exists for women to acquire access to credit, mortgages, loans etc. but in theory women may access all other facilities available to men. In 1989 some women's banks were set up to help women in getting access to economic benefits but it is far from sufficient and has effected no real difference. The main hurdle is the stereotyped role of women in society: women are for the home while business and politics belong to the male domain.

Women do go out of home for jobs except for 'female' jobs such as teaching, nursing, doctors, secretarial work etc.

10.11 RIGHTS OF RURAL WOMEN

Rural women play a significant role in the economic survival of their families and communities but their work receives little or no recognition and they are often denied access to the proceeds of their efforts or the benefits of developmental schemes. The Convention has addressed this phenomenon by making a special provision for rural women, obligating States to ensure that rural women participate in development planning and implementation. They should be able to access adequate health care facilities, family planning, social security, education, etc. The Koran's rules do not make a distinction between rural and urban women. All its teachings are a unified whole applicable to all women. Pakistan is an agricultural country and the bulk of the population is concentrated in rural areas. Women's contribution to the agrarian economy is significant but it goes unrecognised. The level of basic facilities is very poor and women receive the lesser share. There is nothing specifically designed for rural women matching what the Convention is concerned about.

10.12 EQUALITY BEFORE THE LAW AND IN CIVIL MATTERS

The Convention obligates States Parties to ensure women legal autonomy by guaranteeing them equality with men before the law. Women are also to be guaranteed equal legal capacity with men in civil matters with the same opportunities to exercise that capacity. Areas of legal capacity include contracts, property, litigation, representation in the courts. etc. Accordingly, any law that limits the capacity of a woman to conclude contracts, limits her rights to own and deal with her property, or restricts her right to represent her interests in the courts or tribunals contravenes the Convention's principles and should be amended (United Nations, 2000). This article raises four main issues: equality before the law, rights related to property, equal right to represent one's interests in the courts and the right to domicile and residence. These four areas are discussed below in the light of the Koran, first, according to the conservative interpretation, and second, according to the contextual interpretation of the relevant verses and, third, according to the statutory Islamic law of Pakistan to see where they conflict.

The Koran (4:135) stands for complete equality before the law. No distinction is made between poor and rich or between near relations or even parents. As the Koran enjoins everyone not to hide the truth and to be just; therefore to give true evidence and do justice is fulfilling a divine obligation, so the gender of a person cannot justify obstructing the way of justice and truth. However, the *hudood* laws (see chapter 6) in Pakistan do not admit women's evidence in *hadd* cases although the Koran and the constitution do stand for gender equality. The principles of the so-called *hudood* laws are founded on a decontextualised interpretation of the verse 24:4 of the Koran which clashes with human rights standards. If these verses are interpreted within their proper Koranic context, they are gender-neutral and conform to human rights norms (see chapters 2, 6). The verses related to evidence do not mention the gender of the witnesses at all but the male interpreters of the Koran have extended the criterion contained in verse 2:282 to all *hadd* cases. The context and subject matters of the two verses, 24:4 and 2:282, are completely different: the first dealing with adultery and fornication whereas the latter deals with financial matters. The rule and interpretation of 2:282 cannot be extended to other areas of evidence (see chapter 2.6).

Every one has the right to own and manage property according to the Koran (2:188). However, there are two verses, which are interpreted out of their proper context resulting in gender-biased interpretation: one is related to inheritance (4:11-12) and second, to women's testimony in financial matters (2.282). Based on this interpretation, many laws practised in Islamic jurisdictions do not accept the testimony of a woman in financial matters. The evidence law of Pakistan (section 17,*Qanoon-e-Shahadat Order*, 1984) is a case in point wherein the testimony of women is considered insufficient in matters relating to finance and matters involving future obligation. The same is the case of inheritance law where women do not get equal shares in inheritance, no matter what their economic position or contribution to the family is (see chapter 2.5).

Both these legal norms contravene the Convention's principle and need reformation in the light of the contextual interpretation of the pertinent verses. For instance, a woman's share in inheritance is not due to her gender but is tied to her husband's economic responsibility towards his household. If the husband is able to provide his wife with financial support and she chooses to rely on that, then she is not entitled to an equal share. However, in situations where the husband is unable to support his wife or she is without support, then a wife may be allowed an equal share in inherited property (see chapter 2.5). If the inheritance law of Pakistan is reformed on these lines, it would conform to the spirit of the Koran as well as to the Convention. Regarding the testimony of women in financial matters, according to a contextual interpretation, it is the testimony of one woman which the court will accept as the role of the second woman is only to remind. The condition of reminding by a second woman might have been justified in 7th century Arab society on the grounds that women were not well versed in business and financial matters but it may not be necessary today since many women have the requisite information in these areas. The law needs amendment and women should be given equal status to testify in such matters.

Article 15 of the Convention also requires States to accord men and women equal rights in regard to freedom of movement and in the choice of residence and domicile. The Koran places no bar on freedom of movement and choice of domicile and residence. It is available to both men and women. According to the law of Pakistan, 'men and women have the same rights with regard to the law relating to the movement of persons and the freedom to choose their residence and domicile' (Ali, 1995:98). However, in practice the domicile of women is mainly dependent on their parents or their husbands. The choice of residence is also restricted by custom and tradition so that a married woman should stay with her husband whereas unmarried women have to stay with their family. These traditions and customs are commonly attributed to religion but in fact the Koran does not support them.

10.13 EQUALITY IN MARRIAGE AND FAMILY LAW

Article 16 of the Convention is the most significant but the most heavily reserved article, especially by Muslim States Parties. It addresses discrimination against women in the spheres of marriage and the family where they live their lives. It requires States to ensure women, on the basis of equality with men, the rights to enter into marriage with the person of their choice, the same responsibilities during and after dissolution of marriage, bearing equal responsibilities regarding number and upbringing of children, guardianship etc., property rights and minimum age for marriage and registration of marriages. These are all important issues but I will discuss here only those areas in which women do not get equal treatment in the Islamic tradition, e.g. polygamy, divorce, and maintenance for divorcees.

The Koran gives men and women equal status regarding entry into marriage, choice of spouse, number and guardianship of children and ownership of separate or joint property. However, the verses related to polygamy (3:4) and divorce (2:20, 229, 231, 65:2,) are interpreted out of context that places women at a disadvantage. Verse 3:4 is interpreted out of its context allowing a man to marry up to four wives simultaneously contravening the Convention principles. When this verse is put into its proper Koranic context, a man is allowed only one wife at a time. Entitlement to four wives is conditional upon exceptional circumstances and is justified solely for the purpose of protecting the women concerned, not for the gratification of unbridled lust (see chapter 2.3). It is correct that the Convention requires unconditional monogamy but the Koranic conditions attached to polygamy are so rigorous as to make monogamy the norm and polygamy an impossible exception.

The Koran does not give absolute power to a husband to divorce his wife at any time for any reason as it is currently practiced in Pakistan (PLD 1967 Supreme Court 97). Divorce is deemed a detestable thing in the sight of God but is permissible in certain circumstances. When it is not possible for spouses to live within the limits prescribed by God, they should agree on equitable terms to separate with kindness. On the other hand, the Koran does not place any restriction on women's right to divorce their husbands (see chapter 2.4). Women also have the right to stipulate in the marriage contract the delegation of the power of divorce to them. The Koran (2:240) also allows women maintenance: one year in case of a widow – 'those of you who die and leave widows should bequeath for their widows a year's maintenance and residence' – and 'for divorced women maintenance (should be provided) on a reasonable (scale). This is a duty on the righteous' (2:241). According to the law in Pakistan, divorcees are provided maintenance for four months whereas verse 2:241 does not stipulate any such time limit. As argued in chapter 2, remarriage may not happen in four months and in some cultures widows and divorcee are not considered good candidates for remarriage or a woman may be past a marriageable age, i.e. the case of *Shah Bano* (AIR 1985 Supreme Court 1945). It is in these situations where women start suffering after expiration of four months maintenance. The four-month time limit is extraneous to the Koran and against its spirit. For instance, a widow and a divorcee have an equal right to remarry after a waiting period so why is a widow allowed maintenance for one year and a divorcee only four months?

Family law in Pakistan and its judicial interpretation meets Koranic and international standards except in three main areas: polygamy, divorce, and maintenance. The 1961 Muslim Family Law Ordinance (hereinafter, MFLO, section 6) restricts polygamy. For a second marriage, the permission of a first wife is essential. But this restriction is neither compatible with the Koran nor with the Convention standards. Only one wife is allowed when verse 3:4 is interpreted in its proper context (see chapter 2.3). Most Muslim states follow decontextualised and conservative interpretations of the Koran, which is why a majority of them have entered reservations to article 16 of the Convention. According to the Hanafi School of law, which is followed in Pakistan, a man has unilateral power to divorce his wife whereas a wife has to move and establish certain facts in the court of law in order to dissolve her marriage. Women are also allowed to agree on mutual release or ask for the delegation of power to divorce to herself but in practice neither of them happens in Pakistan. It is not considered honourable for a man to delegate to a wife the power of divorce or to agree on mutual release of his wife. So the only common course open to a woman is to get a judicial divorce. But the Koran does not give men absolute power to divorce in the first place and second, it nowhere states that women cannot divorce their husbands in any circumstance. Women do not get maintenance beyond the waiting period of four months, according to the Hanafi School of law. This is again based on an out of context interpretation of the relevant verses and, as argued above, the Koran does not specify the timeframe for maintenance very wisely and leaves it open so that each case is dealt with as the situation demands. The provisions of the MFLO and some principles of uncodified Islamic should be reformed to bring it in line with contextual interpretation of the Koran which meets the international human rights standards.

10.14 CONCLUSION

The foregoing comparative account of laws related to women in three systems, the Convention, the Koran, and the statutory Islamic law of Pakistan, suggests that the rules and spirit of the Koran and the Convention are compatible except in the areas of sexual relations outside marriage. However, certain verses of the Koran are prone to different interpretations and it is here that the conflict crops up. If the decontextualised and conservative interpretation is the basis of laws, then conflict is certain. If laws such as the *hudood* and evidence laws and law of personal status in Pakistan are reformed according to the contextual interpretation, they will be compatible with international human rights standards. The superior courts such as the Federal Shariat Court have declared many provisions of these laws against Islamic teachings.

REFERENCES

Ali, S. S. (1995) *A Comparative Study of the United Nations Convention on the Elimination of all Forms of Discrimination Against Women, Islamic Law and the law of Pakistan*. Peshawar: Shaheen Press.

Ali, Y. (1989) *The Meaning of the Holy Qur'an.* Maryland: Amana Corporation.

Chaudhry, M. S. (1991) *Women's Rights in Islam.* Pakistan.

Hassan, R. (1990) 'Women, Religion and Sexuality' In: Becher (eds.) *An Islamic Perspective.* Geneva: WCC Publication.

Human Rights Commission of Pakistan (2003) *State of Human Rights.* http://www.hrcp-web.org [accessed November 2005].

Human Rights Commission of Pakistan (2004) *State of Human Rights.* http://www.hrcp-web.org [accessed November 2005].

Khaliq, U. (1995-96) 'Beyond the Veil: An Analysis of the Provisions of the Women's Convention in the Law as Stipulated in Shari'ah' *Buffalo Journal of International Law.* 2 pp. 1-47.

Khurshid Bibi (1967) *All Pakistan Legal Decisions* 1967 Supreme Court 97.

Leidholdt, D. (1993-94) 'Prostitution: A Violation of Women's Human Rights' *Cardozo Women's Law Journal.* 1 pp.133-147.

Muslim Women's League (2005) '4th Annual Muslim Women's Games'. http://www.mwlusa.org/muslimwomengames.htm [accessed 1 December 2005].

Naseem Firdos (1995) *All Pakistan Legal Decisions* 1995 Lahore 584.

Pakistan (1973) The Constitution of Pakistan.

Pakistan (1961) The Muslim Family Law Ordinance.

Pakistan (1979) The Offence of Zina (Enforcement of Hudood) Ordinance.

Pakistan (1951) The Pakistan Citizenship Act.
Pakistan (1860) The Pakistan Penal Code.
Pakistan (1984) The Qanun-e-Shahadat Order [Evidence Act].
Pakistan (1997) Commission of Inquiry for Women, *Annual Report.* Pakistan.
Sharifan Bibi (1998) *All Pakistan Legal Decisions* 1998 Lahore 59.
Shah Bano (1985) *All India Review* 1985 Supreme Court 945.
United Nations (1979) Convention on the Elimination of All Forms of Discrimination against Women.
United Nations (2000) *Assessing the Status of Women: A Guide to Reporting Under the Convention on the Elimination of all Forms of Discrimination against Women.* New York: United Nations.

Conclusion

This study has established that an international women's rights regime and Islamic law are dynamic and living phenomena. The international women's rights legal regime started from the United Nations Charter and evolved within decades to a full-fledged independent women's human rights regime. Similarly, Islamic law evolved over 1,400 years informed by several internal and external elements. However, neither human rights law nor statutory Islamic law protect women's rights fully. The statutory Islamic laws of Pakistan are based on an out-of-context interpretation of the Koran which conflicts with the Koran as well as international human rights standards and needs reformation through *ijtihad* (independent individual reasoning). The international human rights regime is gendered and should accommodate the valid concerns of cultural relativists and feminists and address issues specific to women's humanness.

The Koran was revealed in a tribal social structure where men played a dominant role in the protection and survival of tribal interests. Women played a secondary role in the society, except within the upper classes and in big commercial cities such as Mecca. The Koran adopted an egalitarian approach and raised the status of women, endowing them with dignity. The Koran enjoined that women should be treated as full persons with all the attributes attached to this. A woman was declared to be equal with a man in all spheres of life and was afforded similar rights as a man. She was equal with a man morally and spiritually and the Koran declared that every one was responsible for whatever he/she did. No soul should carry the burden of another soul. Women and men were given the right to work and own property, together with other civil and political rights. Several harmful traditions such as female infanticide were abolished at once. Women were declared full legal persons. They were made full partners in marriage and marriage without the free consent of a woman was invalid. Both husband and wife had to consult on familial issues such as the spacing and number of children. Men and women had separate but equal roles and responsibilities in the family. These roles were complementary, not discriminatory. From the analysis of the Koranic treatment of women, it becomes evident that the intention of the Koran was to raise the status of women from subordination to equality. The current perception in some Muslim societies that men and women cannot be equal is based on a decontextualised interpretation of the Koran.

However, the statutory Islamic laws of Pakistan discriminate against women in the areas of criminal law and the law of personal status. These laws conflict with the Koran as well as the 1973 constitution of Pakistan and international human rights law. They require reformation through judicial *ijtihad* according to the contextual interpretation of the Koran to bring them into line, first with the Koranic spirit and second, to achieve greater compatibility with international human rights standards. It is a well-established principle of Islamic law that it can be reformed to meet the exigencies of a given society. It is also a well-established point in the Islamic legal scholarship that the door of *ijithad* is not closed and that the *imam* or those to whom authority is delegated are capable of engaging in *ijtihad*. *Mujtahid* (a person engaged in *ijithad*) must be a Muslim and well-versed in Islamic law and jurisprudence. Non-Muslim jurists or judges cannot be involved in the interpretation of Islamic law. For example, the non-Muslim judges in Pakistan are not competent to engage in *ijtihad*. Otherwise, the result will be the kind of Muslim reaction witnessed in the case of *Shah Bano* (AIR 1985 Supreme Court 945) in India where the interpretation of the Koran by Hindu judges was rejected.

Most judges in Pakistan fulfil the Islamic criterion of *mujtahid* for carrying out *ijtihad*, specifically the judges of the Federal Shariat Court. The cases from the Supreme Court of Pakistan strongly indicate that Muslim judges are capable of interpreting Islamic laws to meet the ends of justice and the needs of Muslims in a nation state. The case of *Khurshid Bibi* (PLD 1967 Supreme Court 97) is a notable example. In this case, the court went beyond the traditional interpretation of the Hanafi law and laid down that a wife can ask the court for dissolution of marriage even if the husband objects to it. The most unique feature of the legal system in Pakistan is the Federal Shariat Court, the highest Islamic constitutional court. The constitution has specifically empowered it to check the Islamic standing of all laws and, in case of conflict, recommend amendment according to Islamic injunctions. The judges of the Federal Shariat Court are well-versed in Islamic law, better equipped and are constitutionally required to be engaged in *ijtihad*. In the case of *Hazoor*

Bakhash (PLD 1981 FSC 145), stoning to death was declared to be extra-Koranic. The Supreme Court overturned the judgment but for different reasons, not that the Federal Shariat Court cannot do so. The Federal Shariat Court can play a vital role in the reformation of Islamic law subject to two conditions. First, political intervention in cases of wider legal importance must be stopped and second, more independent Islamic scholars should be appointed as judges.

The principle of non-discrimination on the basis of sex is as old as the United Nations system itself. Its foundation is laid down in the Charter of the United Nations and is the subject of more than 20 human rights instruments. This principle is also contained in the constitutions of almost all United Nations Member States and seems to be a very strong candidate for becoming a peremptory norm of international human rights law. Human rights advocates urge all countries to conform to the human rights norms and values contained in the human rights instruments. However, the human rights system is not sacrosanct and every human rights norm may not be acceptable to a world full of different cultures and to a greater extent equally valid rights system. Regional human rights regimes such as European, African and Inter-American are good examples of having slightly different but acceptable regimes. To gain wider acceptance for international women's human rights principles and to achieve greater compliance, two important steps are required. First, at normative level and second, at implementation level.

A two-pronged strategy may be followed to make normative changes in the human rights in general and, specifically, in the women's right regime. First, the Women's Convention is not free from cultural biases and should be made receptive to women's rights norms from other and particularly non-Western cultures. For instance, the world's cultures are not unanimous on the subject of sexual relationships between men and women. In Muslim countries sex outside marriage is neither legal nor socially acceptable which seems to be acceptable under the Women's Convention. The process of achieving greater compatibility between human rights and Islamic standards should be two-fold. First, national Islamic laws related to women's rights should be reformed to make them gender-neutral and second, in certain cases the women's human rights system should be sensitised to Islamic human rights principles in a way that does not fundamentally conflict with them but addresses issues in a slightly different way. For instance, women must be given the right to work but in a case a woman chooses to be a housewife instead that must be respected. This is how greater compatibility might be secured. Otherwise serious and impermissible reservations to the Convention will never be withdrawn. Second, the scope of the Women's Convention should be extended to encompass issues of specific concern to women such as abortion, marital rape, domestic violence, pornography, etc. The implied reach of the Convention into the private sphere must be explicit and States Parties must be held responsible for any kind of rights violation taking place behind closed doors by state and non-state agents.

Weak implementation procedures are one of the major failings of the international human rights system. There is no sanction that can implement the decisions of human rights bodies such as the Human Rights Committee, and the Women's Convention is not an exception. By the coming into force of the 1999 Optional Protocol in 2000, the women's human rights regime got its own communication and inquiry procedures but it has only brought it to a par with the mainstream rights system, not beyond that. The Women's Convention needs to address the issues of specific concern to women and provide stronger implementation procedures.

Glossary of Islamic Terms

Alim (pl. *ulemah*): an Islamic religious scholar.

Calip (Arabic: *Khalifa*): the head of an Islamic state. The word *Khalifah* refers to the successor or representative of the Prophet Muhammad or to one of his successors. This person acts as the head of state for the Muslim *Ummah*. Another title for the *Caliph* is *Amir Al-Mumineen*: the leaders of the believers.

Diyat (blood money): is the amount paid by the accused to the relatives of the victim in the case of murder.

Daman: The compensation determined by the court for causing hurt.

Fiqh: means understanding, comprehension, knowledge, and jurisprudence in Islam. *Fiqh* is the product of human understanding that has sought to interpret and apply the Divine Law in space and time. *Faqih* is a person who is an expert in matters of Islamic legal matters.

Huq: truth, right

Huquq Allah: the rights of Allah.

Huquq-al-Abad: rights of man.

Hudud: the limits ordained by Allah. In criminal law, it refers to those cases wherein the court does not have discretion because of the limits set by God. In the legal system of Pakistan, it is spelled as *hudood*.

Imam: any person who leads a congregational prayer is called an *Imam*. A religious leader who also leads his community in the political affairs may be called an *Imam*, an *Amir*, or a *Caliph*.

Islam: Islam is an Arabic word the root of which is *Silm* and *Salam*. It means peace, greeting, salutation, obedience, loyalty, allegiance, and submission to the will of Allah.

Iddah: denotes the waiting period that a woman is required to observe as a consequence of the nullification of her marriage with her husband or because of the husband's death.

Ijma: is the consensus of eminent scholars of Islam on an issue in a given age.

Ila: denotes a husband's vow to abstain from sexual relations with his wife. It was considered a form of divorce in Arab society before Islam.

Khul: dissolution of marriage at the request of wife. In Pakistan, a woman resorts to the judiciary to get her marriage dissolved which is why it is known as 'judicial divorce'.

Madhab: a school of Islamic jurisprudence founded on the opinion of a *faqih*. There are four *madhabs* in Sunnite doctrine: Hanafi, Malaki, Shafi, and Hambali.

Maslahah: public interest.

Medina: the first city-state that came under the banner of Islam when the Prophet migrated from Mecca, his birthplace.

Mubarah: dissolution of marriage by way of mutual agreement between a husband and a wife.

Muta: a temporary marriage.

Nass: literally means something clear. In Islamic law, it means clear injunctions of the Koran and the *Sunnah*.

Qadi (Arabic, qazi): judge.

Qazf: false accusation of adultery, fornication etc.

Qisas: retaliation in kind, an eye for eye.

Qiyas: is a method for reaching a legal decision on the basis of evidence in which a common reason, or an effective cause, is applicable.

Quraish: the Arab tribe to which the Prophet Muhammad belonged.

Sharia: literally means right path or watering place. *Sharia* law is the sum total of laws derived from the Koran and the *Sunnah* of the Prophet Muhammad through human endeavour. *Sharia,* in general terms, deals with every aspect of life: spiritual, man's relation to God and man, ethics, economics, politics, etc.

The Sunnah: the word *Sunnah* means habit, practice, customary procedure, or action, norm and usage sanctioned by tradition. Specifically, it refers to what the Prophet Muhammad said, did, or approved tacitly. The recorded saying/s of the Prophet are known as *hadith/s* (traditions). The word *hadith* literally means communication or narration.

Talaq: man's unilateral power to divorce.

Talaq-e-tafwid: delegated right of power to a wife to repudiate marriage.

Taqlid: to follow a particular *madhab*, i.e. Hanafi or Malaki School

Tazir: discretionary punishment under Islamic law.

Ummah: is a community or a people. It is used in reference to the community of believers or Muslims as whole.

Wali: legal guardian, a friend or protector.

Zakat: alms due or poor due.

Zina: is an Arabic word used both for adultery and fornication.

Zina-bil-Jaber: rape.

Bibliography

PRIMARY SOURCES

Afghanistan (2004) The Constitution of Afghanistan.

Ali, Y. (1989) *The Meaning of the Holy Qur'an*. Maryland: Amana Corporation.

Pakistan (1956) The Constitution of Pakistan [repealed].

Pakistan (1962) The Constitution of Pakistan [repealed].

Pakistan (1973) The Constitution of Pakistan.

Pakistan (1962) The Government Servants (Marriage with Foreign Nationals) Rules.

Pakistan (1961) The Muslim Family Law Ordinance.

Pakistan (1979) The Offence of *Zina* (Enforcement of Hudood) Ordinance.

Pakistan (1979) The Offence of *Qazf* (Enforcement of Hudood) Ordinance.

Pakistan (1951) The Pakistan Citizenship Act.

Pakistan (1860) The Pakistan Penal Code.

Pakistan (1929) The Child Marriage Restraint Act.

Pakistan (1984) The *Qanun-e-Shahadat* Order [Evidence Act].

Pakistan (1939) The Dissolution of Muslim Marriage Act.

Pakistan (1964) The West Pakistan Family Courts Act.

Pakistan (1976) The Dowry and Bridal Gifts (Restriction) Act.

Pakistan (1997) Commission of Inquiry for Women, *Annual Report*. Pakistan.

United Nations (1945) The Charter of the United Nations.

United Nations (1984) Convention against Torture and Other Cruel, Inhuman or Degrading Treatment or Punishment.

United Nations (1992) Declaration on the Rights of Persons Belonging to National or Ethnic, Religious and Linguistic Minorities.

United Nations (1981) Declaration on the Elimination of All Forms of Intolerance and of Discrimination Based on Religion or Belief.

United Nations (1948) Universal Declaration of Human Rights.

United Nations (1966) International Covenant on Economic, Social and Cultural Rights.

United Nations, (1966) International Covenant on Civil and Political Rights.

United Nations (1979) Convention on the Elimination of All Forms of Discrimination against Women.

United Nations (1999) Optional Protocol to the Convention on the Elimination of Discrimination against Women.

United Nations (1969) The Vienna Convention on the Law of Treaties.

United Nations (1993) World Conference on Human Rights 'Vienna Declaration and Programme of Action'.

SECONDARY SOURCES

Afshari, R. (1994) 'An Essay on Islamic Cultural Relativism in the Discourse of Human Rights' *Human Rights Quarterly*. 16 (2) pp.235-276.

Ahmad, L. (1992) Women and Gender in Islam: Historical Roots of a Modern Debate. New Haven: Yale University Press.

Ahmad, M. (1963) 'Islamic Aspects of the New Constitution of Pakistan' *Islamic Studies*. Vol. II.

Alavi, H. (1986) 'Ethnicity, Muslim Society, and the Pakistan's Ideology' In: Weiss (eds.) *Islamic Reassertion in Pakistan*. Syracuse: Syracuse University Press.

Al-Faruqi, I. R. (1962) 'Towards a New Methodology for Qur'anic Exegesis' *Islamic Studies*. pp.35-52.

Al-Hibri, A. (1982) 'A Study of Islamic Herstory: or How did We Ever Get into this Mess' In: *Women and Islam*. Oxford: Pergamon Press.

Al-Hibri, A. (1997) 'Islam, Law and Custom: Redefining Muslim Women's Rights' *American University Journal of International law and Policy*. 12 (1). pp.1-44.

Ali, A. (1969) *The Spirit of Islam*. Pakistan.

Ali, P. S. (1975) *Status of Women in the Muslim World*. Lahore: Aziz Publishers.

Ali, S. S. (1995) A Comparative Study of the United Nations Convention on the Elimination of all Forms of Discrimination Against Women, Islamic Law and the law of Pakistan. Peshawar: Shaheen Press.

Ali, S. S. (2002) 'Testing the Limits of Family Law Reform in Pakistan: A Critical Analysis of the Muslim Family Laws Ordinance 1961' In: Andrew (eds.) *The International Survey of Family Law*. Bainham Andrew International Society of Family Law. pp. 317-335.

Alshech, E. (2004) 'Do Not Enter Houses Other Than Your Own': the Evolution of the Notion of a Private Domestic Sphere in Early Sunni Islamic Thought' *Islamic Law and Society.* 11 (3) p.291-332.

An-Na'im, A. A. (1996) Towards an Islamic Reformation: Civil liberties, Human Rights and International Law. Syracuse: Syracuse University Press.

An-Na'im, A. A. (1994) 'What Do We Mean by Universal?' *Index on Censorship.* 4/5

Anwar, G. (1999) 'Reclaiming the Religious Center from a Muslim Perspective: Theological Alternatives to Religious Fundamentalism' In: Howland (eds.) *Religious Fundamentalisms and the Human Rights of Women.* Macmillan.

Aurat Foundation and Information Services Foundation, (2002) *Citizen's Campaign for Women's Representation in Local Government.* Peshawar: Pakistan.

Badawi, Z. (1976) *The Reformers of Egypt—A Critique of Al-Afghani, Abduh* and *Ridha.* Papers 2, The Muslim Institute: The Open University Press.

Baderin, M. A. (2001) 'A Macroscopic Analysis of the Practice of Muslim State Parties to International Human Rights Treaties: Conflict or Congruence?' *Human Rights Law Review.* 1 (2)

Baderin, M. A. (2003) *International Human Rights and Islamic Law.* Oxford: Oxford University Press.

Badr, G. M. (1978) 'Islamic Law: Its Relation to other Legal Systems' The American Journal of Comparative Law. 26 pp.187-198.

Balchin (eds.) (1994) *A Handbook on Family Law in Pakistan.* Lahore: Shirkat Gah.

Barnett, H. (2002) Britain Unwrapped: Government and Constitution Explained. Penguin Books.

Bayefsky, A. F. (1990) 'The Principles of Equality or Non-discrimination in International Law' *Human Rights Law Journal.* 11 (1-2).

Bielefeldt, H. (1995) 'Muslim Voices in the Human Rights Debate' *Human Rights Quarterly.* 17 (4). pp.287-617.

Boyle, K. and Sheen, J (eds.) (1997) *Freedom of Religion and Belief: A World Report.* London: Routhlege.

Brems, E. (1997) 'Enemies or Allies? Feminism and Cultural Relativism as Dissident Voices in Human Rights Discourse' *Human Rights Quarterly.* 19 (1) pp.136-164.

Brohi, A. K. (1976) 'Islam and Human Rights' *All Pakistan Legal Decisions.*

Brohi, A. K. (1978) 'Islam and Human Rights' In: Gauhar (eds.) *The Challenge of Islam*. London: Islamic Council of Europe. pp.117-195.

Burrows, N. (1986) 'International Law and Human Rights: the Case of Women's Rights' In: Campbell et al (eds.) *Human Rights: From Rhetoric to Reality*. Oxford: Basil Blackwell. pp.80-98.

Burrows, N. (1985) 'The 1979 Convention on the Elimination of All Forms of Discrimination against Women' *Netherlands International Law Review*. 32.

Bunch, C. (1995) 'Transforming Human Rights from Feminist Perspective' In: Peters and Wolper (eds.) *Women's Rights Human Rights: International Feminist Perspectives*. Routledge.

Bulbeck, C. (1996) 'Less Than Overwhelmed by Beijing: Problems Concerning Women's Commonality and Diversity'. 6 pp.31-37.

Byrnes, A. C. (1989) 'The "Other" Human Rights Treaty Body: The Work of the Committee on the Elimination of Discrimination against Women' *The Yale Journal of International Law*. 14 (1) pp.1-67.

Charlesworth, H., and C. Chinkin (1991) 'Feminist Approaches to International Law' *American Journal of International Law*. 85 (4) pp.613-645.

Charlesworth, C. Chinkin. (2000) *The Boundaries of International Law: The Feminist Analysis*. Manchester: Manchester University Press.

Carroll, L. (1982) 'Nizam-i-Islam: Process and Conflict in Pakistan's Programme of Islamisation, with Special Reference to the Position of Women' *Journal of Commonwealth and Comparative Politics*. p.201.

Carroll, L. (1982a) 'Rejoinder to the Proceedings of the Seminar on 'Adultery and Fornication in Islamic Jurisprudence: Dimensions and Perspectives' *Islamic and Comparative Law Quarterly*. 2 (4) pp.57-95.

Carroll, L. (1989) 'Section 4 of the Muslim Family Laws Ordinance: Three Alternative Interpretations' *All Pakistan Legal Decisions*.

Carroll, L. (1986) 'Divorced Muslim Women and Maintenance'*All Pakistan Legal Decisions*.

Carroll, L. (1996) 'Qur'an 2:229: "A Charter Granted to the Wife"? Judicial *Khul* in Pakistan' *Islamic Law and Society*. 3 pp. 91-126.

Chaudhry, Z. (1997) 'The Myth of Misogyny: A Reanalysis of Women's Inheritance in Islamic Law' *Albany Law Review*. 61 pp. 511-555.

Chaudhry, M. S. (1991) *Women's Rights in Islam*. Pakistan.

Clark, B. (1991) 'The Vienna Convention Reservations Regime and the Convention on the Discrimination against Women' *American Journal of International Law*. 85 (2) pp. 281-321.

Cole, J. R. I. (2003) 'The Taliban, Women, and the Hegelian Private Sphere' *Social Research*. 70 (3) Fall pp.771-808.

Cook, R. J. (1994) 'State Responsibility for Violation of Human Rights' *Harvard Human Rights Law Journal.* 7 pp.125-176.

Cook, R. J. (1990) 'Reservation to the Convention on the Elimination of All Forms of Discrimination against Women' *Virginia Journal of International Law*. 30 pp.643-716.

Coulson, N. J. (1957) 'The State and the Individual in Islamic Law' *International and Comparative Law Quarterly*. 6 pp.49-60.

Coulson, N. J. (1964) *A History of Islamic Law*. Edinburgh: Edinburgh University Press.

Daud, Wan Mohd Wan Nor (1989) The Concept of Knowledge in Islam and its Implications for Education in a Developing Country. London: Mansell Publisher.

Dawn (2005) 'CII chief hints at Hudood laws review'. 30 May 2005. Karachi.

Dawn (2005) 'PPP submits resolution against Hudood law in Senate'. 4 January 2005. Karachi.

Donovan, K. O. (1985) *Sexual Division in Law*.

Donnelly, J. (1984) 'Cultural Relativism and Universal Human Rights' *Human Rights Quarterly*. 6 (4) pp.400-420.

El-Nimr, R. (1997) 'Women in Islamic Law' In: Yamani (eds.) *Feminism and Islam: Legal and Literary Perspectives*. University of London: Ittaca Press.

Engineer, A. A. (1996) *The Rights of Women in Islam*. Islamabad: Vanguard Books Limited.

Engineer, A. A. (2004) 'Evolution of Sharia law and its Potentiality for Change' *Islam and Modern Age*. June.

Esposito, J. L. (1998) *Islam: The Straight Path*. New York: Oxford University Press.

Esposito, J. L. (1980) 'Pakistan: Quest for Islamic Identity' In: Esposito (eds.) *Islam and Development*. Syracuse: Syracuse University Press.

Esposito, J. L. (1982) 'Islamisation: Religion and Politics in Pakistan' *The Muslim World*. LXXII, July-October.

Esposito, J. and DeLong-Bas (2001) *Women in Muslim Family Law.* . 2nd ed. Syracuse: Syracuse University Press.

Fadel, M. (1997) 'Two Women, One Man: Knowledge, Power, and Gender in Medieval Sunni Legal Thought' *International Journal of Middle East Studies*. 29 (2) pp.185-204.

Fitzgerald, S. G. V. (1955) 'Nature and the Sources of Sharia' In: Khadduri and Liebseny (eds.) *Law in the Middle East. Vol. 1: Origin and Development of Islamic Law*. Washington, D.C.: The Middle East Institute. pp. 85-112.

Fitzgerald, S. G. V. (1951) 'The Debt of Islamic to Roman Law' *The Law Quarterly Review*. 67.

Fraser, A. S. (1999) 'Becoming Human: The Origins and Development of Women's Human Rights' *Human Rights Quarterly*. 21 (4) pp.853-906.

Freeman, M. (2004) 'The Problem of Secularism in Human Rights Theory' *Human Rights Quarterly*. 26 (2) pp.375-400.

Friedman, E. (1995) 'Women's Human Rights: The Emergence of a Movement' In: Peters (eds.) *Women's Human Rights: International Feminist Perspective*. Routlege. p.18.

Fyzee, A. A. (1999) *Outlines of Mohammedan Law*. 4th ed. Oxford University Press.

Fyzee, A. A. (1955) 'Shia Legal Theories' In: Khadduri and Liebseny (eds.) *Law in the Middle East. Vol. 1: Origin and Development of Islamic Law*. Washington, D.C.: The Middle East Institute.

Ghazali, A. S. (1996) *Islamic Pakistan: Illusions and Reality*. Islamabad: National Book Club.

Goldziher, I. (1967) *Muslim Studies*. Stern (eds.) Barber and Stern (trans.), George Allen & Unwin Ltd. Volume I.

Godziher, I. (1981) *Introduction to Islamic Theology and Law*. Andrea and Ruth (trans.), Princeton University Press.

Gottesman, E. (1991-92) 'The Reemergence of Qisas and Diyat in Pakistan' *Columbia Human Rights Law Review*. 23 pp.433-462.

Greenberg, J. (1984) 'Race, Sex and Religious Discrimination in International Law' In: Meron (eds.) *Human Rights in International Law: Legal and Policy Issues*. Oxford: Clarendon Press.

Halliday, S. (1995) 'Relativism and Universalism in Human Rights: The Islamic Middle East' In: Beetham (eds.) *Politics and Human Rights*. Leeds University Press.

Hallaq, W. B. (1984) 'Was the Gate of Ijtihad Closed?' *International Journal of Middle East Studies*. 16 (1) pp.2-41.

Hamilton (trans.) (1989) *The Hedaya*. Karachi: Darul-Ishaat.

Hassan, A. (1970) *The Early Development of Islamic Jurisprudence*. Islamabad: Islamic Research Institute.

Hassan, R. (2003) Members, One of Another: Gender Equality and Justice in Islam. http://www.religiousconsultation.org/hassan.htm. [Accessed in Nov. 2003].

Hassan, R. (1990) 'Women, Religion and Sexuality' In: Becher (eds.) *An Islamic Perspective*. Geneva: WCC Publication.

Hassan, R. (1982) 'On Human Rights and The Quranic Perspective' In: Swidler (eds.) *Human Rights in Religious Traditions*. New York: The Pilgrim Press.

Hassan, R. (1988) *Feminist Theology and Women in the Muslim World*. Interviewed by Mistead, B. 1988. Women Living Under Muslim Laws (Dossier 4, 1988):
http://www.wluml.org/english/pubsfulltxt.shtml?cmd[87]=i-87-2595. [Accessed Feb. 2005].

Hayden, P. (2001) *The Philosophy of Human Rights*. Paragon House.

Hervener, K. N. (1986) "An Analysis of Gender Based Treaty Law: Contemporary Development in Historical Perspective' *Human Rights Quarterly*. 8 (1) p.70-88

Hessler, K. (2005) 'Resolving Interpretive Conflicts in International Human Rights Law' *The Journal of Political Philosophy*. 13 (1) pp.29-52.

Hidayatullah, M. (1968) *Mullah Principles of Muhammadan Law*. 6th ed. Bombay.

Hitti, P. (1961) *History of the Arabs*. London: McMillan.

Holland, C.W. (1997) 'Women and Religious Fundamentalism' *Columbia Journal of Transnational Law*. 35 pp.217-377.

Holland, C. W. (1999) 'Introduction' In: Holland (eds.) *Religious Fundamentalism and the Human Rights of Women*. Macmillan.

Hosken, F. P. (1981) 'Towards a Definition of Women's Human Rights' *Human Rights Quarterly*. 3 (2) pp.1-10.

Howard, R. E. (1993) 'Cultural Absolutism and the Nostalgia for Community' Human Rights Quarterly. 15 (2) pp.315-338.

Huntington, S. P. (1993) 'The Clash of Civilisations?' *Foreign Affairs*. Summer, pp.22-49.

Huntington, S. P. (1993) 'If Not Civilisations, What?' *Foreign Affairs*. November/December, pp.186-194.

Human Rights Commission of Pakistan (2002) *State of Human Rights*. http://www.hrcp-web.org [accessed November 2005].

Human Rights Commission of Pakistan (2000) *State of Human Rights*. http://www.hrcp-web.org [accessed November 2005].

Hunt, J. (1996) 'Reflections on Beijing' *Australian Feminist Law Journal.* 6 p. 39.

Hussian, A. (1987) *Status of Women in Islam.* Lahore: Law Publisher Company.

Iqbal, M. (1934) Reconstruction of Religious Thought in Islam. Oxford University Press.

Iqbal, A. (1986) *Islamisation of Pakistan.* Islamabad: Vanguard Books Ltd.

India (1975) The Criminal Procedure Code of India.

International Women's Rights Watch (1988) *The Convention on the Elimination of All Forms of Discrimination against Women.* Minneapolis: Humphrey Institute of Public Affairs.

Iqbal, N. (2005) 'FSC suspends LHC verdict: Mukhtar Mai case' *Dawn* 12 March 2005. Islamabad.

Ishaque, K. (1974) 'Human Rights in Islamic Law' *Review of the International Commission of Jurists.* 12 pp.30-39.

Jehangir, A. and Hina, J. (1990) *Hudood Ordinances: A Divine Sanction?* Lahore: Rhotas Books.

Jokisch, B. (1997) 'Ijtihad in Ibn Taymiyya's Fatawas' In: Gleave (eds.) *Islamic Law Theory and Practice.* I. B. Tauris Publishers.

Kadivar, M. (2003) 'An Introduction to the Public and Private Debate in Islam' *Social Research.* 70 (3) Fall pp.659-836.

Kakakhel, N. A. S. (2002) 'Citizenship Act Violates Women's Rights' *Dawn.* 15 July. Karachi.

Kamali, M. H. (2000) 'Law and Society, the Interplay of Revelation and Reason in the Shariah' In: Esposito (eds.) *Oxford History of Islam.* Oxford University Press.

Kar, M. (2003) 'The Invasion of the Private Sphere in Iran' *Social Research.* 70 (3) Fall pp-829-836.

Kennedy, C. H. (1991) 'Islamic Legal Reform and the Status of Women in Pakistan' *Journal of Islamic Studies.* 2 (1) p.45-55.

Khadduri, M. (1946) 'Human Rights in Islam' *The Annals of the American Academy.*

Khaldun, I. (1398) *Al-Moghaddemah.* Beirut.

Khaliq, U. (1995-96) 'Beyond the Veil: An Analysis of the Provisions of the Women's Convention in the Law as Stipulated in Shari'ah' *Buffalo Journal of International Law.* 2 pp. 1-47.

Khan, H. (1980) Islamic Law of Inheritance: A Comparative Study with Emphasis on Contemporary Problem. Lahore: Pakistan Times Law Publication.

Leidholdt, D. (1993-94) 'Prostitution: A Violation of Women's Human Rights' *Cardozo Women's Law Journal.* 1 pp.133-147.

Levy, R. (1979) *The Social structure of Islam.* Cambridge: Cambridge University Press.

Libson, G. (1997) 'The Development of Custom as a Source of Law in Islamic Law' *Islamic Law and Society.* 4 (2) pp131-155.

MacKinnon, C. A. (1987) *Feminism Unmodified: Discourses on Life and Law.* Harvard University Press.

Mahmood, S. (1990) *Constitutional Foundations of Pakistan.* Lahore: Jang Publisher.

Mahmood, M. (2003) *The Constitution of Islamic Republic of Pakistan.* Pakistan: Law Times Publication.

Mansfield, A. (1990) *The Arabs.* Penguin Books.

Maududi, S. A. (1995) *Human Rights in Islam.* 2nd ed. Lahore: Islamic Publication.

Maududi, S. A. (1987) *Tafeheem-ul-Quran.* 6th ed. Lahore: Adara Turjuman-nul-Quran.

Mayer, A. E. (1990) 'Current Muslim Thinking on Human Rights' In: An-Na'im and Deng (eds.) *Human Rights in Africa: Cross Cultural Perspectives.* Washington: Brooking Institutions.

Mayer, A. E. (1994) 'Universal versus Islamic Human Rights: A Clash of Cultures or a Clash with a Construct?' *Michigan Journal of International Law.* 15 (2) pp.307-404.

Mehdi, R. (1994) The Islamisation of the Law in Pakistan. Curzon Press Ltd.

Mehdi, R. (1990) 'The Offence of Rape Law in the Islamic Law of Pakistan' *International Journal of the Sociology of Law.* 18 pp.19-28.

Mernissi, F. (1985) Beyond the Veil: Male-Female Dynamics in the Modern Muslim Society. Indiana University Press.

Meron, T. (1986) Human Rights Law-Making in the United Nations: A Critique of Instruments and Process. Clarendon Press.

Mill, J. S. (1998) *The Subjection of Women.* Oxford World Classic.

Minai, N. (1981) Women in Islam: Tradition and Transition in the Middle East. New York: Seaview Books.

Minor, J. A. (1994) 'An Analysis of Structural Weaknesses in the Convention on the Elimination of All Forms of Discrimination against Women' *Georgia Journal of International and Comparative Law.* 24 (1) pp.137-153.

Mirza, Q. (2000) 'Islamic Feminism and the Exemplary Past' In: Richardson (eds.) *Feminist Perspectives on Law and Theory*. Cavendish Publishing Limited.

Monshipouri, M. (1998) Islamism, Secularism and Human Rights in the Middle East. Lynne Rienner.

Moosa, E. (2000-2001) 'The Dilemma of Islamic Human Rights Schemes' *Journal of Law and Religion*. 15 pp.185.

Mottaheda R., and Stilt, K. (2003) 'Public and Private as Viewed through the Work of the *Muhtasib*' *Social Research*. 70 (3) Fall pp.735-748.

Morsink, J. (1991) 'Women's Rights in the Universal Declaration' *Human Rights Quarterly*. 13 (2) pp.229-256.

Mortimer. (1983) 'Islam and Human Rights' *Index on Censorship*. 12.

Mushriq 27 May 2001 Peshawar (Pakistan).

Muslim Women's League (2002) 'Women in Pre-Islamic Arabia' http.islamfortoday.org. [Accessed Nov. 2002].

Muslim Women's League (2005) '4th Annual Muslim Women's Games'. http://www.mwlusa.org/muslimwomengames.htm [accessed 1 December 2005].

Mutahhery, M. (1982) *Woman and Her Rights*. Karachi: Islamic Seminary.

National Commission on the Status of Women of Pakistan (2003) Draft Report on the Meetings of the Special Committee To Review The (Enforcement of Hudood Ordinances, 1979.
http://new.ncsw.gov.pk/index.php [Accessed March 2005).

Nicholson, R. A. (1996) *A Literary History of the Arabs*. Cambridge University Press.

Otto, D. (1999) 'A Post-Beijing Reflection on the Limitations and Potential of Human Rights Discourse for Women' In: Askin and Keoing (eds.) Vol. 1 *Women and International Human Rights Law*. New York: Transnational Publishers, Inc. Ardsley, p 128.

Panikkar, R. (1982) 'Is the Notion of Human Rights a Western Concept?' *DIOGENES*. 120 pp. 28-42.

Pearl, P. (1979) A *Textbook on Muslim Law*. London: Croom Helm.

Piscotri, J. P. (1980) 'Human Rights in Islamic Political Culture' In: Thompson (eds.) *The Moral Imperatives of Human Rights: A World Survey*.

Polis, A., and Peter Schwab (1979) 'Human Rights: A Western Construct with Limited Applicability' In: Polis and Schwab (eds.) *Human Rights: Cultural and Ideological Perspectives*. Praeger Publishers.

Quraishi, A. (2000) 'Book Review of Islamism, Secularism and Human Rights in the Middle East By Mahmood Monshipouri'*Human Rights Quarterly*. 22 (2) pp.625-629.

Quraishi, A. (1997) 'Her Honour: An Islamic Critique of the Rape Laws in Pakistan from a Woman-Sensitive Perspective' *Michigan Journal of International Law*. 18 (2) pp.287-320.

Qutb, M. (1964) *Islam the Misunderstood Religion*. Kuwait: Darul Bayan Bookshop.

Rahim, A. (1911) *Muhammadan Jurisprudence*. Lahore: PLD Publishers.

Rahman, F. (1982) Islam & Modernity: Transformation of an Intellectual Tradition. Chicago University Press.

Rahman, F. (1982) *Major Themes in the Quran*. 2nd ed. Bibliotheca Islamica: Minneapolis.

Rahman, F. (1966) *History of Religion Islam*. London.

Rahman, F. (1965) *Islamic Methodology in History*. Karachi: Central Institute of Islamic Research.

Rahman, F. (1979) 'Towards Reformulating the Methodology of Islamic Law' *New York University Journal of International Law and Politics*. 12 (2) pp.219-224.

Rahman, T. (1997) *Essays on Islam*. Lahore: Islamic Publication.

Rahman, T. (1968) 'Maintenance of Wife in Islamic Law' *All Pakistan Legal Decisions:* Lahore.

Redding, J. A. (2004) 'Constitutionalsing Islam: Theory and Pakistan' *Virginia Journal of International Law*. 44 (3) pp.759-827.

Rida, M. R. (1966) 'Muhammad Rashid Rida: Legal Doctrines' In: Kerr (eds.) *Islamic Reform: The Political and Legal Theories of Muhammad Abduh and Rashid Rida*. University of California Press.

Roberts, R. (1980) *The Social Laws of Koran*. 5th ed. London: Curzon Press.

Romany, C. (1993) 'Women as Aliens: A Feminist Critique of the Public/Private Distinction in International Human Rights Law' *Harvard Human Rights Law Journal*. 6 p.87-125.

Sachedina, A. (1999) 'The Ideal and Real in Islamic Law' In: Khare (eds.) *Perspective on Islamic Law, Justice, and Society*. Rowman and Littlefield Publishers.

Said, A. A. (1979) 'Precepts and Practice of Human Rights in Islam' *Universal Human Rights*. 1 (1) pp.1-18.

Sayeh, and Morse (1996) 'Islam and the Treatment of Women: An Incomplete Understanding of Gradualism' *Texas International Law Journal*. 30 (2) pp.311-334.

Schacht, J. (1955) 'Pre-Islamic Background and Early Development of Jurisprudence' In: Khadduri and Liebseny (eds.) *Law in the Middle East. Vol. 1: Origin and Development of Islamic Law*. Washington, D.C.: The Middle East Institute.

Schacht, J. (1950) 'Foreign Elements in Ancient Islamic Law' *Journal of Comparative Legislation and International law*. 32 pp.9-17.

Schwab and Polis (eds.) (1982) *Towards a Human Rights Framework*. New York: Praeger.

Shahab, R. U. (1984) 'Proposed Law on Qisas and Diyat' *All Pakistan Legal Decisions*. Lahore.

Shah, N. (1990) 'Rights of Women before Courts of Law' *All Pakistan Legal Decisions*. p.80.

Shah, N.A. (2005) 'The Constitution of Afghanistan and Women's Rights' *Feminist Legal Studies*. 13 (2) pp.239-258).

Shakespeare, W. (1983) *Julius Caesar*. Penguin Classics.

Smith, W. R. (1903) *Kinship and Marriage in Early Arabia*. Cook (eds.) London: Adam and Charles Black.

Stowasser, B. (1994) Women in the Quran, Traditions and Interpretation. Oxford University Press.

Stowasser, B. (1998) 'Gender Issues and Contemporary Quran Interpretation' In: Haddad (eds.) *Islam, Gender and Social Change*. Oxford University Press.

Stowasser, B. (1987) 'Liberated Equals or Protected Dependent? Contemporary Religious Paradigms on Women's Status in Islam' *Arab Studies Quarterly*. 9 (3) pp.260-283.

Streeter, N. (1996) 'Beijing and Beyond' *Berkeley Women's Law Journal*. 11 p.200.

Sullivan, D. (1994) 'Women's Human Rights and the 1993 World Conference on Human Rights' *American Journal of International Law*. 88 (1) p.164.

Sullivan, D. (1992) 'Gender Equality and Religious Freedom: Towards a Framework for Conflict Resolution' *New York Journal of International Law and Politics*. 24, p.800.

Taha, M. M. (1987) *The Second Message of Islam*. An-Na'im, (trans.) Syracuse University Press.

Taperell, K. (1985) 'Islam and Human Rights' *Australian Foreign Affairs*. 56.

Taylor, D. (1983) 'The Politics of Islam and Islamisation in Pakistan' In: Piscatori (eds.) *Islam in the Political Process*. Cambridge University Press.

Teson, F. (1985) 'International Human Rights and Cultural Relativism' *Virginia Journal of International Law*. 25 (4) pp.869-898.

Tibi, B. (1992) 'Review of Mayer's, 'Islam and Human Rights' *Harvard Human Rights Journal*. 5 pp.221-226.

Tibi, B. (1999) 'The European Tradition of Human Rights and the Culture of Islam' In: An-Na'im and Deng (eds.) *Human Rights in Africa: Cross Cultural Perspectives*. Washington: Brooking Institutions.

Tibi, B. (1994) 'Islamic Law/*Shari'a*, Human Rights, Universal Morality and International Relations' *Human Rights Quarterly*. 16 (2) pp.277-299.

Tinker, C. (1981) 'Human Rights for Women: The UN Convention on the Elimination of All Forms of Discrimination against Women' *Human Rights Quarterly*. 3 (1), pp.32-43.

Tolbat, I. (1998) *Pakistan: A Modern History*. London: C. Hurst.

United Nations, Human Rights Committee (1978) *Shirin Aumeeruddy-Cziffra v. Mauritius* Communication No. R.9/35 (2 May 1978).

United Nations High Commissioner for Human Rights (1993) CCPR General Comment No. 22: The right to freedom of thought, conscience and religion (Art. 18).

United Nations, High Commissioner for Human Rights (1989) *CCPR General Comment No. 18: Non-discrimination*.

United Nations, Human Rights Committee (1984) 'Communication No. 172/1984: *Brooks v. Netherlands*. 09/04/87'.

United Nations, Committee on the Elimination of Discrimination against Women (1989) *General Recommendation No. 12*.

United Nations, Committee on the Elimination of Discrimination against Women, (1992) '*General Recommendation No. 19, Violence against Women*'.

United Nations (1993) Fact Sheet No 22, 'Discrimination against Women: The Convention and the Committee.

United Nations (2000) Assessing the Status of Women: A Guide to Reporting Under the Convention on the Elimination of all Forms of Discrimination against Women. New York: United Nations.

United Nations (1996) Fact Sheet No. 2 (Rev. 1), The International Bill of Rights.

United Nations (1994) Fact Sheet No 23 'Harmful Traditional Practices Affecting the Health of Women and Children.

United Nations, Division for the Advancement of Women '*General Recommendation No. 8*, 1988.

United Nations, Division for the Advancement of Women (2005) '*Text of the Convention/States Parties/Reservations*'..

United Nations, Division for the Advancement of Women (2005a) '*Text of the Optional Protocol/Signatures and Ratifications*'.

United Nations (1993) World Conference on Human Rights 'Vienna Declaration and Programme of Action'.

United Nations, Department of Public Information (1996) *Platform for Action and the Beijing Declaration.* New York.

Usmani, M. T. (1999) *Islam and Modernism.* Siddiqui's trans. Pakistan: Darul Ishaat.

Vincent, R. J. (1986) *Human Rights and International Relations.* Cambridge University Press.

Vogel, F. E. (2003) 'The Public and Private in Saudi Arabia: Restrictions on the Powers of Committees for Ordering the Good and Forbidding the Evil' *Social Research.* 70 (3) Fall pp.749.

Wadud, A. (1999) Quran and Woman: Rereading the Sacred Text from the Woman Perspective. New York: Oxford University Press.

Waltz, S. (2004) 'Universal Human Rights: The Contribution of Muslim States' *Human Rights Quarterly.* 26 (4) pp.799-844.

Waring, M. (1988-89) 'Gender and International Law: Women and the Right to Development' *Australian Year Book of International Law.* 12 p.177-189.

Watson, J. S. (1998) Theory & Reality in the International Protection of Human Rights. New York: Transnational Publisher.

Watt, W. M. (1969) *Muhammad at Median.* Karachi: Oxford University Press.

Weiss, B. (1978) 'Interpretation in Islamic Law: the Theory of *Ijtihad*' *The American Journal of Comparative Law.* 26 pp.199-212.

Weiss, B. (1998) *The Spirit of Islamic Law.* London: Georgia University Press.

Wright, S. (1989-90) 'Economic Rights and Social Justice: A Feminist Analysis of Some International Human Rights Conventions' *Australian Year Book of international Law.* 12 pp.241-264.

Yost, B. (1995) 'Women's World Conference Was Eye-Opener for Attendees From Valley' *Phoenix Gazette.* September 23.

Zein En-Din, N. (1982) 'Removing the Veil and Veiling' In: Al-Hibri (eds.) *Women's Studies International Forum.* Pergamon Press.

Zearfoss, S. C. (1991-92) 'The Convention on the Elimination of All Forms of Discrimination against Women: Radical, Reasonable, or Reactionary? *Michigan Journal of International Law*. 12 pp.903-942.

SELECTED INTERNET SITES

Muslim Women's League: http.islamfortoday.org

Women Living Under Muslim Laws: http://www.wluml.org/english/index.shtml

United Nations High Commissioner for Human Rights: http://www.unhchr.ch/html/menu3/b/treaty9_asp.htm

United Nations, Division for the Advancement of Women, New York. http://www.un.org/womenwatch/daw/cedaw/states.htm

CASES FROM OTHER JURISDICTIONS

(1986) 9 European Human Rights Review 203.

47 (1995) Dhaka Law Reports 54.

All India Review 1985 Supreme Court 945.

CASES CITED (PAKISTAN)

All Pakistan Law Decisions 1960 Lahore 1142 (It is more commonly cited as PLD).

PLD 1981 Federal Sharait Court 145.

PLD 2004 Supreme Court 219.

PLD 1981 Federal Shariat Court 145.

PLD 2004 Federal Shariat Court 1.

2004 Supreme Court Monthly Review 432.

2004 Supreme Court Monthly Review 1701.

PLD 1967 Supreme Court 97.

PLD 1990 Supreme Court 295.

PLD 1993 Supreme Court 341.

2004 Supreme Court Monthly Review 1903.

PLD 1998 Lahore 59.

1999 Monthly Law Digest 1250.

PLD 1995 Lahore 584.

PLD 2003 Lahore 474.

PLD 1989 Federal Shariat Court 95
PLD 1989 Federal Shariat Court 95
Pakistan Law Journal 1996 Federal Shariat Court 138.
1994 Pakistan Criminal Law Journal 2210.
1990 Supreme Court Monthly Review 886.
1997 Pakistan Criminal Law Journal 1095
1997 Pakistan Criminal Law Journal 546.
Pakistan Law Journal 1983 Federal Shariat Court 134.
PLD 1984 Federal Shariat Court 121.
PLD 1996 Karachi 316.
1995 Supreme Court Monthly Review 1403.
National Law Reporter 1986 Shariat Decisions 61.
PLD 1982 Federal Shariat Court 11.
National Law Reporter 1985 Supreme Court 367.
PLD 1981 Federal Shariat Court 308.
PLD 1981 Federal Shariat Court 308.
1994 Pakistan Criminal Law Journal 1111.
1997 Pakistan Criminal Law Journal 416.
1994 Supreme Court Monthly Review 475.
1997 Pakistan Criminal Law Journal 543.
National Law Reporter 1986 Shariat Decisions 575.
National Law Reporter 1986 Shariat Decisions 30.
National Law Reporter 1986 Shariat Decisions 60.
2004 Pakistan Criminal Law Journal 1175.
National Law Reporter 1986 Shariat Decisions 240 (2).
PLD 1989 Federal Shariat Court 95.
PLD 1996 Lahore 50.
1997 Supreme Court Monthly Review 897.
1993 Pakistan Criminal Law Journal 1872.
1996 Shariat Decisions 335.
1997 Pakistan Criminal Law Journal 313.
Karachi Law Reporter 1997 Shariat Cases 121.
PLD 1981 Supreme Court 120.
PLD 1980 Peshawar 4.7.
PLD 1981 Supreme Court 120.
PLD 2000 Federal Shariat Court 1.
National Law Reporter 1992 Shariate Decisions 502.
1993 Civil Law Cases 219.
2003 Yearly Law Reporter 2623.

1984 Supreme Court Monthly Review 583.
1995 Pakistan Criminal Law Journal 1657.
PLD 2000 Federal Shariat Court 63.
1992 Monthly Law Digest 93.
PLD 1995 Lahore 475.
PLD 2004 Supreme Court 219.
PLD 1999 Lahore 479.
1995 Monthly Law Digest 1439.
PLD 1969 Lahore 108.
PLD 1995 Federal Shariat Court 1.
2003 Civil Law Cases 1213.
PLD 1995 Lahore 98.
PLD 1992 Karachi 46.
1998 Civil Law Cases 1054.
PLD 1991 Lahore 251.
2003 Monthly Law Digest 1077.
2002 Supreme Court Monthly Review 1563.
2003 Civil Law Cases 214.
PLD 2003 Peshawar 146.
PLD 1967 Supreme Court 97.
National Law Reporter 1995 Shariate Decisions 558.
PLD 1957 Dacca 245.
PLD 1978 Quetta 117.
PLD 1971 Lahore 151.
1990 Civil Law Cases 1908.
PLD 1972 Supreme Court 302.

Index

U

W

Z

STUDIES IN RELIGION, SECULAR BELIEFS AND HUMAN RIGHTS

1. Amanda Whiting and Carolyn Evans (eds.), *Mixed Blessings: Laws, Religions, and Women's Rights in the Asia-Pacific Region*, 2006, ISBN 90 04 15141 9

2. Natan Lerner, *Religion, Secular Beliefs and Human Rights: 25 Years After the 1981 Declaration*, 2006, ISBN 90 04 15209 1

3. Anne F. Bayefsky and Arieh Waldman (eds.), *State Support for Religious Education: Canada versus the United Nations*, 2006, ISBN 90 04 14980 5